The Boy from Hammersmith

Henry Darling

Published by New Generation Publishing in 2021

Copyright © Henry Darling 2021

First Edition

The author asserts the moral right under the Copyright, Designs and Patents Act 1988 to be identified as the author of this work.

All Rights reserved. No part of this publication may be reproduced, stored in a retrieval system or transmitted, in any form or by any means without the prior consent of the author, nor be otherwise circulated in any form of binding or cover other than that which it is published and without a similar condition being imposed on the subsequent purchaser.

ISBN
            Paperback   978-1-80031-201-2
            Hardback   978-1-80031-200-5

www.newgeneration-publishing.com

New Generation Publishing

Foreword

This book is an inspirational story of a journey through life, sharing a boy's painful childhood upbringing without love or care, yet a determined little survivor whose incredible ability to bring humour into such a dire day-to-day existence without self-pity has to be admired.

The ups and downs of many career changes, meeting his adorable wife, and seeing his children flourish into professional people in their own right are a testament to the writer's fortitude.

The sadness, enlightenment, and especially humour, woven into almost every part of this story, is lightly to send the reader into spontaneous bouts of laughter. The writer is a brilliant raconteur; his phonetic writing of dialects also brilliant. It's all there for us to share, and, like all good childhood fairy tales, it's a story with a happy outcome as the author enjoys his mellowing years without a single regret. A must-read story for everyone, not least those, who through birth or circumstances not of their making, see themselves disenfranchised from society without hope.

Pamela Forrester

Contents

Early Days	1
Hard Times	12
School Days	46
Mischievous Meanderings	59
Australian Goodness	76
Nigh-on Neighbours	85
On the Up	91
Step-change	121
Northern Ireland	136
County of Angels	143
Warming Up	147
The Orkney Bomber	158
Home Again	167
A Butcher's Hook (Colloq.)	173
Between the Lines	180
Back Again	186
Allo, Allo, Allo	194
Maidenhead Calling	199
In the Sticks	215
Brighter Eyes	226
Rain in Vain	230
Bendy Bobbies	236
Moving On	243
Out and About	257
An Indulgence	266

Preface

One year and eleven months after the end of the Second World War, twins were born in Paddington General Hospital to a mother of three other children, living in temporary accommodation in Paddington, London, before being rehoused in Hammersmith. Their father, an ex-Royal Naval sailor deserter during the First World War, of ill-health suffering the effects of diabetes and its associated issues, and therefore unable to work. Abject poverty was the 'norm', with little income other than that given under the Government's National Assistance programme, living within a two-bedroom maisonette on the second floor of an old Victorian building that was two years short of being demolished. It was during a period of national food rationing before and shortly after the introduction of Social Security and the National Health Service.

This book is a personal account of the recollections of life as perceived, experienced, and remembered by the surviving twin from that time right up to writing the last paragraph.

This is Henry's story.

Gertcha! A rhetorical utterance often heard from my mother, who would, at the same time, raise her forearm as a gesture for me to get out of her way or else risk the back of her hand.

"The power of accurate observation is commonly called cynicism by those who have not got it."
(George Bernard Shaw)

Oh, dear!

Early Days

On the morning of 18th August 1947, my sister Ann Marie was born, and, to the shock and horror of my mother and the dismay of others, I too arrived a little later at 12.20 p.m. the same day. My twin and I left Paddington General Hospital with our mother, Kathleen Lilian Darling, who took us back to her residence at 17 Park Place Villas in Paddington to join our two sisters and my father, Henry Gilbert Hawes. After a relatively short time, our family moved to Hammersmith. Five months later, Ann Marie was dead after suffering from the effects of severe chronic gastroenteritis. I was the smaller and weaker of the two with the same life-threatening condition, with the expectation that I too would succumb to the illness. All through my adult years, through lack of information and doubt, I hoped against hope that maybe my twin sister hadn't died but instead had been given away in infancy through unbearable poverty and hardship and that one day I might find her, but that was not to be the case. In later years, I discovered that Ann Marie Darling's name appeared in Fulham Palace Road's cemetery records (near to where we had lived in Hammersmith), having had a pauper's burial way back in February 1948.

My earliest recollections of life were while living at No.6 Marguerite Mansions, Caroline Street (now Queen Caroline Street), Hammersmith, just off Hammersmith Broadway, past what was then the Gaumont Cinema, later to become the Odeon, but more recently; The Hammersmith Apollo. Queen Caroline Street led off away from the Apollo down to the River Thames' north bank adjacent to Hammersmith Bridge. Marguerite Mansions was as much as I remember an old Victorian dilapidated austere-looking building that faced onto the road directly opposite what was then newly built blocks of three or four storey council flats, each block of a different name. Our maisonette was on the second floor, accessed via a communal open entrance leading to a flight of well-trodden worn-smooth grey/black stone stairs. The local authority provided the accommodation under the terms of the National Assistance Act of 1948, which superseded the 'Poor Law', a system that existed since the reign of the first Queen Elizabeth and became an Act of Parliament later passed in the United Kingdom by the Labour Government of Clement Attlee.

The maisonette our family occupied in Hammersmith consisted of two tiny bedrooms, a living area-cum-kitchen with a black metal grated coal-fuelled range, and the only heat source to boil water, cook food and warm the home. A bare wooden table-top with three chairs and a single mustard-coloured rectangular sink with a cold-water tap was the only means of sanitation. The door leading out onto the concrete floor balcony from the central part of the accommodation led onto the scullery area where the washing of clothes took place, all contained within a galvanised oval washtub alongside a wooden-framed metal 'washboard' used to force out grime. The laundry then passed through a twin roller hand-operated 'cranked wheel' mangle to extract the remaining water before being hung out to dry on a horizontal clothesline attached to opposing walls. For me, the washboard doubled as a Skiffle board as I ran my thimble-covered fingers up and down on the galvanised fluted metal surface to an imaginary tune before boredom moved me onto the hand-operated clothes mangle. I would then put my fingers between the rollers to see if they would appear on the other side without having had to endure too much pain. That done, I would play about with the Sunlight household soap and Izal carbolic soap used to disinfect hard surfaces, table-tops or foul-mouthed individuals uttering expletives (or so my mother said) before the slippery bars went over the balcony. Why I didn't go over the top along with the soap, I'll never know. I didn't play with any toys other than a wooden train loaned for a photo opportunity, as I do not remember ever having any.

My family group at Hammersmith included Henry Gilbert Hawes (my dad), aged fifty-seven and born in 1894 in the district of St. Georges' in The East, London (The East End). My great paternal grandfather, a master baker 'Journeyman' (defined as someone who completed his or her apprenticeship term and therefore became unaffordable to the employer), was drawn to the bustling London docks at the time of the Industrial Revolution in the 1860s.

According to his naval record, my father was 5ft 5ins tall and, from what I recall, of a rotund build. My mother, Kathleen Lilian Darling, was aged thirty-six years and appeared much taller than my father. I had two sisters (quite possibly step-sisters), both older than me by two years ten months and the other one year five months respectively. There was also mention of another sibling five or six years older than me, who I later learned was my step-brother on my mother's side. Luckily, this boy was not living with us, having been brought up by my maternal grandmother in Kensal Rise, North London, and so not part of the overcrowding problem we experienced in Hammersmith. I never knew who Peter's father was, or anything about my step-brother for that matter other than regarded as 'backward' - whatever that meant.

As I grew older, I became increasingly curious about the world around me, often asking my mother about my step-brother, his father and other topics that took my interest, but the rhetorical answer was always, "I forget" after every question. For all the secrets my mother kept to herself, there might well have been other siblings lurking about somewhere on the planet. Genealogy searches are what's needed at this point, although I doubt the relevance for this story.

When Henry Gilbert was at home and not in the nearby hospital in the Hammersmith Road, he would sit me on his lap puffing away on rolled-up cigarettes, the smoke of which always caused a stinging sensation in my eyes. Margarine would be smeared onto my head during such times, creating flat shiny hair finished off with a distinct 'navy style parting on one side. It should come as no surprise that I started to go bald at the age of nineteen. Thank you, Dad. And thank you, the makers of Echo margarine! Whenever the hordes of Musca Domestica were unable to land on the overcrowded brown sticky 'flypaper' hanging down below the only light bulb in the room, would form an 'airport flight stacking pattern' above and behind my head, waiting to land once I sat down or stood still for a nano-second. My dad and I got to know our resident flies on first name terms such as 'Flat-Stanley', a name given to successive generations not quick enough to get out of the way of a slap to one's head.

Henry Gilbert had little to no time for my older sisters, one of who reminded me of a broad leather belt with a large brass buckle that my father wore around the waistline of his trousers, periodically removing it to give both of them a wallop. I recall the belt's visual memories from times spent sat on my father's lap while looking down through tear streamed eyes from his constant smoking. The trouser belt never did come my way. I do not know why he singled my sisters out for a 'belting'; I can only speculate. Maybe, just maybe, they weren't his.

My mother and two sisters often went out of the maisonette, leaving me to be looked after by my father. On one such occasion, when Henry Gilbert and I were alone, two very thick slices of bread (doorstops), so thick you couldn't see through them, were set in front of me. Both portions had copious amounts of margarine smeared onto them that came from the same paper wrapper of the stuff plopped on my head with monotonous regularity. My father would then sit down to watch with obvious delight as I devoured them, both slices, every single crumb. I might even have managed a small, satisfying 'burp'. It was a real treat I had to keep secret from my mother and siblings, who might otherwise have dared to ask why the only loaf of bread on the premises had reduced in size.

I learned in later life, long after my father had died, that he had served in the Royal Navy as a Stoker First Class from 1913 until the end of hostilities in 1918 when discharged from HMS Pembroke, a land-based Naval Prison, having served three different periods of internment for 'Desertion'. An estimated thirty-seven million people died across the globe during WW1, but, thank-goodness, Henry Gilbert was in the Royal Navy when he jumped ship. If my father had instead been in the Army, there's little doubt he would have been subject to summary execution, and of course, neither I, my two lovely children, nor my adorable three grandchildren would ever have existed. If Henry Gilbert continued to serve overseas during the First World War aboard a naval ship, as he did on two occasions between internment periods, it was 'odds-on' that he most likely would not have survived.

My father's task aboard a naval vessel within the belly of a ship was either shovelling or supervising the shovelling of coal into the furnaces that kept the propellers turning and the ship functioning; a perfect and preferred target for German U-boats, second only to the ship's ammunition magazine. Instead of remembering my father as a 'runner' (as recorded in his historical Royal Navy records), I would like to think he was a sort of 'Jack-the-lad' who visited hospitality establishments during ports of call. After all, I'm his son. Missing his ship's departure by sleeping over rather than cowardice is what I would like to think as the most likely reason for my father's absence as his ship sailed off over the horizon without him. My dad's relative short-term three months periods of detention suggest that his absence might well have been unintentional. My mother never mentioned Henry Gilbert at all other than telling me he had diabetes (cheery soul, my mother), even up until her death in 1976 when so many untold secrets died with her. My father's Royal Naval experience came as a complete revelation because I somehow thought he was a baker, bricklayer, and many other things, but never a sailor – and a 'Runner' at that. Hey-ho.

Daily life for me as a child in Hammersmith was often spent playing outside on the road as a sort of 'Billy-no-mates'. Other children of a similar age were nowhere to be seen, probably safely indoors under parents' watchful eyes. Not me; even at the age of four and five, I would often meander down some two hundred yards or so on my own to the River Thames water-edge towpath by Hammersmith Bridge, only to stare into the grey/green soup of the river water. Massive amounts of litter and other debris ebbing and flowing from the waves created by passing boats was a constant sight. It wasn't uncommon to see partially decomposed domestic animals, swans, beer bottles and human excrement large enough to be worthy of comment bobbing up and down among the detritus flowing backwards and forwards between the two bridges of Hammersmith and Putney. Sometimes, I would be in the company of both sisters when we were each the recipient of a penny piece to be spent in the nearby shop in Crisp Lane on the way to the River Thames, ironically, on a 'Penny packet of broken crisps. Depending on how hungry we were, an Arrowroot biscuit that cost the same but the size of a dinner plate (at least that how it appeared to me) would be the option. The bribe of one penny to each of us was probably to get us out of the way so that Mum and Henry Gilbert could concentrate on finding a way to provide us with a baby brother. No surprise then that we later had an addition to the family: our younger brother, John Gilbert who arrived on 14th February 1952 and probably the catalyst for getting us moving very soon afterwards to a reinstated derelict council house; 52 Faroe Road W14. All hail Smith's crisps, especially the broken packets that contained twice as many crushed crisps as fully priced unbroken ones, which, along with the bonus of two or more blue paper twists, suggested a baby boy was on the way. There was enough rock salt in each packet of blue paper to clear the pavements of ice along the entire length of Queen Caroline Street and enough left over to season Mum's overcooked spuds. All hail.

It was one dark early evening in the middle of winter, when, at the age of five, I remember my eldest sister having to run an errand into Hammersmith Broadway to buy the London Evening Standard newspaper from a newsstand outside the

London Underground Station. Returning home in a distressed state, my sister said a man had taken her down into a basement of a block of mansions opposite the Gaumont Cinema and attempted to do things to her. Henry Gilbert, so enraged, immediately marched off into the rain looking for the culprit, wearing nothing more than his off-white collar-less shirt, baggy trousers held together with Echo margarine and fag-ash, the ominous broad leather belt with the large brass buckle he wore around his waist, and broad-span trouser-supporting braces. It was probably the only time he had left the maisonette other than periodically visit the local hospital or go to the toilet. As far as I was aware, the police were not involved as I do not remember seeing a very tall man in a very dark uniform darkening our doorway. Perhaps the incident wasn't as dangerous as it could have been - thank goodness. I never did get to know the outcome and doubt that my father found the culprit. He didn't get his newspaper either.

During the time of living in Hammersmith with my father's addiction to smoking recycled tobacco, my two sisters and I had to trawl King Street's gutters in Hammersmith, picking up 'dog ends or 'fag ends' (cigarette butts) from the street gutters. Once home, my father would empty the contents onto a large sheet of the 'News of The World' newspaper before hand-rolling the accumulated 'nicotine dense' tobacco into 'Rizla' cigarette papers before sealing them along the edge with a lick of his tongue. So used were we to the dreadful task of collecting those lip-stained cartridges of unimaginable carcinogenic contents, we didn't bat an eyelid when passing under the noses of people waiting at bus stops; after all, that's where we would find concentrations of the wretched things. If we found a sweet among the fag-ends, it was a bonus, wrapped, unwrapped, or even sucked.

There was a café at the top end of King Street, Hammersmith, on the left side before entering Chiswick High Street that appeared to be owned and run by an Italian family. The staff always seemed to be busy, noticeable by their fashionable white shirts, smart trousers, and shiny black hair -

an opportunity in the waiting. My sisters and I (or whoever was with me at the time) would peer through the street-fronted large window during cold, wet nights, watching the goings-on within the shop of so much food in the hope of being noticed, as we invariably were. Following several glances by the staff toward the window, a treat in the form of what we knew as a cheesecake (a pastry festooned with desiccated coconut that had nothing to do with cheese at all, as far as I knew) was always forthcoming. So too was the Italian utterance of "Piss off stai rimandando I miei clienti." My interpretation was that the staff said we were making their clients uncomfortable with us gawping and depositing smears of nasal mucus on the window, made worse by the rain. Compassionate chaps, those Italians; must have come from Naples. I like the Italians. We tried the same tactic outside an Italian Café at the far end of Kensington High Street in the shadow of Kensington Palace, but the verbal response there was loaded with expletives and noticeably different from the Hammersmith lot. Not from Naples – obviously. No cakes.

I must have been relatively small, as I recall being in a bed very high off the floor in a hospital isolation ward with a glass panelled observation partition. I must have been there for a considerable time as I had forgotten where I lived. I do not know why I had been hospitalised as my mother always rolled out the same rhetorical answer when asked; "I forget". Hot milk was given every evening and consumed with gusto. I had never had warm milk before as a nightcap; even today, some seventy-plus years, the smell of it evokes memories of that hospital experience.

The day I left the hospital, I could not walk unaided and had to be assisted by my mother on one side (the only time I recall having had physical contact with her), and my older sister, Joyce, who supported me on the other as I walked along a corridor of highly polished brown linoleum floors that would have been any health 'n' safety inspector's nightmare in modern times. Two ambulancemen dressed in official-looking dark uniforms with flat-peaked caps similar to London bus inspectors, policemen in cars, door attendants at the Olympia, and postmen, crouched down in front of me and smiled as they condescendingly rubbed my hair as they said, "Hello, Sonny boy" before wishing me well and moving on. As I grew older, I became aware of five horizontal incision marks on my arms and legs, indicative of surgical intervention. I also have two scars, one on the calf of my right leg – in the exact shape of a clothes iron hotplate – and another scar indicative of scalding running from just above the rear of my knee up to my right buttock. The scarring will be with me for life and remain unaccountable. Many years later, after forty-something years, my siblings and I got together to reminisce on our upbringing only to discover that each of us had a variety of unaccountable scars, with one sister, in particular, having scars across her chest, indicative of scalding.

Visitors rarely ever came to our home at No.6 Marguerite Mansions, although I suppose there must have been what with the advent of the National Health Service and our family needing particular attention, especially after the arrival of our 'Smith's Crisps' baby brother. Visits of relatives from both sides of the family were almost non-existent, no uncles, no aunts - no one. I had several uncles and aunts on both sides of the family but only ever saw two of my mother's sisters during my lifetime, and even then, only on two or three occasions. My father had heaps of siblings, some of whom perished in the London Blitz in 1940-1941 when most of the East End had been blown to smithereens, but unaware of any of my father's surviving siblings ever existed until a search on the Ancestry website scores of years later revealed there had been at least a dozen of them still scattered around London during the time I grew up.

Early one evening, when our family was cosily settled in, there was a knock on the front door of our maisonette; my father opened the door only to be confronted by a very tall metropolitan police constable. The officer was dressed from head-to-toe in a dark blue uniform sporting large shiny silver buttons, a ginormous shiny badge on the front of his helmet, and a 'pedestrian crossing' patterned band around his lower left sleeve signifying he was on duty but, sadly, not going home. The officer appeared to be at least 6ft (1,82m) tall, the minimum height required for a copper (or peeler) in those days, and, with the extra twelve inches or so of the helmet added on, his appearance made me feel as if we were in the imaginary world of Gulliver's Travels, Alice in Wonderland – or both. A window had been broken at the flats opposite and, apparently, I was the culprit. Henry Gilbert dragged one of the three kitchen chairs across to where the policeman was left waiting, lifted me onto it in an attempt to align my face with the officer's, at which point instructed me to give an account of myself. Following that encounter, I experienced a bout of almost constant diarrhoea, relief coming only after several days of sleepless nights and nightmare images of convict ships, transportation, Botany Bay and all that stuff. The police constable didn't stay long after observing that I must have noticed his fly-buttons were open as I was at or about his waist height. He was gone! Gertcha! I protested my innocence but to no avail. The broken window had to be paid for, which probably meant all of us going without something or other. The ominous broad leather belt with the large brass buckle stayed around Henry Gilbert's waist.

Some years later, after my family had moved to Faroe Road, ground preparations were underway to build the Hammersmith flyover that was completed in 1961. Much of the burial ground to one side of St Paul's Church had to be excavated with many graves exhumed and taken elsewhere or popped onto the garden allotments in Barnes a mile or two away, providing much-needed potassium for growing potatoes and tomatoes after years of soil neglect. Thankfully, I was unaware at that time of being born a twin and would not have known if my sister's body had been interred there or elsewhere, so the moving of graves was not an issue for me and certainly wouldn't have been for my mother who didn't seem to show any emotions.

Halloween was not celebrated or even heard of by most of us at the time of the grave excavations, but spooky stories of ghosts running amok did the trick instead. As boys, I and a couple of others would invent our entertainment in an attempt to scare each other witless by timing ourselves to see how long it took to pass through the newly built pedestrian underpass where the graves had previously been. The cycling activity through the subway usually ended in screaming, falling off bikes, and losing bowel control, just as I nearly did when peddling like fury on a downward stretch of the newly completed Hammersmith Fly-over. Reaching speeds above 30mph standing on the pedals of an adult ladies framed bicycle that caused me to bob up and down faster than a bobbin on a sewing machine, I heard the noise of a police chrome bell behind me clanging as quickly as I was peddling. It was another award-winning 'Bollocking' from a very tall man in blue. I read a report once that suggested that at least one victim of the Kray brothers went in with the wet concrete as part of a vertical supporting pillar during the flyover's construction. How scary is that? I often wondered if the victim's body, and maybe scores of others, had been plopped in the concrete vertically with arms extended skywards to lend extra support. Kids, eh?

Hard Times

I was five years old when our family moved to Faroe Road. One can only imagine what the residents must have thought when an impoverished family of six took up residence in a reinstated derelict house within their midst while they struggled to shed the memories of austerity and hardship after World War Two. An intent to better themselves usually meant casting dispersions on the ability of those less fortunate to erase memories of their own past experiences. And who can blame them? I do not remember the actual move to the house in Faroe Road, only being there.

Faroe Road consisted of some seventy-something houses with a bombsite at the top end. The open-spaced area was devoid of anything other than flattened brick debris hosting weeds, where there previously must have stood three or four houses. The last remaining home at the top end of the road adjacent to and on the same side as the bombsite had been propped up with a wooden buttress framework, presumably to stop it tumbling down.

Directly opposite the bombsite that faced out onto Blythe Road were derelict houses that had also been wrecked by the German Luftwaffe some years earlier. Demolition was underway, but no-one thought of disconnecting the electricity from the bare hanging wires protruding from the walls. Curiosity was to get the better of me as I mooched around looking for anything of interest. I happened to see and was drawn to some electrical cables with bare wires protruding from them. I grasped the shiny metal ends of the threads and almost electrocuted myself in the process. No amalgam mercury tooth fillings, thank goodness - at least not then. I didn't dare tell my mum. I didn't tell my mum either when knocked flying off my bike by someone riding a motorbike. There didn't seem to be any point. Over the years that followed, the bombsite adjacent to the house propped-up to stop it falling down provided a recreational area for me and others to build opposing shelters of corrugated sheets, protecting us all as we threw stones at each other. We usually arrived in makeshift go-karts made up of four pram wheels roughly fixed to a scaffolding board with a three-sided box on top that served as a cockpit. The makeshift contraption was controlled by the rider sitting within the three-sided box using leg movements and lengths of rope tied to the protruding front axles.

Faroe Road extended from the junction with Blythe Road at the top to Milsom Road at the bottom. Two gas-powered street lights were lit every evening at twilight and extinguished each morning at sunrise by the 'The Lamplighter', a London County Council employee, charged with the job of keeping the use of gas to a minimum. The London County Council later replaced the lamp standards with electrically powered ones, each with a dim single filament lightbulb. Both lamp posts were regular focal points for straying dogs and other dogs out on 'walkies' with their owners to dump copious amounts of their bowel contents around them, enough to cover the Isle of Wight's entire land surface, as would, apparently, the Christmas wrapping paper purchased every year in the United Kingdom. After ridding themselves of their repugnant offerings onto the pavement, the dogs would adopt the sitting position with their rear legs pointed forward and upward, dragging themselves along the ground in search of relief from their over-sensitive anal glands. The pavement offered the only means of comfort for the unfortunate Canis Lupus Familiaris as their rear-ends passed over the mortar joints. Thwaaaack!

    Parked alongside each lamppost were the only two cars in the street, both black with one in a perpetual state of rust and disintegration. Each of the two vehicles provided a focal point for children to clamber over until chased off either by the owners or passing police patrols. There was also a large solitary green-painted ex-army Aerial motorbike chained to one of the lampposts in the road that somehow managed to survive the war and plethora of scrap-metal merchants that appeared to have come out of nowhere, many of whom had become wealthy buying obsolete armaments brought back to the United Kingdom after the war. Such weapons, tanks, etc., probably started life as railings fronting houses only to end up as 'gun-metal' fettled into toy soldiers, along with endless quantities of Lead used to repair water pipes. I never did get to know who owned the strange contraption chained to the lamppost, although a rumour circulated that he had been a deserter from the British Army who was too frightened to come out of his house. The image I still have in my mind is of a saddle so big the rider must have had an arse the size of an African Bull Elephant, which had to have been the most plausible reason why the owner didn't manage to get out through his front door!

From time-to-time, Faroe Road would be lit up at night by a yellow light emanating from an illuminated badge affixed to the top of a radiator grill of a Wolseley police car as it turned into the road, slowly proceeding along to the end before disappearing around the corner. As children, we were instinctively aware that a small illuminated badge at the front of a black car bonnet signified trouble and, after spotting the chrome bell affixed to the front bumper confirming the worst - scarpered. I cannot help think the constables inside the vehicle must have extracted great delight touring our street and others nearby, creating a Mexican wave effect of children disappearing in front of them as they went, while viewing their reappearance in the rear-view mirror very soon after. I vowed that one day I would be a police officer. I just loved the effect.

Our house in Faroe Road was a three-storey run-down Victorian building, not too dissimilar to a few others in streets elsewhere in some parts of London. Fifty-two Faroe Road consisted of a basement below pavement level with two upper levels, all with large pane sash windows fronted by iron grill balconies that were just wide enough to accommodate two small children standing shoulder-to-shoulder facing out towards the road. Of course, the exception was the basement window which faced forward within the basement area with a view up towards the pavement-level iron railings that had remained intact after the war. In contrast, metal fences fronting other houses along the street at ground level without basements had been requisitioned and taken off as scrap to provide much-needed metal for the war effort a few years earlier. The cement-mortar holding the ornate iron grilled balcony in place had deteriorated over many years, much of which had fallen away, rendering the terraces extremely dangerous; however, that didn't stop me standing on them in the absence of anyone telling me not to do so. Why the ironwork had not been requisitioned was beyond my comprehension at the time, but if it had been, it was highly likely I would have ended up in the basement much quicker than I would have liked.

The front outside area within the basement of our house consisted of stone steps that led down from the pavement to a small enclosed courtyard with a coal cellar and a padlocked entry-door for gaining entry into the lower part of the building. Access to the coal-cellar for the delivery of coal was through a steel-capped aperture at pavement level. Getting into the house's lower level via the padlocked door was for the exclusive use of council workers who had unfettered access to two of the three basement-level rooms to deposit debris and other building waste brought in from elsewhere. We were effectively living above a builder's waste dump. The third room in the basement served as a 'scullery' with a square sink and a cold water tap beside a copper basin set within a concrete block at waist height, under which was a fire grate for the burning of coal and the remains of wood from Orange boxes to heat water. There was no means of smoke extraction from the fire when lit other than opening the only sash window in the room. My family must have come out of the place blacker than when we went in and probably one step away from carbon monoxide poisoning, especially during winter months when it was too cold even to contemplate opening the window at all. A long rectangular shaped galvanised bath, placed on the floor in the scullery with hot water poured into it from the copper basin, was where we would take it, in turn, to bathe. I was always the last ever to be allowed to enter the grey scum-ridden water; seniority of age never came into it; my mother's preferences did. The sharing of the bathwater stopped altogether after my eldest sister Joyce reached puberty. So too did bathing, especially for me. The only time I experienced all-over cleanliness after family bathing had ceased was either on sports days or physical training at school, or else the London County Council's swimming pool in Lime Green, somewhere near Shepherds Bush. After a session of swimming, I would meander back home with a wet towel tightly rolled under one arm and all of my important little places squeaking at every step. Goodness knows what I left behind in the water.

The only toilet for our house's occupants happened to be in the garden; gaining access to it was through a side door leading out of the scullery into a small courtyard. Getting to the W.C. involved having to run the gauntlet of a dark rodent infested stairway past the rooms full of builders' rubble,' The 'Loo' consisted of a single-tier brick outhouse with a corrugated roof and an old wooden door with gaps above and below offering views of the occupant therein if one was inclined to look. Creepy-crawlies were always in attendance, taking shelter to avoid predatory birds and the perishing cold of winter, along with what appeared to be giant spiders hiding behind torn square sheets of the Daily Mirror or the News of the World newspapers that had been cut into manageable squares and impaled on a metal butcher's hook to serve as toilet paper – so soothing! The toilet bowl itself was of a perfect funnel shape, devoid of an 'S' bend but instead had a central aperture that appeared to disappear down into the bowels of the earth (forgive the pun).

The stairway that led down from the first floor to the basement level was devoid of any light source. Getting to the toilet was, as far as possible, confined to daylight hours; even then, the entire basement area was as dark as night with boarded-up windows. Descending the stairs' depths to the basement meant having to run the gauntlet between the landing at the top and the back-yard door at the bottom as fast as was humanly possible. Simultaneously, it was prudent to create as much noise as possible to scatter the resident rats and mice who might well have thought they had more of a right to be there than any of us; they probably did. Still, the local council rat catcher, not to be confused with the school's truancy officer patrolling the streets every day, would often remind successive generations of the dreadful things that their territorial claims had been misplaced. By the time any of us arrived at the outhouse, the funnel-shaped W.C. bowl was almost superfluous to requirements.

At the front of the house, the first storey above the front basement room was the so-called sitting room. The room had a sash window with a horizontal crack across the entire width, held together with putty to reduce draughts and stop further slip. An aperture the size of a child's clenched fist remained between the upper and lower panes of glass. To reduce draughts and prevent the escape of 'Joey' the budgerigar, my mother would place a rolled-up sock into the hole allowing our birdie to fly around the room at leisure depositing excrement wherever he or she fancied, whether it be on the mantelpiece, the piano, the windowsill or upon one's head. Initially, 'Joey' was yellow, latterly blue, but later still, turquoise. Funny that; either Joey was a flying chameleon in drag or a cross-dressing 'Melopsittacus Undulatus' (a budgerigar to me at least). When I posed the question 'Who's a pretty boy then?' I didn't always get the response I was expecting.

It was in the sitting room of our house that Henry Gilbert slept in a large bed, and for the time I remember him being at home, he was almost always there. There was an occasion when I happened upon my parents who were in the process of providing yet another sibling when I asked them what they were up to, but, in the absence of a plausible reply, asked if I could have a packet of Smith's crisps that had a blue-twist wrapper of salt. Later that day, my siblings and I found ourselves sat on the steps of the Havelock Arms pub at the end of Milson Road, Hammersmith, munching packets of Smith's crisps while our parents were inside doing what grown-ups did in public houses. One of the very few times my father ventured beyond our home's sitting room was when he wandered down to the same Havelock Arms with my mother while I followed behind, angling for yet another packet of crisps. I have always been able to recognise opportunities!

There was a time when I inadvertently walked into the kitchen at the precise moment my father gave my mother a tremendous wallop, causing her to fall to the floor. They both looked aghast at my sudden presence, with Mum pulling an expression not unlike Picasso's portrait 'The Scream'. I was quickly ushered out through the door and left to wonder the cause of the altercation.

In the years that followed, it was in the sitting room that our family (minus my father) huddled together in front of an open-grated fireplace to ward off the winter months' extreme cold. My mother always took pride of place, sat with her legs wide open, covered with a blanket, capturing almost all the radiant heat emitted from the orange glow of large diminishing chunks of coal as the rest of us jostled to get a glimpse of the flames. Payment for coal, by instalments, was given to a bloke who appeared each week brandishing a record of payment booklet in anticipation of extracting a shilling (5p) from my mother. Sometimes, if everyone in the house remained silent and out-of-view, the geezer would go away empty-handed. Gertcha!

Inside the front sitting room of our house was a walnut veneered radio that my mum had on perpetual rent from Radio Rentals at a shilling (5p) per week. The set had a volume control knob on one side and a tuning knob on the other with a couple of knobs in between, the use of which I was never able to fathom. The radio, powered from the mains electricity supply through a connection to the non-earthed central light socket hanging from the ceiling, became our only media entertainment source. The BBC Light Programme's programmes included a riveting serial story of a fictional family experiencing the London Blitz that we avidly listened to while sat around the fire in almost total darkness. Apart from the small green light of the radio, the only other source of light came from the flames of the open-grate fire, the heat from which had the effect of creating a red mottled pattern on my mother's legs. Beams of light from the headlights of occasional passing vehicles, which oddly at times seemed to sweep across the room in the opposite direction to where the car was travelling, would sometimes momentarily light up the room, and those of us huddled around the fire. The lampposts in the street provided little or no meaningful light towards our house as both were too far away in opposite directions.

To the rear of the sitting room, facing out towards the garden above the second basement room, was the kitchen. Furnishings within the kitchen consisted of a grey gas cooker that we often huddled around with its oven door open to keep warm and a built-in waist-high cupboard on each side of a chimney stack, both always full of discarded worn-out shoes and other junk. The same table and chairs we had in Hammersmith became the main focal point in the kitchen, next to a single Belfast-style sink with a wooden draining board mounted onto a rigid wooden framework. The sink assembly, along with a cold water tap and a bucket underneath used for catching drips and other extraneous matter, had been hurriedly affixed onto a wall in one corner of the kitchen by council workers. Hot water taps were non-existent.

Inside the kitchen to the left of the doorway could be found the food cupboard, a single tall unit with a width of about 900mm that had formerly been a 'Tall-boy' clothes wardrobe acquired from goodness-knows where.

What little food we had would have been found on the one high-level shelf of the food storage unit. For two or three years each Christmas, a Capon (a cock chicken more than a year old and chemically or physically castrated to enhance rapid growth) hung from the clothes rail under the high-level shelf. The adapted food cupboard became the focal point for hordes of mice who would party at will, their gatherings scattering in all directions when disturbed by someone looking to rob them of what they were eating. Such was the infestation of mice, in a futile attempt to keep the blighters under some sort of control, my mother partially filled buckets of water, strategically placing them around the kitchen before retiring to bed. The following morning, dozens of mice would be found swimming around the inside rim of each bucket in a futile attempt to get out. The Pied Piper of Hamelin would have had a one-stop-shop at our house if he had chosen to target mice instead of rats. As in the storybook, the pied fellow wouldn't have been paid either. To the delight of my mother and a certain Mr Baggs, the visitor from Hamelin might well have emptied the streets of kids with me trailing on close behind.

In the absence of effective birth control in earlier times, it became accepted that children were often unplanned and unwanted to the extent that their mere presence became an encumbrance to everyday adult life. The term often uttered 'Children should be seen and not heard' meant children always had to keep their place. It wasn't uncommon to see small children sat on the stone steps of pavement-fronted public houses in all weathers, getting soaked through while their parents were inside 'whopping it up (or down)'. There were so many condescending utterances directed at children of all ages (a legacy from by-gone Victorian times) and far too many to list, but here's a few of them: -

- "Don't speak until spoken to - imbecile."
- "Get off the wall, or you'll get Piles."
- "Tuck yourself in, or you'll get kidney disease."
- To keep children on their toes and fearful of everything, the term 'Bogeyman' was often used that encompassed anything or everything; or perhaps a solitary policeman in dark clothing that would appear out of the darkness

from around a corner at any given moment to nobble any child that crossed his path.
- "It's time you were circumcised, my lad. Pardon?
- Any complaints made about having a sore throat usually resulted in one's tonsils being whipped out to stop any future grizzling.
- And, to boys of a certain age: "Keep your hands where people can see them or else, you'll go blind." Sorry? I never did understand why more men than women disproportionately wore spectacles. My dad did.
- And of course, the immortal phrase: 'Gertcha', usually followed-up with a 'clout' to the head…and all for doing absolutely nothing.

And, just to put a finer point on the subject; researching the topic of attitudes towards children in earlier times, I came across this: -

'During the first half of the 20th Century, many psychologists believed that showing affection to children was simply a sentimental gesture that served no real purpose - even cautioning that displays of affection risked spreading diseases and contributing to adult psychological problems.

Wherever they went, children of a particular 'class' in society such as mine were made to feel as welcome as Blowflies at a Butcher's picnic. Happy days.

Back at the house in Faroe road, council employees had decorated the kitchen walls with wallpaper applied halfway down with gloss paint to floor level for easy cleaning – if it ever was. At a slightly lower level and facing out towards the rear garden, behind the house's kitchen, was my bedroom - at least initially. The room had dry-rot floorboards that failed to support anyone approaching adult weight walking over them and, when broken or crumbled, stayed that way. I vividly recall accessing my bedroom by having to pass the bannister rails to the stairs which led down to the ever-derelict basement, although soon after moving in, council workers boarded up the access with a hardboard partition with a door to facilitate relatively safe access to the basement level. It was the same place at the top of the stairs that I remember my father chasing me with his thick-rimmed glasses that covered his intentionally crossed-eyes along with a complete set of false teeth protruding from his mouth in an attempt to frighten the life out of me, which he invariably managed to do.

Ascending the first flight of stairs in our house, away from the kitchen was the bedroom, occupied by my sister June, which, for the time she was sharing family experiences, remained out-of-bounds for the rest of us - including my mother. The second flight of stairs led to a landing with a door leading to my mother's bedroom, who shared the same bed as our younger brother, John. Adjacent to the door leading to my mother's bedroom was the door leading to a more oversized bedroom I later had to share with my eldest sister, Joyce, after my mother had inadvertently set the floorboards on fire from a heater that, through design, dripped paraffin directly onto a burning flame. There wasn't a wick of any sorts, so if anyone inadvertently knocked themselves against the heater, paraffin would spill out onto the floor. By the time I arrived home one late afternoon after school, I felt a tightening in the pit of my stomach as I witnessed firefighters from the London Fire Brigade swarming all over our house. Large water hoses trailed out from the front door down to a fire tender where a small group of onlookers were gawping and chatting to each other. Another humiliation. Gertcha!

In the large shared bedroom at the top of the stairs that I shared with my older sister were two eight-paned sash windows facing out towards the road, which as time went on forfeited several panes of glass that were replaced with bits of cardboard. My eldest sister and I slept at opposite ends of the room on black metal utility beds with stripe-patterned mattresses stuffed with horse-hair, covered over with two blankets. The coverings were coarse woven material with three institutional-style blue parallel pin-striped lines running down the centre; charity issued without a doubt. During winter months, what with the cold, lack of heating and draughts rattling through loose-fitting window frames, it was not unusual to go to bed fully clothed to keep warm. Whenever it was, bedtime always kicked off with a rush to grab the biggest overcoat previously placed on the handrail at the bottom of the stairs. Whoever was lucky enough to get the garment would then take it up the stairs and put it on top of the two blankets for added warmth. However, racing to grab one of the only coats large enough to be of any benefit became a source of conflict between the younger of my two sisters and the rest of us.

There was a gas and an electric pre-payment meter in our house's hallway that only accepted single shilling coins (5p). When the money ran out, usually without warning, off would go the lights, and so too the supply of gas. Many-a-time I recall going to bed holding a candle to see myself up the stairs with hot melting candle-wax dripping onto my clenched fist as I went. If the electricity supply terminated during the day, one of my other siblings or I would have to run to the local newsagent's shop to swap handfuls of copper coins for shilling pieces. Such coins were in plentiful supply when the gas and electric meter man emptied the cash box of money and gave some back in the form of a rebate.

If things weren't bad enough living at or below the poverty line, our house became the subject of a burglary when the cash contents of the gas and electricity meters in the hall became a target. My mum had to replace the loss by buying fewer power units at an inflated price. Frequent journeys to the shops to obtain shilling pieces, along with strips of six 'Aspro' (Aspirin) painkiller tablets from an outdoor vending machine and very, very occasionally, a rock-hard block of Neapolitan ice cream wrapped in newspaper, must have appeared as if my siblings and I were from the cast of the late comedian's Benny Hill's fast-forward films.

Reddish-brown bed bugs (Cimex Lectularious) were constant companions, often found crawling out of whatever I had been wearing during the night, their extended abdomens filled with my blood. Such was the infestation scale, in the forlorn hope of eliminating or keeping the wretched parasites under some sort of control, I often applied the flame of a lit candle to the springs that tensioned the metal slats of the bed supporting the mattress where the repulsive parasites had retreated. The smell of burning bugs was reminiscent of ground Almonds that put me off marzipan for life. My mother and younger brother were always cosily tucked up each night with a thick feather eiderdown quilt and, as far as I know, were spared the constant onslaught of bedbugs. I have no account of the younger of my older sisters' predicament in this regard; by the time I was fifteen years of age, she had long left the family home.

Our garden in Faroe Road consisted of 'make-do' boundary fences with easy access for marauding dogs to come and go at will. I recall being in our garden on one occasion when I happened upon three dogs, one mounted on the other with a third sitting nearby, manicuring his paws. Next door to us, the neighbour owned a breed of British Bulldog called Peggy that stood alongside him as he became transfixed watching the spectacle over the garden fence until he became aware of my presence. The neighbour quickly explained that the dog underneath wasn't feeling well and that the dog on top was pushing it to the hospital. Yeah, right! The promiscuous duo was obviously in a hurry, evident by the enthusiasm shown. I did my best to help the copulating couple by running toward them at lightning speed while at the same time chucking a house brick and shouting the fearful phrase – Gertcha! The dogs dismounted in a nano-second and found themselves standing back-to-back, unable to uncouple and, by the expressions on their faces, probably wondering what day it was. I reminded them that it was still Saturday and that the hospital was still open by proffering the contents of a bucket of cold water. That did the trick. To the sound of what I thought was the pop of a champagne cork, followed by a whelp, the 'Good Samaritan' dog and his spectating mate cowardly disappeared over the garden fence in opposite directions at supersonic speed. At the same time, the dog subject of their attention and in need of urgent hospital attention exited the garden through a small gap in the fence, rendering the hole much more significant than before. They would probably have pissed on my mum's strawberries if she had had any - bloody embarrassing.

While the threesome spectacle was on the go, Peggy, the bulldog next door, kept running up and down on the other side of the boundary fence, leaving slobber in its wake while at the same time making an almighty racket in a determined but unsuccessful attempt to be part of the action. What with the bulldog's physic of expanded chest and diddy legs more in keeping with a Queen Anne fireside armchair, there was little chance of a liaison with the lanky boys in our garden without knowledgeable guidance from someone at Crufts, or at least someone with biceps the size of rugby balls.

As you would have no doubt gathered, dogs were a regular feature of life throughout my time in Faroe Road. A common sight was seeing Canibus vigorously mounting each other as they hurriedly went about restocking their own kind after World War Two losses when countless numbers of Fidos' were unfortunately blown to smithereens during the London Blitz in 1940 and 1941. Another regular sight was of dogs crapping with impunity on street corners and on bombsites conveying a message: 'Have some of this sunshine'. With a flicking of the back legs and a brief look left and right, the culprits would then disappear into the next road. It wasn't unusual to see grown-ups and children alike scraping the stuff off from the instep of shoes against kerb edges or else discovering that one or other of us carried a surprise or two indoors. No doggie-bags back in the 1950s to collect dog waste or very little plastic of any sort for that matter. How we, as children, managed to avoid becoming blind from

Toxocariasis, a parasite worm in dog excrement that yearns to be in the environment of a human eye, was a marvel to behold.

Of course, most dog owners are responsible people in these modern times, but back in the 1950s and 1960s - not so. It was a regular sight to see dogs copulating on almost every street corner with residents running out and tipping buckets of cold water over them, just as I did in our garden. There was a bad-tempered paranoid elderly lady at the bottom of Faroe Road who became so obsessed throwing buckets of cold water over unscrupulous dogs, inadvertently took to throwing water over passing cyclists on tandem bicycles as they cycled past her front door. Mad Madam's impulsive actions probably stemmed from the idea that if the dogs and tandem cyclists were getting what she was not getting, they ain't getting it too - Oi! Sploooooosh!

During the summer months of the 1950s, I would stand on the outside balcony of the kitchen window with nothing much to do other than torment the bulldog next door that had been confined to its owner's backyard, but, luckily, I never got close enough to exchange greetings or anything else for that matter.

I had a friend with a one-sided Mohican haircut called Arfer Mow (I've changed Toby's name to protect his identity), who became a landscape gardener with a propensity of leaving jobs half-finished, significantly when cutting grass. Toby had the unfortunate experience of having dog excrement stuffed into his mouth when he was about twelve years old by a bully from the next street. The horrendous experience resulted in my friend acquiring a perpetual habit of rolling his top lip upwards while at the same time sniffing his fingers before then exhaling loudly through his nostrils. I can imagine he and I going on a trip to Germany with someone proffering a bratwurst with utterances of, "Diese sowsidge ist like, ow you say, Hotdog. Nein? Und, Voud you like vun?" At which point, my friend's top lip would instantaneously and involuntarily tremble while at the same time curl upwards before replying, "Nah – no fanks!" The sniffing 'n' banging went on for years and might still be going on for all I know. Poor sod. Woof!

On 2nd June 1953, Queen Elizabeth II's coronation took place, and it is, of course, well documented. Almost all streets in the land had been closed to traffic, allowing for street parties to take place in celebration. Some weeks earlier, I recall someone knocking at our front door asking for a contribution towards the street party's cost, but my father would not, or more likely, could not contribute. On the big day, I also remember enviously standing on the front steps of our house looking on as other children in the street sat on both sides of a long row of tables. The seemingly endless food adorned platform with red, white, and blue decorations stretched from one end of the road to the other, with the attendees getting stuck into all manner of colourful edible delights as I sat and watched.

During the time of moving from Hammersmith to Faroe Road, or the months that followed, I was taken by my mother to visit my father to what I knew as Fulham Palace Road Hospital, where he remained due to on-going health issues. The ward my dad occupied was part of a two-level wooden structure like a wartime military billet with a wooden staircase leading from a back door of the upper storey to an outside grassed area at ground level. Back then, children were never allowed into hospitals to visit, so I had to be content standing on the lawn, looking up at my father as he smiled, waved, and threw sweets down to me. That was the last time I would see him.

On 4th September 1953, I found myself sitting on the doorstep of our house, having nothing more to do other than be on the lookout for the bully from the next road. My mother appeared on the top step behind where I was sitting and told me my dad had died and promptly retreated back inside the house, closing the door behind her. There were no hugs or kisses, and no signs of emotions either. There had to be reasons why my mother treated me with a degree of indifference; it was just that I didn't know them. I had just turned six years of age and felt very alone. The moment is still with me. Somebody once said that if I looked skywards and spotted the brightest star, it would be my father watching over me. My mother's lack of interest made it highly unlikely that it was her that proffered such words. Even in my seventies, I still look upwards on crystal clear nights in search of the brightest star, knowing, of course, that it had to be a distant planet, probably Mars or Saturn; or quite possibly, Henry Gilbert. My father's body was buried in Ealing Cemetery, London, England, in an unmarked pauper's grave in the same fashion as my twin sister Ann Marie's body had been some five years earlier in Fulham.

After the death of my father, events for me took a downward turn; I became vulnerable. Hunger was a constant companion with little income coming into the house. John, my little brother, reminded me of the time he was sucking his shirt collar, brought on by being desperately hungry. A woman living opposite us, a refugee from Nazi-occupied Poland, recognising extreme poverty when she saw it, tied a necklace of chicken bones around his neck to ward off hunger pangs. Cornflakes or puffed wheat with watered-down milk so diluted it appeared blue around the edges was all we had for breakfast, although free milk and free lunches were always available at school during the school term. I was lucky enough to become eligible to return to school during the non-term time from Monday to Friday for free dinners too. I don't know how my siblings fared as none of us attended the same schools.

Weekends at home were always a bit hit 'n' miss; if I wasn't around at mealtimes, I either went without or else found myself scratching about in the 'tall boy' food cupboard looking for an old piece of rock-cake or portion of bread pudding that didn't have mouse droppings on it. Minced-beef stew was sometimes available, or else a neck-of-mutton concoction with ivory-coloured sinews floating at the surface that took ages to chew. Once cooled, the homemade stews would form a hard layer of fat at the top, so thick they could easily have been entered into the annual Gloucester cheese rolling contest. If my mother's creations had been in that cheese-rolling event, they probably would have reached the bottom of the hill first, inflicting severe injury upon anyone unfortunate enough to get in the way of her creations as they rolled and bounced down to the bottom.

The exception to grease-laden weekday food was Sunday lunch, usually available at home and always consisted of roast beef or pre-frozen New Zealand lamb, shipped from halfway around the world became as cheap-as-chips; that was until the U.K. joined the then EEC. The press of the time warned the British public that prices would at least double after joining, and they were right. Tariffs slapped on products imported from the British Commonwealth made them much more expensive than before, putting much of it beyond the reach to the likes of my family. While it was affordable, lamb or beef for Sunday lunch was usually followed by apple pie prepared from apples collected from reject piles in Hammersmith market, just off King Street. The few times my mother ever tolerated my presence was on a Sunday while peeling those apples. I was always hungry and would wait in anticipation of eating the peel as it came away from the knife. Eggs were purchased from a grocer's shop nearby and almost always cracked, but then they were bought cheaply, along with an assortment of broken biscuits bought by ounce weight. Who could complain? It was the only way we could afford food at all. Packets of perfectly shaped undamaged biscuits were the preserve of those who were more fortunate than us.

Fruit and vegetables obtained from a fruit and vegetable market just off King's Street, Hammersmith on a Saturday, was by way of raking through piles of unsold or rotting fruit and vegetables left behind by street traders after closing time. It was always a race to collect as much edible stuff that was available before being cleared by the local authority after trading had ceased. The collected bounty was dragged home in an 'orange box', effectively a makeshift pram without wheels, tied at the front with some string that undoubtedly made an awful noise when dragged along the pavement - even more humiliation. Nothing went to waste, including the orange boxes that became kindling wood for the front room fire if any of it remained after surviving the journey home. Cringe, if you will – I still do!

Sar-fend-on-Sea (colloq.). I remember two occasions when my mother, siblings and I presented ourselves at a bus stop in front of the BBC studios in Shepherds Bush Green, bound for a day out at the seaside. Images of old coaches depicted in children's seaside storybooks came to mind when an old single-decker bus of similar appearance arrived to take us on a day trip to Southend-On-Sea in Essex. While waiting for the 'Cronk' to appear, I noticed large quantities of cigarette-ends spread over a wide area on the pavement and gutter around us. My instinct was to pick up those small white lipped-stained fag-ends, but they were of no interest to me by this time as my father was no longer with us.

Off we went in the bus to the sounds of gear-grinding, along with the sight of black smoke belching from the vehicle's exhaust pipes that remained suspended in the air long after we had disappeared into the distance. The bus coughed and spluttered its way along the entire route, groaning at the weight of crate-upon-crate of Barclays Best Bitter and Watney's Pale Ale, piled high in the luggage compartment. The entire contents of crated beers heard jingling below was destined for consumption whenever the bus stopped along the route and arrived at the pebble-stone beach of Southend-On-Sea. And it was.

While serious boozing was well underway next to wooden beer-crates stacked alongside the bus, our family meandered down onto the beach, sat down and swiftly gobbled-up homemade egg sandwiches followed by a jam tart that had been snatched from the marauding mice in the 'Tall-boy' food cupboard. Nothing else - that was it. We then headed off to the Kurzaal, a fairground complex of numerous stalls of entertainment. One such booth at the fairground, entitled

'Knock the Lady Out of Bed', invited lecherous punters to part with money in exchange for three wooden balls to chuck at a bullseye sign. Once hit, the target would release a locking mechanism causing a well-made divan-type bed to be tipped, and out would pop a scantily dressed beautiful young lady onto the floor for all to leer. Although the men were always throwing the balls with extreme gusto, the womenfolk provided the money to goad them. It was a good job the fire-buckets were empty of water, otherwise, instinct would have got the better of me. I wanted to hire three balls myself, but all I had was a penny, so instead had to settle for a stick of seaside rock riddled throughout with the words: 'Southend-On-Sea'.

All along the avenues of the entertainment stalls within the Kursaal, fights spontaneously broke out with the sickly sound of flesh hitting flesh as slobber and blood-laden mucus flew everywhere. Frightening. It was time to depart and board the bus for the return journey home, leaving a couple of would-be passengers in the care of the local police before they would have to find their own way back to London a day or two later.

Back on the bus on the return journey to Shepherds Bush, the sound of loud adult chuntering could be heard from within the rows of seats as I developed a bout of motion sickness that caused me to uncontrollably heave. At the point of vomiting, someone from behind where I sat shoved smelling-salts under my nose. Christ almighty, if I had been wearing a hat, it would have shot clean through the roof! It worked; I was as 'right as rain' afterwards and turned to slurp my stick of seaside rock. What remained of the beer had been finished off as the coach arrived back at Shepherds Bush before all day-trippers stepped down onto the pavements where even more fag-ends had accumulated. One of only two so-called annual holidays was over. I often wondered who got the deposit money back from the beer bottles.

I only once returned to Southend-on-Sea, which was after my first child Justin's birth. Wanting to share my childhood experiences with my wife, off we went with our son bundled up in a Terylene cotton-towelled nappy that made him look twice his actual size, his legs horizontally stuck out each side because of it. After telling my wife about munching egg sandwiches and all that, we found ourselves at the far end of the 1.33 miles of the Southend pier. It was a chilly day with pensioners sat warming themselves in the autumn sunshine, blankets covering their legs to keep warm. One elderly Lady, knowing how famous our son was (more on that later), asked if she could hold him. While sat on the stranger's lap, happy to oblige, Justin promptly relieved himself, saturating the blanket beneath. Following profound apologies, the lady lifted the blanket from her lap without getting up as urine gushed through the material onto the wooden planks of the pier's decking below, a scene reminiscent of trawlers nets being drawn onto a fishing vessel. Thankfully, strawberries were out of season. A marathon sprint back to the start of the pier, picking up a peppermint-flavoured stick of candied seaside rock on the way that bore the words 'Southend-on-Sea' within its core, along with a giant flat disc-shaped red lollipop the size of a dinner plate, and we were homeward bound.

****

Back home after the day-trip to the seaside, it was life as usual with merchants of all descriptions vying for business every weekend, touring the streets of London to sell their produce. Costermongers (always referred to as barrow boys) would turn up having pushed their carts from wholesale markets scattered around London laden with fresh seasonal fruit, which, of course, for us was price-prohibitive, but it didn't matter as we had our own supply from Hammersmith market anyway. Fresh fish was also available, along with offerings of jellied eels and a wide variety of other shellfish. My mother referred to the young costermonger fish-seller as 'The Winkle Man - can't think why. Knowing that someone in our house was partial to a winkle or two, the fishy bloke would always stop by our front door expecting an almighty rush to his cart to collect a full pint-size glass of the foul-tasting ominous-looking dark-shelled molluscs. After the winkle-seller departed, what remained of the afternoon was spent removing the winkles' protective caps using a sewing needle to gain access to the disgusting contents within.

There were occasions when a bloke would turn up riding an adapted tricycle offering to sharpen knives, shears or almost anything else. Such was the poor chap's positioning when peddling like fury to turn the sharpening wheel; it was a wonder he didn't end up with a double-strangulated lower-abdominal hernia.

Brewery horse-carts were a regular feature during my time in Faroe Road, as the Watney's Shire Horses trundled past our house on their way to the brewery-owned pub in the next road, or else seeing the Charrington's brewery drays doing the same thing on the way to their brewery-owned pubs. The drays' drivers always seemed to be inebriated, all sporting rosy-red cheeks and scarlet-coloured noses that would have been more in keeping on Father Christmas's Rudolf. It must have seemed like Christmas every day for the beer chaps, downing pint after pint of ale after completing each delivery. The draught horses had their share of alcohol, always drinking beer slops from a bucket only to end up as pissed as their handlers.

Initially, horse-carts delivered bread, although the transport mode changed to electric vehicles in line with the mid-fifties' milk floats. The sound of someone hollering 'ANY OLD IRON, RAG-BONE' rang out and more prevalent than the sound of garden birds twittering their stuff. The horse-carts, dragging bones for processing into wood-glue, rags for recycling into 'shoddy' (a term used to describe anything poorly made), and household items for selling-on, would stop at the same places in the road including directly outside the White tide Lady's flat until its 'Totter' handler reappeared and caught up on foot. The whole shebang would then move off to a horse-recognised stopping place further along the route. The upside to all the stopping and starting resulted in copious amounts of horse manure being left along the way, ready to be scooped up by anyone not too concerned about what others might have thought. All I can say is that our garden was always full of colour – and dogs. Some savvy totters would suspend a canvas sheet 'hammock-style between their horses' legs to collect rear-end offerings for sale. The most likely of customers would have been anyone not quick enough to obtain their samples from the surface of the road or else considered themselves to be above such a degrading act.

Two ice cream vans appeared each weekend and every day during school holidays, jostling to be the first to off-load their creations. Scala ice cream vendors, Italians by name and Italian by nature, offered the most delicious of all ice creams, always over-generous with portions to ensure their trading name remained at the forefront of children's minds. The rival to Scala, a well-known purveyor of whipped-up fluffy white creations of fat and sugar, tempered with a trace of vanilla, would race to take up the most popular position in the street, but the uptake compared to Scala was minuscule. Children were always savvy, instantly recognising the jingle that emanated from the van of choice as it turned into the road and parked up in the same place every day. The logo on many ice cream vans used to be: 'Watch that child, it may be deaf', or 'Stop me and buy one'. A similar sign appeared within the local barber's shop premises read: 'Buy me and stop one', referring to the purchase of condoms or 'Johnnies'. I often found myself sitting in a barber's chair, having a crew-cut hairstyle that consisted of a 'short-back-and-sides', finished off with a trimmed platform top, so flat as to allow me to stand on my head unsupported by my arms if I had chosen to do so. Almost everyone leaving the barber's shop would be invited to buy something for the weekend, but those words were lost on me. I paid the princely sum equivalent to two-and-a-half-pence and was out the door.

At the age of twelve, I realised that if I were to make changes to better myself, I would have to strike out independently. And so, I did. Bertram Mill's Circus came to the Olympia in Kensington (just a few minutes' walk from where I lived) every year for a few weeks over Christmas. I worked on a stall selling balloons, assisting in the making-up of balloon dolls with cellophane skirts attached to sticks inserted into the configurations to serve as handles. Apart from fetching copious amounts of tea from the canteen for my employer and her business partner, it was my job to apply adhesive tape to conical-shaped hats and insert the tasselled sticks. The retail business owner, a Mrs Shafi, and her Indian nephew Rashid, would then draw a smiley face onto each balloon and place it on a rack of tensioned string along with hundreds of others awaiting the outpouring of circus spectators at the end of each performance. The world-famous Coco the Clown would collect two of the dolls from us during each performance and give them away as part of his activities while in the circus ring. The result: a complete sell-out of balloon dolls – every time. The punters got their balloons, and I got some pocket money.

Honest John by name - honest John by nature; at least that's how many of the fairground stallholders would have you believe. Working for the Balloon Lady within the Grand Hall of the indoor funfair of Bertram Mills' Big Top Circus provided ample opportunities to observe how some of the shysters among the stallholders managed to extricate money and profit from unsuspecting fairground patrons.
    A stall with five buckets in a row, set up at knee-height and tilted forward in such a way to ensure that wooden balls thrown into them swirled around the inner walls before flying back out again and landing on the floor. Five balls for a shilling (5p) gave fun-seeking people the chance to win a stuffed teddy bear or a chalk ornamental Alsatian dog. I never did get to see anyone walking away with a prize, and no wonder; the guy who ran the stall had a convex-shaped solid disc that he applied to the underside of each bucket before proceeding to whack it with a lump hammer. The result was a more concave bottom

than before, ensuring that almost every wooden ball bounced back out again.

Another entertainment stand had plastic ducks with a magnet strip stuck to the ducks' beaks' underside. The trick was to dangle magnets from a makeshift rod in an attempt to 'oik' a duck out of the moving water to claim a prize. Unbeknown to those taking part, the metal strips applied to almost all the ducks were not magnetic at all. The stallholder would create a distraction by mechanically agitating the water as it whizzed around, causing the yellow plastic darlings to bob up and down, giving the impression that the choppy water was the cause of failure.

A stall sporting a coconut shy had a few 'target' coconuts that were darker than the rest and as hard as granite, each packed onto a pedestal with a back higher than its front to prevent the coconuts from falling backwards. Each nut was well-seated into tightly compacted sand to prevent them from being dislodged. Very few coconuts became trophies, but, 'hang on a minute', there was always the opportunity to buy one or two hairy balls to impress accompanying lady friends.

'Roll-up - roll-up, everyone's a winner' is what one stallholder kept bawling out, the sound of which penetrated the air from somewhere way off in the distance within the Grand Hall of the Olympia. This particular stall of entertainment with the vocal proprietor had plastic ducks floating around a central pillar festooned with an assortment of stuffed teddy-bears and the like, one of which was the size of the rotund-looking lady herself who perpetually circumvented the whole display. Instead of a magnetic strip of metal, each duck had a large cup-hook affixed to the upper part of its head. Every duck had a black painted number on its underside that guaranteed a prize every time and nearly always a pencil with a fluffy coloured faux-feather stuck on the top. Big Teddy on top never did achieve his freedom, and I'm not so sure if the circumventing Teddy below did either.

A rifle range had a gallery of moving targets and rifles with sights that were way off-kilter. If the stallholder saw a punter hitting too many targets, the weapon would be withdrawn after use and replaced by an even wonkier one. Many of the menfolk taking a pop at whatever was in front of them were likely to have been ex-servicemen, experts at downing an enemy at five-hundred yards, but there they were, finding themselves scratching their heads wondering why they were unable to down a tin duck passing in front of their eyes at fifteen feet. Still, the wonderment of it all was to see many of those sharpshooters leaving the fairground with gleeful facial expressions, sporting crimson-red lipstick on their cheeks and shirt collars along with remanets of pink candyfloss stuck to their hair. Eagerly clutching something fluffy in one hand and a pair of coconuts in the other, macho-man headed home, and, as the 'King of Coconuts' stepped down off bus numbers 9, 27 or 73, or from an overcrowded underground train at Earls Court, the love and pleasure hormones Oxytocin and Dopamine coursing through his veins was a reminder that he was in for a special treat - just for being soooooo smart. Gertcha!

I suspect that when Bertram Mill's Circus had long disappeared into the distance, some of the non-professional fairground stallholders reverted to being Rag 'n' Bone men or 'Knife & Scissor Sharpers' on contraptions that risked giving them yet another strangulated hernia. And, of course, it was all for the fun of the fair.

Back home after the circus had moved on, I was on the lookout for some other means to earn a bob or two. Here are some activities I got up to: -

1. Collected discarded newspapers, taking them in bundles to a shop at the end of the road to weigh and be paid according to weight. However, sometimes I would get less than expected after broken bits of paving slabs mysteriously appeared amongst the papers. Gertcha! The local chip shop would also take newspapers off my hands in exchange for a bag of chips. The newspapers

would be lined with semi-grease-proofed paper to accept the fish and chips, which were then wrapped-up together and handed over to customers.

2. Collecting empty glass Coca-Cola, lemonade and Tizer bottles, returning them to different confectionary shops to retrieve the deposit someone else would have paid.

3. Travelled to the posh parts of the west end of London with a bucket, sponge, and chamois leather, knocking on doors inviting the occupants to have their cars washed. Although I only managed to retain two regular customers who were willing to allow me unfettered access to their most expensive motor cars, it worked.

4. I loaded potatoes into a spud-peeler at the local café, although the employment didn't last long. I would tip the potatoes that looked like disfigured gargoyles into the automatic potato peeling machine, but what came out the other end was nothing short of marbles, no training, and no further prospects of future employment in that café, that was for sure. No worries.

5. After school and on Saturdays, I worked in the local greengrocers while eating my way through chests of bananas and cooked beetroot that had to be boiled in a galvanised bucket. If people could turn purple by over-eating beetroot, as one can turn orange by eating too many carrots, I would indeed have been one of them, exiting the main door on my way home looking not unlike a burgundy-coloured Smurf. After munching a few bananas, I would discard the skins by throwing them over the back wall onto a pathway leading to residential flats above the shops. I do not recall ever hearing the thud of flesh hitting hard surfaces or the uttering of expletives so assumed that some well-meaning public-spirited individual picked up the skins and disposed of

them accordingly - most likely back over the wall. When all the tasks I had to do were complete, I would enter the shop's front and serve customers, tipping their choice of fruit and vegetables directly into their shopping bags while making a mental note of the total amount of money to collect. I was good at serving customers and so allowed to do the same every Saturday.

6. Milk and paper delivery rounds. Every morning, six days a week, come rain or shine, I would be up and out of bed at 6 am to present myself at the nearby 'Turners' newsagent's shop that formed part of a small parade of other shops in Blythe Road. The loading-up of vast amounts of newspapers complete, I would be off on my rounds, pushing customers' choice of reading material through their letterboxes before hurrying off to school.

7. Helping the milk delivery bloke deliver his products was always on a Saturday after completing the newspaper deliveries. Off we'd go, the milkman and I, in an electrically powered 'Milk-float' loaded up to the gunnels with metal-capped bottles of sterilised milk as well as red, silver and gold-topped bottles of pasteurised milk, fresh cream and glass jars filled with unflavoured yoghurts - whatever they were. The door-stop deliveries were carried out over a wide area and took up almost the entire day.

8. I sold newspapers, cigarettes, and tobacco on Sunday mornings from behind the same local newsagent counter that I delivered newspapers. Almost everything in the shop apart from newspapers was subject to Sunday trading laws and should not have been sold. Sleight-of-hand ensured other products were available to customers, passed over the counter beneath purchased copies of Sunday newspapers.

9. I delivered customers' shoes for a chain-smoking nicotine-finger-stained cobbler. The business's proprietor always took immense delight flatulating and laughing, seemingly in a state of terminal decline because of it. It was a relief to deliver customers shoes to escape the workshop's putrid atmosphere, not to mention the bonus of receiving monetary tips.

10. Carol-singing in Kensington and Knightsbridge had mixed results. Only half of the premises visited had occupants that bothered to open their doors. Those who have it, keep it, I guess. One apartment our small group of carol-singers (me and my two sisters) called upon happened to be the home of a wealthy middle-eastern foreign dignitary who invited us in to perform in front of his family. The reward for singing ourselves hoarse after reciting every Christmas Carol known to man was a small box of wooden dolls decorated in their country's traditional costumes or some foul-tasting dates that could only have come from the back-end of a donkey. Merry bloody Christmas!

11. 'Penny-for-the-Guy' begging outside the Odeon cinema in Kensington High Street - now that was a real earner. American tourists, drawn to the presence of a stuffed effigy of Guy Fawkes sporting a paper-mâché facemask and ragged clothes plonked in an old pram, would often inquire about its origins. When the story of 'Gunpowder, treason and plot' rolled out, the money would roll in as I helped myself to coins from their outstretched hands. Taking money from the foreign tourists was easy, especially from the Americans, as those I met had no comprehension of pounds, shilling, and pence – or anything else for that matter, other than knowing how to get to the moon some years later as the rest of the world looked on in disbelief. Half-a-crown pieces (two shillings and sixpence) were always my coin of

preference, but in the absence of any relatively high denominational coins, I focused on anything silver. "God bless America".

12. We were setting up as a skiffle duo (my brother and I) outside a pub in Blythe Road at the top end of Faroe Road, equipped with nothing more than a washboard, sewing thimbles on the tips of each finger, and an old tea-chest with a large hole at its centre. The chest, turned upside down with a broom handle inserted vertically into one corner, had string affixed to the top of the broom-handle, tensioned and diagonally tied down to one of the tea-chest corners. My brother and I twanged and twanged our made-do instrument to create a deep bass sound while singing our hearts out for no more than a few witty comments and a belly full of laughs from the patrons within the pub. At least we tried.

13. I scrubbed the stone steps fronting a chapel in Kensington Church Street, London (opposite what was then the Queen's Household Cavalry's barracks) to remove algae and urine stains of both man and dogs. I came home smelling of a sewer rat with an attitude to match. I only did it once and earned little more than my bus-fare home. Bless you, my child. Halle-blummin-lu-iah.

Visitors hardly ever called at our house, although occasionally one would knock on the front door to hand over discarded clothes. If I answered, I would refuse the offerings as pride would not allow me to accept them. My mother would go ballistic if and when she found out only for me to be chased up the stairs and given a 'bloody good hiding' with an iron fire-grate poker for doing so, without ever listening to my reasoning. Many-a-time I recall running up the stairs to my bedroom and barricading the door, holding out for as long as I could with my legs pushing against whatever I had put behind it in a vain attempt to stop 'Poker Girl' crashing through; poker in hand.

The beatings I had to endure from my mother went on until I was big and strong enough to keep the door shut or until my mother, tired of pushing and unable to gain access, retreated downstairs. After such encounters, I usually stayed out of the way, choosing to remain in my bedroom or else dashed to the front door until things calmed down. Apart from my brother and the chicken bones necklace episode, there were a couple of other noticeable acts of kindness. Whenever I hurt, cut, or grazed myself getting up to all kinds of mischief, I would always have to deal with the issues myself except on one occasion when I developed a large boil on the temple of my head, so large as to be visible from the rooftop of the nearby block of flats. It was a lady further down Faroe Road that tended to the infection by applying a poultice of bread soaked in hot milk, held together with a bandage wrapped around my head starting from under my chin. I arrived back home looking like the Dutch artist Meneer Vincent van Gogh after he cut off his left ear's bottom half. My mother didn't even know I had a boil and didn't seem to care. An elderly couple who lived next door (the other side to Peggy the Bulldog) gave me four three-penny pieces every Saturday morning that I was required to share with my siblings. I habitually sat on the dividing wall at the front of our house at the same time each Saturday every week until the money was forthcoming – then I'd be gone.

Other acts of kindness were sometimes shown by others, none more so than the old 'battle-axe' lady further down the road, the same person who threw buckets of water at copulating dogs and tandem bicycle riders. Enraged at being the recipient of my constant larrup each time I sped past on my bicycle, the fiery lady was determined that I should receive a free gift. The unexpected present came in the form of a long-handled broom that went straight through the front-wheel spokes of my bike, sending me 'Arse-over-head' crashing to the ground. Every part of me hurt, especially my knees, the fall having inflicted a deep graze laceration after coming into contact with the newly laid fine-stone road surface applied by the council to deter children from drawing chalk patterns on an otherwise smooth tarmac surface. I steered a wide berth afterwards that encounter - that was for sure. There was no point telling my mother as I might well have received a so-called 'Bloody-good-hiding' just for upsetting the neighbours.

At the age of nine, or ten, I remember being accompanied by two charming people who took me by train to Orpington in Kent, where Mrs Daish, one of several hosts, offered her home and family life experience as part of a charitable scheme for underprivileged London children. I spent a long hot summer's week as part of the family, going to various places, sharing meals, and attending church on the one Sunday I was there. Rumour spread that after I walked out of the church, two or three roof rafters collapsed. I experienced kindness and understanding, even to the point of being allowed to pick raspberries from their garden to eat at will. After I left and returned home, the raspberry canes looked as though they had been got at by a swarm of locusts. Staying with my host family was the first time I had used a toothbrush and the first time I felt wanted since my father's death. It was an experience I shall never, ever forget. And I love raspberries. Thank you, Mr, and Mrs Daish, wherever or whichever one of the seven planes of existence you currently find yourselves, and, if you're able to read this book over my shoulder, please do not make me aware of your presence as I am too easily spooked.

One of the very few boys I dared call a friend lived further down the road on the opposite side to where I lived. The boy was none-other than Arfer Mow, who became a specialist grass-cutter. Arfer, hereinafter referred to as Toby, had a fascination with German wartime paraphernalia, owning an endless collection of pictures, tin helmets, gas-masks, Nazi badges and bayonets affixed to his bedroom walls. There was even a German Lugar pistol under his bed, an experience he allowed me to share. That was nice. His parents were also kind by inviting me to join them on a trip to Brighton in their old red coloured look-alike Brooke Bond Tea van. Off we went one Saturday morning, their son and I sat on a mattress in the back, during which time I developed a bout of uncontrollable flatulence. I blamed their son Toby (a trick learnt from my mother), which raised such an almighty stink, with arguments going on-and-on and the boy's mother vowing never to take me on a seaside trip again. Despite the protestations, my friend's dad, who was giving up taxi driving, invited a couple of other children and me to join him on a 'lap of honour' around London in his old grey spoked-wheeled Hackney Carriage. The taxi was of the type with a squeezable rubber 'honker' instead of a car battery operated warning horn. As a final act of celebration after completing a tour of 'The West End', we were all treated to one of those pseudo cheesecakes that didn't have a trace of cheese and a cup of tea at the Lyons Corner House near the Odeon cinema in Kensington High Street.

Of course, Christmas is a time for giving except for our family, the giving was to ourselves. As children, any money we managed to save throughout the year went to buy presents, but only for ourselves. I usually bought two cardboard boxes from Woolworths that contained a sweet shop and a toy post office. A cardboard box depicting the front view of a post office and pop-up shelves within, along with a similar package with a picture of a sweetshop that contained miniature bottles of bead-like sweets, was my only treat. I recall my mother using some of the money I had saved throughout the year to buy myself a Christmas present of a Timex wrist. Curious as always, it wasn't long before I had the back off to find out about its workings, damaging the watch beyond repair in the process. My siblings and I were never encouraged to buy for each other, so we didn't.

 The late Mr Baggs, a married gentleman who lived in Faroe Road next to Toby, took a shine to my mother, probing my mother's reaction for every salacious detail of her interaction when spending time with her in the passage-way of our house. Eavesdropping at every opportunity, my brother and I would hear the words 'Dik-Dik' (what-what?) often repeated, believing that our exploitative licentious visitor's first name must have been a double-barrelled version of Richard. It wasn't until years later it dawned on me that one or other of them must have been referring to a National Geographic story about the small Dik-Dik (what-what?) antelope that lives and hides in the woodlands and forests of eastern Kenya and Southern Africa; it being a small animal, knee-high to a grasshopper relative to its larger cousins that roam the African plains.

Mr Baggs's enormous generosity extended to Christmas Day one year when my mother was invited over to his house next to the boy with the Lugar pistol, to share a 'tipple' with him and his wife, leaving us children alone at home wondering when we were going to get our Christmas dinner. By his compassionate nature, Mr Baggs must have given my mother something special because she came rolling home sometime after lunchtime, looking the worse for wear and promptly went up the stairs to bed. The capon hanging upside down in the 'Tall-boy' cupboard remained hanging upside down in the 'Tall-boy' cupboard, stripped bare – with one eye open!

One final act of compassion and generosity was afforded to us a few days before Christmas when we were visited by my mother's youngest of four siblings and her boyfriend, whose name I didn't get to know. During the brief moment at our house, Auntie Nora gave each of us children a bundled packet of four 'Spangles' hard-boiled multi-flavoured square-shaped sweets as a Christmas present before wishing us a 'Merry Christmas' and beating a hasty retreat. Her visit was an act of bravery. My mother's other siblings and grandmother had very little or nothing to do with us and might well have confronted our visitors on their return back to wherever they came.

School Days

I had just turned five years of age when school beckoned. Off I went at the start of my first term in September 1952 to St Paul's Church of England Infant School, part of the church of the same name in Hammersmith Broadway. As I remember, the only classroom happened to be down some very steep stone steps on the side of the church's main building, which led into some dark, austere rooms. It was probably obvious I was the youngest, smallest, poorest but best-groomed looking toddler in the class, with a hairstyle that even Adolf what's his-name would have envied. I was my father's pride and joy.

Sundays involved having to attend Bible Classes at St. Paul's church, accompanied by my two sisters while our parents were at home. My mum would probably be looking after baby John, habitually boiling the guts out of potatoes and cabbage in preparation for lunch while at the same time Henry Gilbert might well have been rolling cigarettes using recycled tobacco as we made our way to and from Sunday school. Returning home from church, we had to show my dad a stamp depicting a religious figure or scene adhered within the pages of a small Sunday school attendance book to prove we had been there. I do not have any other recollections of the church or Sunday school for that matter, as our family must have been on the move some months later. Hallelujah!

After attending St Paul's Church of England Infants' School in Hammersmith, having moved to Faroe Road, I found myself at Addison Gardens Infants School's school gates. The building had been sub-divided from the secondary school of the same name, where I was to spend eighteen unremarkable months.

From the age of seven, I attended Lena Gardens Primary School on a Road called Lena Gardens! The school was just metres from the London Underground route on the

Metropolitan Line from Shepherd's Bush to Hammersmith, close to an engineering workshop that emanated loud noises throughout the day and heard in every classroom. How we ever got past A, B & Clickety-clack in the alphabet was a mystery.

Miss Grilles was my school teacher at Lena Gardens, and I recall her as a kind person, always tying my shoelaces when I arrived at school. There was a little-used rear entrance to the school playground with an open wooden gate where a man selling toffee apples would appear, holding a wooden tomato tray supported by a length of string that had been looped around his neck. Inside the tray were his creations stacked high, ready to sell to the children in the playground. Not having any money to buy a toffee apple, I would hang around until the school hand-bell sounded to summon everyone back into a single file before being led off to their respective classrooms. If there was ever one toffee apple remaining, I had hoped to have been the recipient, but that never the case. The toffee apple man smelled.

It was a typical day at school at Lena Gardens (or so I thought) when the whole class went off in a coach somewhere for the day on an excursion paid for by their parents. I was left behind. After the coach departed, the teachers who stayed back at school were left wondering what to do with me. With few options open to them, I found myself in a lower-year all-girls sewing class where I made a pin-cushion in the shape of a fish. I received some sympathetic recognition for my efforts, but little interest shown by my mother when I arrived home with it.

Four years at Lena Gardens Primary School came and went, punctuated with regular visits to the dentist. I, along with a multitude of other children, were lined-up and seated, only to be gassed to a state of delirious stupidity, coming back to our senses at some unfathomable time later holding a white enamelled bowl with a blue rim that contained blood and sputum while at the same time vomiting and looking like happy demented pumpkins on their way to a Halloween party.

Fillings of any kind did not happen. When it came to dental treatment, it was always a case of 'Out or nowt'. Yorkshire, you'll understand.

Impetigo, a bacterial infection of the skin, usually manifested itself around the nose and mouth of those afflicted and a scourge for some of the more poverty-stricken amongst us that required visits to the local clinic during school time. A person dressed in medical clothing applied mauve ink-like iodine to puss-filled scabs before those of us that were afflicted returned to school looking like psychedelic pufferfish with clown-like expressions around the noses of those whose bacterial infection was rampant. The only tangible items I took away from school after four years of learning was the art of silent begging for toffee apples and the hand-made paper-chain Christmas decorations that nobody else wanted. I left Lena Gardens Primary School at the age of ten years and eleven months without ever knowing how many teeth I left behind or if I had even sat the Eleven Plus exam that determined whether I should go to a grammar school if I passed or secondary school if I didn't.

I had just turned eleven when I found myself walking through a Secondary School's gates for the first time. I wore a free school uniform which had the school's crest emblazoned on the jacket. The school was situated on the road called Addison Gardens, the same place where I had attended as an infant and very conveniently just a few streets away from where I lived. As a generalisation, it always seemed odd to me that only private, grammar or high schools had names of famous people other than that of the streets they occupied.

Addison Gardens school, a Victorian building set amongst residential houses, looked formidable enough with its oversized windows and iron-grill gates leading from the road into the playground. Above each entry point into the playground were the words 'Boys' and 'Girls' cast in stone, although any girls had long gone; too dangerous for them, I suspect – at least then. From memory, the school's upper floors were accessible from the outside via dark stone stairways that led down to the tarmac surfaced playground outside.

The September intake of 1958, of which I was part, consisted of about a hundred or so pupils divided into four groups, selected to attend classes 1a, 1b, 1c or 1d depending on some obscure assessment unbeknown to man – or me. I found myself in level 1b but within two weeks moved to level 1a. I don't know if the teacher of the former was unable to put up with my intemperate habits or that I demonstrated a modicum of intelligence. In any event, I moved up and, being the youngest and smallest of my class, soon became the target of bullies. There was an occasion when rushing up one of the stone stairways of the school, a boy in front turned and pushed me back down the first flight. I received a broken wrist but conditioned as I was to accept pain and violence, did not report the incident for fear of retribution. Physical pain was no stranger to me, so I was able to nurse my arm in silence throughout the remaining part of the afternoon before taking myself off to the hospital in Hammersmith, some thirty minutes or so walk away. Once home, sporting a plaster-cast on my left forearm, I told my mum what had happened, but nothing came of my experience, and no-one held to account. I think I was still twelve.

After school, extra-curricular activities were non-existent (for me anyway) except choir practice which I thoroughly enjoyed, probably because of the absence of anyone trying to make my life a misery. The music teacher alone gave me encouragement to demonstrate the best of what I had to offer, which led to being part of the school choir singing my heart out in Hammersmith Town Hall to some dignitaries or other and choir members' proud parents. My mother was not there.

There was a time, and only the one time as far as I can remember, when the entire class had an away-day visiting The Victoria & Albert Museum in Kensington, London. Packed lunches were the order of the day, requiring all pupils to bring their food from home. All kinds of edible delights were tumbling out of wrappers, including fruit, chocolate bars and

Smith's Crisps with the blue salt twists lovingly packed by mums. My lunch consisted of two rounds of thinly sliced white bread from the Co-op 'filled' with a smearing of plum jam that I had put together myself – nothing else, not even margarine, but it didn't matter - I was used to it.

At school, being the victim of physical and violent bullying was an everyday occurrence. I was often the recipient of physical abuse for reasons that I can only assume was being small for my age, showing physical signs of poverty and neglect, known to come from a family whose mother was less than caring but, more poignantly; didn't have a father. I was less able to physically stand up for myself and, without the support and help from anyone, became a punch-bag to a select few who chose to see me that way. I stood out from others of my class in other ways as I seemed to have had a perpetual cold, constantly wiping my nose on the sleeve of a second-hand woven ginger-coloured overcoat or else ripping out the black lining of it to be used as a handkerchief. I became known as 'Snotty-nosed Henry' in need of some unorthodox attention by some tough guys. I spent most of each day ignoring the lessons, pre-occupied and worrying about how I would avoid a bashing at the school gates following a stream of threats. I almost always managed to outwit my pursuers by planning escape routes during lesson time, often exiting the school via the 'prohibited' teachers' stairway, except on one occasion when, coming out of that very stairway, I was spotted by a couple of older boys who were out looking for me. The same two boys chased me from the school gates to the front door of our house. Terrified and frantically hammering on the front door, my mother opened it and gave me a wallop in front of my pursuers as punishment for banging so hard, pulled me into the house and closed the door. Win-win for a couple of thugs, I'd say.

When I was about fourteen, I was at school and remember being pounced upon by a couple of the usual bullies, one of whom drew up copious amounts of phlegm from as far down as the membrane separating his guts from his scrotum before spitting the accumulated mass into my face. I had had enough by then and found enough courage and determination to do something about it by promptly marching up to the headmaster's office with phlegm still hanging on my face. I appeared at the headmaster's secretary's office, uttering the two culprits' names, but it was a wrong move. I was given some toilet paper by the secretary to remove the offending sputum and told to 'Buggar off'. That was that. I went back to the playground straight into the arms of the perpetrators who would teach me not to 'grouse'.

There were only two other occasions I had cause to go to the headmaster's office, one of which was to collect two sheets of light-tan coloured toilet paper impregnated with Izal disinfectant that sometimes doubled-up as tracing paper, along with a key for gaining access to the toilet block. The toilets were always locked, denying access to pupils that smoked cigarettes, although that didn't stop them from smoking them anyway. Ironically, the school's back-end by the teacher's entrance was the area of choice for smoking after the toilet block, presumably because there was so much cigarette smoke wafting from the teachers' staff-room, boys smoking close-by would have gone unnoticed. The second visit to the headmaster's office was for a less favourable reason.

The cigarettes of choice for the intrepid under-age smokers congregating at the teachers' entrance consisted of low-grade factory-floor sweepings of tobacco, marketed as 'Dominoes' and could be purchased by anyone regardless of age from a small tuck-shop just yards away from the school gates. The short paper open-ended wallets that contained four cigarettes were of a red and cream colour that resembled a domino in every detail. The school playground would occasionally be awash with Domino cigarettes following a burglary at the shop selling them. Very few parents were ever seen at the school gates, although the police were often in attendance.

To say Addison Gardens school was rough would have been a gross understatement. My form classroom was the science laboratory with benches serving as desk-tops. The only scientific experiments that I remember were always undertaken by the teacher and not the pupils. One such experience was to demonstrate the conductivity of different materials, glass in particular. A cold glass bottle was partially submerged in boiling water, and, 'Crack', the bottle shattered. I was tempted to tell the science teacher that an easier way to achieve a more spectacular result would have been to insert a 2d tuppenny banger firework into the bottle, but that would have resulted in a caning. Anyway, I wasn't impressed with the experiment as I'd seen the same result countless times at home. The second experiment involved each pupil being handed a dessert-spoon full of mercury just to demonstrate how heavy the stuff was. Forget mercury poisoning. The third experiment showed how an electric current could only flow by creating a complete circuit. To illustrate a cause and effect, pupils had to form a continuous line by holding each other's hand in a way that only boys were prepared to do. A hand-operated generator affixed to a bench had two protruding metal terminals, one positively charged and the other negatively charged. The circuit became complete when boys on both ends of the handline grasped the generator's two terminals as the teacher vigorously cranked the generator to create a current. As each individual broke the circuit when the electric shock became too much to bear, the teacher would mention Ohms Law, but that was lost on most of us. The only Ohms Law anyone was interested in was the one that involved going home.

    The worktops within the science laboratory were higher than standard school desks, which provided an opportunity for all kinds of skulduggery while experiments were going on. One particular individual who appeared to look much older and physically more advanced for his years took to unbuttoning his trousers to expose himself in all his glory. Boys otherwise engaged turning on gas-taps and showing little interest in what the science teacher was doing had a stark reminder about what growing-up would be all about. It really did happen. It was rumoured that the boy in question later suffered rapid eyesight failure, although, to be fair, he did get to work in an unlicenced Kennels and might well have hosted parasite worms usually found in dog excrement. Gertcha!

Some pupils' deeds in the playground in the absence of teacher supervision of any kind included setting fire to bits of paper and unattended clothing items by intensifying sunlight through a magnifying glass. Some individuals even made hand-held darts by binding four matchsticks to a sewing needle with strong cotton thread, finished off with a paper flight at the end. The darts were then thrown towards the backs and calf-muscles of unsuspecting hapless individuals as they passed by.

Violence was an everyday occurrence and not just the preserve of school bullies. Teachers were also privileged to indiscriminately dishing out summary justice at their own discretion when not huddled together in the all-male smoke-filled staff-room drinking tea or whatever else, having little regard or concern about what was going on in the playground.

For the whole four years at Addison Gardens, my form teacher was a tall man with feet so large he would have been unable to fall forward flat on his face if any of us had succeeded in tripping him up. The teacher had what must easily have been size thirteen or fourteen gym-shoes that he kept in his desk drawer. Whenever the teacher felt the need to punish someone (usually me), the dreaded over-sized plimsole would appear from a drawer with utterings of "Come here, Darling." Ordered to bend over in full view of the class, I received whacks across the backside that were always extremely painful, mainly as I did not wear underpants. Humiliating. If caught doing anything untoward, which could have been as little as not applying due diligence, the punishment was a whip of the cane across both hands, administered as hard as possible, noticeable by the teacher's jaw muscles rippling as the blows rained down. This same teacher sent me to the headmaster on one occasion to receive 'Six-of-the-best', the dreaded terminology for receiving three whacks to each hand from a cane. The punishment meted out away from pupils' gaze by the headmaster Mr Jenkins was for reasons I have never been able to fathom. The pain inflicted was excruciating to the point I could not grasp anything with my hands for a considerable amount of time afterwards. Other teachers would throw a blackboard duster made up of hard felt-like material affixed to a wooden block at any boy not paying sufficient attention. In itself, the projectile did not present a hazard if the start-point of trajectory was by the blackboard, as it was easy to see it coming - but not always. There was an ever-present threat of a teacher approaching from behind to mete out a hard slap to the back of one's head, for goodness knows what. I can only guess the teacher must have spotted headlice as he passed by. Gertcha!

Mr Gardener was our woodwork teacher and the least-violent staff member, tolerant of almost everything except if a boy cut himself while incorrectly using a hand-tool. A whack across one hand with a length of wood dowel would be the reward before the unfortunate soul would be given a first-aid sticking plaster or bandage to stem the bleeding. No-one ever mentioned the violence dished out by the teachers to their parents for fear of a thrashing for having misbehaved in the first place. The authority of adults was never questioned or challenged, whosoever they happened to be.

Mr Steel (I'm guessing) was a chap that held lessons on working with metal. Oh, be joyful. He wasn't a teacher as such and not cloned to mete out physical punishment. However, if any boy injured himself when working with metal, as a penalty, the hapless individual would be denied access to the first-aid cabinet. No pain of punishment, but no sympathy either. It was rumoured that Mr Steel took the first-aid plasters home with him, but I'm not sure about that.

During my final year at school, new subjects were added to the school curriculum, including metalwork (as mentioned), working with plastic and last but not least, the French language. Apart from everyday lessons in history, geography, maths, and English, other than those mentioned, no new or meaningful academic subjects were available. A few weeks into metalwork, I achieved nothing more than a multitude of cuts, often coming out of the classroom, looking as if I had been to an Abattoirs convention. I turned my back on the subject and returned to woodwork. I did pretty well in fiddling about with wood, making a couple of coffee tables and an upright dining chair, which, when taken home, ended up as firewood very soon afterwards.

Plastic Engineering classes; now, they were a laugh. The future is plastic, or so our teacher told us. The instructor, an aged gentleman of about one-hundred-and-fifty years (I'm guessing again), 'oiked in' from God-knows-where, or else resurrected from the church cemetery in Hammersmith, gave each class two hours a week of his time. We learned how to make an envelope-opening paper-knife. Four or five different coloured laminated sheets would be stuck together and fashioned into the shape of a dagger (a dagger, for Christ's sake – at our school of all places) using a fret-saw and files before being sanded-down and polished to perfection. That was it, a year's work. I took my creation home and promptly lost sight of it.

History lessons had to be taken seriously. The teacher of the subject was a very stern chap demanding diligence from all those present. I did learn quite a bit about past events, especially about feudal systems in early times. The history of the Royalty was of little interest to me, so too was the events of the American Civil War of 1861, until someone in the class blurted out that his Great, Great somebody or other was killed there. When challenged to explain how the boy's relative became caught up in an event so far from British shores, the wag replied' "He went over there to complain about the noise". Whoops!

French language lessons were introduced into the school for the first time during my last year at Addison Gardens. A certain Mademoiselle Fleur Blancmange was in for a rude awakening. Two weeks into the curriculum, Mlle. Fleur made a monumental error by addressing a boy who was being disruptive as a 'Nincompoop' and 'silly arse'. Well, the whole class erupted into chaos. Control of the classroom became history as the teacher exited the classroom quicker than she came in – never to return. The only French picked up by any of us sounded remarkedly similar to English spoken profane expletives. Even condoms became known as 'French Letters, although, in the absence of any girls, their only use was to be filled with water and used as projectiles. Once thrown, the condoms bounced around the tarmac surfaced playground until reaching an intended target, or else became snagged on the corner of the school's jagged brick walls, discharging the contents over a wide area and whoever happened to be in the vicinity. It was, after all, a 'boys only' school.

Every now and again, without prior warning of what was to come, impromptu visits by a team of stern-looking people in white 'doctor coats' would summon every boy, class by class, to have their hair inspected for headlice and nits. Once examined, the class members would return from whence they came, minus me, of course. One of the attending nurses would then escort me onto an old St. John's-type ambulance before being taken to a London County Council treatment station somewhere near to the Lime Grove public baths and subjected to a de-lousing process. I would be returned in the same former ambulance that was so obvious to everyone what it was; the only thing missing that could have drawn a more extensive crowd would have been a marching band. Once back at school, I was placed back into class with my hair looking like I had just returned from a Carnival in Rio De Janeiro, stinking of something akin to creosote. Thank goodness there was only ever an hour or so remaining before the school bell would go off, signifying that we could all go home. I could then retrieve a modicum of personal dignity by doing a disappearing act in the hope that by the following morning, my classmates had forgotten about the previous day's events. At home, scrambling to get up the stairs to bed with the stench of medication wafting from my hair, the bed bugs would allow me some respite by going off and organising a bed-bug convention in someone else's bed. But they always came back.

Sports days at Addison Gardens involved climbing aboard a bus and transported to some far-off playing fields through a lack of sports facilities within the school's tarmac-surfaced compound. Football was the 'Be-all and end-all' of activities during winter months, or cross-country running by default. While on the football pitch, I often found myself the unwanted recipient of a football with a couple of thugs intentionally kicking the ball in my direction as they made a bee-line towards me from further down the field. In an attempt to distance me from the ball and approaching adversaries, wearing smooth-soled plimsoll shoes instead of football boots, I would slip 'arse-over-head' in the mud before being trampled on by someone's studded football boots. No surprise then that I opted out of football in favour of cross-country running, where I would be left alone.

Cricket replaced football during the summer months, but after the gangly waving of a cricket bat with little coordination and looking like a demented praying mantis, I received a cricket ball in my groin and fell to the ground writhing in agony. The sports teacher decided that team sport, and in particular, cricket was not for me. Cross country running was back on the list, which amounted to nothing more than being sent off along a country track with instructions to be back at the shower block after whatever was going on in the playing fields had finished.

The very last weeks at school were underway, although there were more than one-hundred or so boys due to leave, only twelve places were available for the best of the bunch to move up to Class 5T the following year to gain one or more GCE examinations. From the thirteenth boy onwards, everyone else, regardless of their potential or academic achievements, had to attend the 'Careers Advisory Officer' to be allocated a job from a list of willing employers. Only fourteen years of age at the time of the job selection, I had been assigned to be a 'Van Driver's Assistant'.

"Sorry, sir, I don't want to do that," I remember saying. "I'm going into the Army."

"You're not old enough, Sonny," came a patronising response.

I stoically looked on before being shown the exit. "Next!"

Mischievous Meanderings

Memories of London 1958 – 1962 were traffic-jammed streets with trolleybuses, black cab taxis and red diesel buses spewing out masses of black smoke onto everything and everyone standing at bus stops. I suspect, as almost everyone smoked cigarettes or pipes, a little bit of extra pollution added to the mix would have gone unnoticed as people wretched and coughed their guts out waiting for the next bus, like the one that had left them standing at the bus stop would have been packed. When buses were half-full, passengers would almost always be on the smokers' upper deck, leaving the lower-level empty. It must have been a nightmare for the driver struggling to prevent his or her bus from tipping over as they steered it around every corner, sucking in every breath of smoke-filled air from the passengers on the upper deck and the toxic fumes of London traffic pouring in through an open side window of the driver's cab. It came as no surprise that cardiac arrest was the primary cause of premature deaths among bus drivers.

Bombsites and derelict houses were common-place, as were one-legged men propped up on almost every street corner, supported by upside-down 'A' shaped wooden crutches topped with leather, tucked under their armpits, the vacant trouser leg neatly pressed and pinned up. These men must have been casualties of war, as there were so many of them. Proudly standing bolt upright on street corners or outside large public buildings, habitually smoking hand-rolled cigarettes, those veterans appeared as if they yearned to be part of the bustle of everyday life.

Vagrants, men and women, also referred to as 'Tramps', were common-place, often seen pushing old prams loaded up to the gunnels with their worldly belongings. Very occasionally, I would stumble across lonely souls settled in amongst the debris of bombed-out houses or under railway arches with only themselves and a pet dog or cat for company.

Perhaps the songwriter Ralph McTell took his inspiration to write the song Streets of London in 1969 by seeing many of the things I and others would have also seen throughout the 1950s and 1960s.

The year 1958 saw the start of an all-out bus strike in London for reasons of no importance to me at the age of ten. The strike lasted from 5th May to 20th June of that year, causing absolute mayhem to the travelling public, especially commuters getting in and out of London. Hordes of would-be passengers used to assemble in Hammersmith Broadway by the main bus stops when public-spirited drivers of cars would pull in alongside hordes of impatient passengers, displaying a cardboard sign indicating the destination of the vehicle that could be easily seen through the car windscreen. A mad scramble would ensue with people piling into strangers' cars to get home as quickly as possible. The effort as a whole was akin to the Dunkirk Spirit, with everyone everywhere pulling together for the common good. Throughout the strike, it was not unusual for me and someone from my class at school to take advantage of the situation by joining the weary homeward-bound crowds at Hammersmith Broadway, cadging lifts that invariably took us to Richmond Park. I would return home soon after dark each evening, hungry and often soaking wet, having walked back without so much as being asked, "Where have you been?"

It was on one such trip to Richmond Park when I happened upon four fledgeling jackdaws scampering around on the grass under the tree from where they had fallen. I picked one up, intending to take it home but, while walking towards the nearby road within the park, a car drove up; the driver got out and said he would take the jackdaw from me and hand it over to the park warden at the gatehouse on his way out. Obedient as always to grown-ups, I handed over the little mite only to see the car swiftly leave the park without stopping. I went back to the tree and picked up another fledgeling but, this time managed to get it home. Unlike the name I called the man that nicked my first fledgeling, I called my jackdaw - Jack! Jack was a trusting friend to me during the summer months of 1958, staying close by or perched on my shoulder wherever I went. He was untethered and free to fly whenever he or she chose, even going with me to school sat on my shoulder pirate style only to end up being placed in a cardboard box on a window sill for the duration of each day. I kept my dickie bird in a cage within my former bedroom that had the burnt floor before my mum demanded its removal out into the garden. I took Jack down to the scullery at the bottom of the stairs, but that was not enough – he or she had to go to the garden. The cage ended up outside in full view of neighbouring cats and endless streams of doggie-swingers, which must have frightened my friend witless.

One Saturday morning towards the end of summer, I had gone out, leaving Jack behind only to return and find the cage empty with the door wide open. One of my family members must have been responsible, probably my mother. It didn't take long to see my feathered friend on the ridge of the roof, making an almighty racket as cats circled below. Up I went to the slate roof via the first storey balcony and then the second, before inching my way over the guttering towards the ridge where I half expected the entire cast of 'Mary Poppins' to jump out from behind the chimney pots, but the only other thing moving around apart from me, was my birdie. I managed to grab Jack before heading back down, slithering over the eave gutter as I went. Using my feet to feel for the drainpipes that guided me down to safety, I managed to get to the balcony below, narrowly missing a fall into next door's backyard where Peggy the Bulldog was eagerly awaiting my acquaintance. 'Phew'- it was close. Two weeks later, Jack was dead, having been left out in the cold and probably terrorised by ever-present marauding cats and the perpetual spectacle of doggie goings-on.

We didn't have a television as far as I remember for most or all of my time living in Faroe Road. Still, my mother, one of my sisters and younger brother were often invited into a house further along the road to watch someone else's television instead. On one particular evening after arriving home soaking wet, having trudged all the way back from Richmond Park, I was starving hungry and vainly attempted to find something to munch by letting myself into our house using the oversized mortice key hanging on a piece of string behind the door. No-one was at home, and I found nothing that I could eat. As darkness fell, I set off back up the road when I spotted my mother sitting in comfort inside someone's house watching television. Everyone in that room, including my mother, my eldest sister, and my younger brother, knew I was outside but most likely chose to ignore me on my mother's instructions. I sat down on a rain-sodden pavement with my back to the railings of the house until my family came out after the BBC television channel had come to a close. The sound of the National Anthem, along with a test-card appearing in the centre of the screen, followed by a diminishing black dot that morphed into a blank screen, was an indication my mother and siblings were on the move.

Running amok around London, was usually with my little brother John who followed me like a bad smell (his words not mine). I always seemed to wear the same school uniform with my arse hanging out the back of torn trousers and bits of cornflakes packets visible through holes in the soles of my shoes. The image of the Kellogg's red cockerel flashing into view at each alternate step when walking at speed must have been enough to induce an epileptic fit to anyone watching. And never with neatly tied shoelaces.

    My first pair of 'decent' non-school uniform trousers was a pair of denim jeans I bought from Shepherd's Bush market using the money earned from my endeavours. I was thirteen. The jeans cost a princely sum of ten shillings (50p). The fashion of the time was to wear denim jeans with turned-up trouser bottoms, not to be trendy, you'll understand, it was just that there was only ever one length available – long. The shorter the legs of the wearer, the larger the turn-up. During the cold months of winter, I often wore a multi-coloured jumper made up of unravelled wool from previously worn garments that had seen better days or had become too small for any of my family to wear.

In and around London, especially at weekends and during school holidays, usually involved my brother and I jumping on and off London Underground trains with a set target of visiting as many stations as possible without being grabbed by a ticket inspector. However, we always managed to evade getting caught whenever we completed our journeys through the entire underground network. Whatever train we were on as we arrived at a station, my brother and I would always alight and make our way up to ground-level to ascertain our whereabouts before diving back down again into the underground network. Our behaviour was not unlike meerkats on the African Serengeti Plains or the 'Wurthefukarwe' nomadic tribe of Borneo. The jungle guys of the far-flung isles in the Pacific Ocean were known to become disorientated as they moved about under the forest canopies, so much so that whenever they came across a clearing in the forest floor, they would always shout out their tribal identity:

"Wurthefukarwe!!?"

Running after London Transport buses and hopping onto the passenger rear access boarding platform just as the buses pulled away became a regular pastime. My brother John and I would test the bus conductor's observation powers to see how far we could get before being noticed, only to jump off when speed allowed. It was great fun. In the 1950s, when new immigrants arrived from the Caribbean on the Windrush passenger ship to help fulfil the acute shortage of workers, many became bus conductors. It was these same guys we had to watch as they were always swift to spot non-fare payers, unlike the regular ones who didn't seem to care less as they stood on the rear boarding platform with an arm and leg crooked around a vertical pole, smoking rolled-up cigarettes. Electrically powered trolleybuses were a different challenge altogether, in that they went from a stop position to 35mph in a micro-second, making boarding on-the-move almost impossible. The trolleybus drivers were always on the lookout for children like us, peering in their rear-view mirrors, waiting until the last moment before flooring the accelerator pedal. Whooooooosh! It wouldn't have been the first time I left the remains of cornflakes packets, nasal mucus and the occasional 'biological skiddy' on the road. I desperately wanted to be a trolleybus driver.

Skedaddling on bicycles was also a regular activity facilitating the means to cause mischief somewhere. Apart from the lady at the bottom of the road that caused me to come off my bicycle, Mr Baggs, a close friend of my mother that I mentioned earlier, was often the recipient of derisory verbal comments from me, especially about his thick Yorkshire accent. He would do nothing other than exclaim, "I'll 'ave thee for thy cheek", which of course was not going to happen because he knew that I knew of his clandestine goings-on with my mother. Aye-oup, Mister Baggs, aye-oup! Gertcha!

Bicycles I took possession of came and went; all of them made up of spare parts from discarded or abandoned frames supplemented with bits from Halfords, Woolworths, and the like. I always painted my bikes with Valspar 2-4 hours lacquer bought from Woolworths along with transfers to make them look as near as possible to the new ones that other boys had. Later, I became the proud owner of a tandem bicycle that I obtained from a pile of junk dumped on a nearby bombsite when, on one particular occasion, my brother and I used to trail uninvited behind some other boys on their posh brand-spanking-new bikes. I was the rider at the front of the tandem with my younger brother seated behind peddling like fury in an attempt to keep up as the group disappeared into the distance. It didn't help to have the wrong sized pedals and chain cogs which caused the chains to repeatedly come off, leaving us isolated from the leading group. My brother and I got home late, much later than anyone else, our hands covered in dirty grease as a result of having to repeatedly put the chains back onto the gear-cogs. Of course, my brother was to blame each time we came to a stop, accused of not peddling on occasions, which in later life admitted was the case.

Towards the end of my time in Faroe Road, I recall having what must have been my best bicycle, painted and polished to perfection, secured to the railings fronting our house. The same older boy that stuffed dog excrement into Toby's mouth appeared one Saturday morning shouting for me to come out onto the road. Choosing not to for fear of being fed a hotdog sandwich, I watched from the front room window as he wrenched my bicycle from its anchor point, trashing it right in front of my eyes. I called for my mother to come and help, but she was having none of it, preferring instead to stay indoors and not cause a fuss. The bike was a complete wreck. The outcome might have been very different if my dad had been alive, who might well have gone out in his collar-less shirt, margarine ash-sodden trousers held up by broad strapped braces and broad waistline belt to confront the perpetrator, but who would by which time have long disappeared.

And still on the subject of bicycles: there was a friendly family that came over from Ireland to move into a house further up the road. The family included two grown sons, one of whom used to ride a bicycle to and from his workplace, habitually leaning it against his house's front railings once he had arrived home. Early one dark winter's evening, a total stranger appeared on a bicycle as I passed the same bike leant against the railings. The stranger explained that the unattended bicycle owner was at work and needed someone to take it to him. As I trusted all grown-ups, I fell hook, line and sinker for his story and obediently took the bike and followed the stranger to 'Charles House', a tower block of offices in Kensington, where I knew the owner of the bike worked. The thief gave me two shillings (10p) for my help and literally told me to piss-off, not caring in the least about the consequences I would have to face when I got back home. There was a welcome party waiting for me when I got back to Faroe Road from the family whose bike had gone missing. I was promptly frog-marched down to Hammersmith Police Station on the Shepherds Bush Road to give an account of my actions. My mother did not attend the police station, and nothing came of it. I do not remember what happened to the two shillings except wonder if it went towards purchasing a set of spare brake-blocks for a new bicycle the aggrieved had to acquire. There it is.

There was an old Victorian single-storey red-brick building further down Faroe Road, opposite to where I lived, an Art Studio at the time of writing. My mother worked in the same building when it had been a central cooking depot preparing school meals, tasked with having to mash potatoes for local schools – that was until she had a 'little accident' in the ladies' toilets, leaving it for others to find.

She would have got away with her indiscretion if she'd had the presence-of-mind to clear it up (whatever it was) instead of cart-wheeling her way back in triumph to her workstation next to where the potatoes were boiling away. When challenged, my mother put the blame firmly on the only Afro-Caribbean lady on the premises. Shocking!

The centre remained closed for the remainder of the day, just as it would have been at weekends and during school holidays. There were no spuds for the kids that day. My mother came home in disgrace, looking for another job.

Full-sized milk-churns were placed outside the Victorian Cookhouse's main entrance where my mother had worked, safely hidden behind very tall, almost intruder-proof railings to prevent them from being stolen. The churns became the focus of attention by me and another boy who both considered it necessary to get them out on the road for a bit of fun. We were, of course, going to return them afterwards. My friend and I went over the gates into the compound and, while I lifted one of the churns above head-height using the railings as support, realised it was too heavy to take any further, dropped it in a timely fashion while taking a measured step backwards and tripped over the gates' anchorage point. I fell to the ground and fractured my wrist – again! Somehow, I managed to climb the tall gates and get back over to my house before taking myself off on another unaccompanied journey to the hospital.

On another occasion, while attempting to repeat the rolling churn trick, the same boy with me got both of his legs jammed in some horizontal bars covering a basement area on the wrong side of the railings within the building's boundary. Unable to help, I got out of the way 'sharpish' only to calmly and innocently witness the arrival of the London fire brigade, who managed to extricate the unfortunate soul from his predicament at the precise moment he embarrassed himself.

December 1952 saw the 'Great Smog' of London, which lasted five days, killing 12,000 people. It was either during or not long after the time tarmac-covered hardwood blocks that formed the road surface of Hammersmith Bridge had been lifted and stacked each end, accessible to anyone prepared to take them away for burning in fire-grates in homes across

Hammersmith and beyond. The blocks created so much black smoke when burned, it always looked as if our house was the Titanic's engine room.

Smog-filled air was a common feature throughout the fifties, as I remember well, never more so when, on a rare occasion, my mother took us on a couple of bus journeys to Kensal Rise to see her mother. However, the reception when we got there was as cold and empty as the foggy nights themselves.

On one of only a very few visits to my maternal grandmother's house, I briefly saw our step-brother named Peter, and only on two or three occasions after that. During one such visit, my siblings and I sat in front of an open grate fireplace at the same time as my grandmother bent forward to stoke the flames. Granny then promptly relieved herself of flatulence before stroking her dress's material over her buttocks as if to settle her feathers. Well, we all burst into uncontrollable fits of the giggles that came to an abrupt end when grandmother railed against us, shaking the poker at us while at the same time pulled a facial expression not too dissimilar to a smacked arse. My mother was to inherit the same traits. We couldn't wait to get out. Love you, Granny, and sadly, goodbye. We, as a family, didn't get to visit our grandmother after that fretful experience ever again.

Whatever happened to my maternal grandfather, I will never know except wonder if Henry William Darling fell off his perch before my Nan's budgie did. I note from the Old Bailey Court records of 1875 that a person of the same name who lived in my mothers' family's vicinity became a victim of an employee's theft of ribbons. Henry himself (if it was him or indeed his father, also Henry William Darling) is on record as a 'Catcher of Rats'. Oh, dear! My grandchildren and hopefully great-grandchildren will love it when they learn of the genetics coursing through their veins. But at least 'Ratty' was the business owner!

As a family group, we waited at a bus stop for the return journey from my grandmother's home in Kensal Rise, straining our eyes searching for a number six bus. Suddenly out of the smog, one would arrive as if from nowhere, the jagged shafts of light emanating from the side windows reaching out into the foggy darkness. I could even have been picking my nose to remove the accumulations of soot-encrusted dried mucus without anyone ever knowing; not even the person stood next to me.

The first bus to arrive at the bus stop was packed to the gunnels with passengers, probably on account of nothing else venturing out for fear of a collision. Our family boarded the bus and occupied the only remaining vacant seats, which happened to be just inside the boarding platform running parallel to the centre footway. As the bus chuntered further along the route, an elderly but able lady came aboard, which prompted me to instinctively stand up and offer my seat. I received praise and a shilling from the grateful person as she sat down, but looks of jealousy from my two sisters as I pocketed the money. At times like these, my mother would refer to me as 'Goody-bloody-two-shoes', but the shoes I wore were anything but.

There was a Co-op departmental store in King Street, Hammersmith, where I would be taken to be fitted out with a new pair of 'Tuff' black shoes, courtesy of whoever supplied the free school uniform.

Fog or smog-ridden days and nights were always good fun, providing an opportunity to become almost invisible. The nearly impenetrable smog enabled me, a friend and probably my brother John to go out and involve ourselves in some sort of tomfoolery. 'Knockdown Ginger', a term to describe knocking on someone's door and running away, would last well into the night, as happened on numerous occasions. Not too far from our house lived a West-Indian Caribbean family who did not escape our attention, which, for no other reason other than knowing that they rarely ventured out of the house, the chances of getting caught were very slim. They too were subject to 'Knockdown Ginger', but in their case, a friend and I obtained an inner-tube from a bicycle wheel, cut it to form one length, tied one end to the knocker on the front door and, under considerable tension, tied the other end to the railings. We would bang the heavy cast-iron knocker against the door as loudly as we could before taking a few steps back into the smog and disappear from view. Within seconds, we could hear someone from within the house coming to the door but unable to open it, sought the help of two or three others from within who together made a further unsuccessful attempt to do so. We then saw fingers protruding through the door's partial opening, followed by half images of peering faces. Unable to fully open the door, the occupants retired only to appear from the basement below and proceeded to untie the offending article. We had a good giggle and even had the gall to knock on their door the next day, asking if they had any unwanted lemonade or coke bottles that we could take back to the local shop for a deposit refund.

While attempting to make myself scarce after knocking on someone's door during one of many forays, I slipped over a kerb edge, seriously spraining my ankle. I hobbled and hopped home in search of sympathy, but as usual, none was forthcoming. The next day involved a trip to the doctor's surgery in an old pram, having been pushed there by the boy that had over indulged eating doggie stuff. Thick black smelly ointment the density of car axle grease applied to the injured ankle, bound by crepe bandage and mumbling threats from my mum was my reward. The neighbourhood fell silent for a considerable amount of time afterwards.

Guy Fawkes Night on 5th November each year was the first opportunity to celebrate anything once the cold nights had crept in. Massive amounts of combustible material, including orange boxes, tea-chests, pallets, and dead grannies, were collected up to four weeks ahead of the big day and heaped up in the centre of the 'bombsite' at the top of our road. The bigger the heap, the better, although if it were too big when lit, as was often the case, the fire brigade would turn up and spoil the fun.

Shops everywhere had large display cabinets packed full of fireworks from small inoffensive hand-held Roman candles right up to rockets that would give a dazzling display of colours, none of which had age-related restrictions. Some of the money collected from 'Penny-for-the-Guy' sessions outside the Kensington Odeon wasn't wasted buying 'sissy' Roman Candles, Fire-crackers, Jumping-jacks, dazzling Volcanoes or Rockets, but instead used to buy 1d, 2d and 3d Bangers – and I mean 'Bangers'! One penny (1d) bought a banger that went off with a noticeable 'poof' (depending on who lit it) and strong enough to wreck a paper bag. Bangers marketed as 'Cannonballs' were loud enough to get the Russians out of bed in Moscow during the time of the Cold War and, in confusion, would run amok shouting 'что это за хрень?' along with no-end of other eye-watering expletives.

It wasn't unusual to set a flame to the blue touch paper of fireworks placed on the balconies of nearby blocks of flats above the shops and scarper before the things went off, the sound of which reverberated throughout the entire building, causing consternation and general mayhem. The women from within the apartments would be the first to appear, dressed in powder-blue or pink candlewick dressing gowns bought as job-lots from 'Brentford Nylons' in Hounslow. Oh, and tightly fitting wire hair curlers forged into their heads in an attempt to make the wearer look glamorous. The menfolk would appear wearing nothing more than Lyle & Scots 'Y' front underpants and string vests sporting cocoa dribble stains. One particular boy ramped up the deed by putting so-called 'Cannonball' fireworks inside glass milk bottles that had been left out for collection the following morning by the milkman. Unbelievable! It couldn't have been me as I was at home with my feet pressed firmly against the bedroom door.

It was a day or two before Guy Fawkes night; I was with a boy who lived opposite to me in Faroe Road when his mother called for him to go indoors, at which point, he blurted out,
"Mum, I saw a boy stick a banger up a dog's arse", to which she exclaimed loudly,
"Toby! You mean rectum!"
"Wrecked him?" I quipped, "Nor arf - it blew him to smithereens!"
No more trips in the 'look-alike' Brook Bond Tea van for me - that was for sure. I assumed that the boy who put bangers in bottles was the same delinquent called Bertie that lived not too far away and known for his psychopathic behaviour. He was the sort of person who would swing a cat from a central light fitting just for the fun of it. There was a derelict house in the nearby Blythe Road which sported such a spectacle – it had to be Bertie.
The 'cowboy' fashion during the 1950s was for every boy to wear a replica furry hat of the type worn by Davy Crocket, an American folk hero, frontiersman, and politician. The animal-skin furred hat worn by Davy was a natural pelt of a raccoon with the tail hanging at the back. Still, the one sitting atop a certain boy's head somehow looked more like a domestic tabby cat with dull fazed eyes and a bulge protruding out from

under the tail. The wearer of the cat-like crown covering became known as Tom on account of the hat, although I was sure it was Bertie.

On reflection, there must have been no-end of juvenile tearaways around during my time as a young boy. Modern-day media reports of juveniles using drugs, knives, guns, and other weapons must give the impression that my generation were angels, as indeed most of us were.

One foggy night in Paddington, another boy and I, while raking the streets looking for something to do, happened upon a policeman who appeared out of the mist. The law enforcement officer seemed to be much shorter in height than the regular tall guys of his calling. Taken-aback by his appearance, we both fell about laughing, but that all came to an abrupt halt when [he] 'Shortie' gave us both an almighty slap across the side of our faces. We didn't tell anyone about our experience, and neither did the diddy police officer. "Evening all."

Always on the look-out for more mischief, I was never going to be disappointed. A lady resident in the same block of flats that had been the subject of so many bangs in the run-up to Guy Fawkes night co-existed with a bloke who was often away delivering bottles of Coca-Cola. In the absence of the lady's husband, a dog-walker would appear heading towards the building waving a white handkerchief in anticipation of a similar response. When that was done, the dog was then free to sniff out its own flag-waving totty at the bombsite opposite before wending its way to our back garden where he could be sure of a welcome pack of a bucket of water and a house-brick when caught eagerly attempting to mount one of his mates. At the same time, flag-waving matey would tuck his handkerchief back into the top pocket of his dapper-looking jacket before nipping up the stairway of the building to indulge in all things Coca Cola. Such goings-on became the gossip amongst the women-folk, although I suspected there had been an element of jealousy. That all changed to hatred when the 'White Tide Man' came to call.

During the late 1950s, whoever owned the brand name of the washing powder 'Tide' (America's favourite washing powder at the time and later branded as 'Daz'), launched a campaign by randomly calling on households in the U.K. with a representative dressed from head to toe in white, accompanied by a television camera crew. If the occupant of the house or flat, visited produced a packet of the same name's washing powder and espoused superlatives associated with the product, the householder received five-pounds sterling - in cash. The reciprocal handkerchief-waving lady told the man in a white suit that she washed absolutely everything using 'Tide', including her hair and a multitude of white handkerchiefs. What she failed to mention was that her morals had been excluded from the process, as she gleefully offered our man in white an opportunity to slake his thirst with a sip or two of the slurpy stuff. I'm sure that every time I passed the block of flats long after Bonfire Night, I could hear the sound of banging resonating throughout the building. 'Aye-oup, odd is that' is what Mr Baggs would have said; after all, he knew all about such matters.

    Clandestine goings-on of people having extra-marital affairs was not confined to the White Tide lady. One sister reminded me of when we were walking as a family group after Henry Gilbert had died or had been admitted to the hospital in Hammersmith. My mother told us to wait outside someone's house as she popped in to collect some groceries. Among the items our mum came out with, apart from a packet of tea, were packets of dried egg powder shipped over from the United States during and after World War Two, much of which was discovered years later hidden in store cupboards across the nation. I dread to think what was in the mix, but whatever it was bloody-well worked, sending not only American servicemen into overdrive but many a good girl too. We had a quantity of the grey powdery stuff stored away in a cupboard in our house's sitting room that seemed to diminish in quantity, periodically replenished from goodness-knows where. More doors were opening and closing in and around Hammersmith in any given week than the doors on the entire stock of cuckoo-clocks in production at an Austrian factory. Cuckoo! Cuckoo! Gertcha!

Australian Goodness

The Ideal Home Exhibition at the Olympia in Kensington, London, came around every spring with newly-built state-of-the-art houses appearing inside the Grand Hall, with a plethora of supporting trade stands at its periphery. The 'Ideal Homes' were of little interest to me, but what did attract my attention was the food hall with all the big brands, represented by household names such as Hovis, Marmite, HP Sauce and Ryvella, to name but a few. Getting access to the Grand Hall of the Olympia then on to the food required a great deal of cunning after gaining unpaid access. 'Bunking-in' was the term used to describe slipping in through any exit door, which usually meant dodging the door attendant on the inside and casually mingling with the droves of visitors while at the same time seeking out freshly presented free food samples on counters. Mind you, some of the stallholders were savvy, rightly thinking that I or whoever was with me was about to sweep the counters clear of food in the same way as fishing trawler nets do on the seabed and, as a result, would withdraw the samples in a flash before we were able to get to them.

 The girls on the Australian food stand in the Grand Hall of the Olympia were different from everyone else and always my first port-of-call. The lovely all-female staff were ultra-friendly and consistently offering food samples of cheese, honeycomb, and honey, spread onto biscuits already topped with upside-down butter, cheerily smiling, and wanting to talk about anything and everything English. Of course, I obliged - naturally. It was my first attempt at flirting, and I was surprised how easy it was, although I didn't understand the term. I suspect the girls, having seen the film David Copperfield back home, might well have thought I was one of those filthy dirty lovable scruffy characters mooching about town waiting to take advantage of whatever presented itself. Nah, not me, Luv.

To get some respite from the ever-present threat of being punched, kicked in the groin, or spat on, I would skip school when 'Australia' was in town, returning to the Olympia to visit their stand almost daily. I was on first-name terms with the staff, so much so, one of the girls wrote a letter addressed to my school purporting to be my mother, setting out dubious reasons why I was not there.

Having over-indulged in cheese and all things saucy, I succumbed to the delicious smell of frying sausages wafting on the air. The 'Walls' food-stand was staffed by yet more good-looking young ladies, all of whom had complexions of 'Peaches and cream' in contrast to the tanned complexions of the Aussie girls. On one occasion, one of the ladies on the 'Walls' stand was deftly and tantalizingly turning sausages with her fingers to achieve an all-around consistent colour. I always thought sausages had a gentle curve, but all I could see in the frying pan were straight ones. The mind boggled. In a sales environment, I long learned that to sell a product successfully, one had to sell the sizzle, sausages being a prime example of something grey and flaccid that would be of little interest until seen to be sizzling, then everyone would want a piece of the action. Unlike the Aussie beauties, the girls on the 'Walls' stand fiddling about with the sausages were adamant that urchins like me should be denied free samples. Attempts to snatch portions of whatever was being fried usually resulted in a rap across the knuckles with a hot spatula before being told to piss-off. Charming!

Back over on the Australian stand, one of the girls said to me,

"Would I like to go 'daaan-ander', Bruce? "Down-under?" "Where's that?" I enquired.

The tallest of the girls listening to what I had to say, while at the same time giving me a wink of her eye, said,

"Well, you know Bruce, Daaan-aander, aander, bladdy aander!"

Oops. "Pardon," I said. " Not bloody likely", I said. "Anyway, my name's not Bruce, Shelia (or Shelagh); it's Darling - Henry Darling".

I then told her and others listening that I was a descendant of the famous Darling Dynasty that owned the land they walked on back in Australia, including the rivers they swam in and every bottle of wine they've ever had the privilege of drinking. Further into the conversation, I told my captivated audience that my genetic connection probably came about after a clandestine encounter with a member of the Darling family at the back of an estate owner's equivalent of a modern-day bike-shed way back in the 1700s, but that didn't necessarily exclude me from an inheritance. I also told those very nice young ladies there are so many birds of prey in England because of the vast number of churches. Judging by the look of astonishment on the faces of those listening, I could have got them to believe any old codswallop.

"Got any cheese?" I asked.

Anyway, referring back to going 'daaan-aander'; having never-ever ventured beyond the resort of Southend-on-Sea in Essex, I would not have known what to do if I did venture south although I know Mr Baggs would have been undoubtedly willing - God rest his soul. For my part, I had to explain that I was only fourteen-and-a-half and, in any event, didn't have a passport (whatever that was). Oh, be joyful.

I was into my third slug of Australian Cheddar when one of the Ozzie girls on Australia stand headed towards me and said,

"I meant to ask you, Bruce, no, sorry, Henry, why are so many people called Henry in and around London?".

"Well,", I said, "Most mothers wanted their sons to be acknowledged as direct descendants of King Henry VIII, especially the peasant-folk who lived near to Hampton Court Palace where all kinds of shenanigans went on; all of the mothers calling their bastard sons Henry, hoping against hope of an inheritance in some form or other when His Royal Highness finally popped his clogs".

I then went on to say that 'Good King Harry' was reputed to have had a predilection for procreating whenever and wherever he went.

The girls from 'daaan-aander' then said in unison, "O'Riley?"

"Yes, Oh, really," I said.

I then told them that although my name-sake was reputed to have had six wives, depending on who was asking at the time, the Catholic Pope maintained four legal ones while the head of the new protestant church, King Henry himself, insisted there were just two incontestable marriages. I then went on to say,

"There was so much confusion and changing of laws surrounding the king's marriages at the time, his so-called fourth wife had her head chopped off for committing adultery when in fact his majesty wasn't legally married to her anyway. Odd, was that".

"O'Riley?" said one of the girls.

"Yes, really", I said.

"Mind you", I continued, "Our lad, 'Enerey' was a bit of a rascal, having had an endless stream of mistresses to sate his voracious appetite. All Henry wanted to achieve was a male heir to the throne and stopped at nothing to do what he had set out to do. Always ever-ready, His Majesty dismissed the wearing of the then fashionable dan-fangled triangular piece of material affectionally known as a 'Codpiece' that was usually worn at the crutch and held in place by string. Not wanting to risk getting his 'Hampton' caught by following the fashion of the time when some gentlemen resorted to padding out their codpieces to emphasize whatever was lurking within, our lubricious royal gentleman was ahead of the game. His Royal Highness wore leggings that terminated just above his knees and an outer garment with a hemline that hid not only his garters but also His Majesty's Royal Staff that would have put any Australian Aboriginal's Didgeridoo in the shade".

"So, there you are, ladies", I said, "That's why there are so many Henrys about the place".

Enthralled by the whole story about my origins and the King himself, my captive audience fed me every one of their product lines, including a couple of sips of their Australian 'Big Red' wine. Having consumed rather more than I should have considering my age, and in a delirious fog of confusion, I thought I heard something about one or two of the girls saying they were about to go 'daaan-aander'. The following day, fearing the worst, I found myself doing a head-count relieved to learn that everyone was still there. Phew!

Two days had passed, and I longed to go back and be among the girls from Oz. Off I went to the Olympia, slipping through a gap in one of the fire-exit doors while the attendant in an overall brown coat had gone away to get a cup of tea, scratch his arse and buy a packet of Woodbine cigarettes, or else a 4ozs packet of Old Holborn tobacco for yet another rolled-up fag. As I approached the Australian stand, I noticed all the girls looking towards me with knowing smiles on their faces, their expressions suggesting that they knew something that I didn't.

Within minutes of arriving at the Ozzie stand, someone let slip that Shelia (or Shelagh), who I had seen only a couple of days earlier, had just been daaan-aander, which puzzled me as I thought a one-way voyage aboard a steamship took six weeks - it did in the 1950s. The ladies, with knowing looks of expression on their faces, gathered around to hear more stories, the same person that had given me the last bit of cheese on my earlier trip said, "Henry, (bingo!) what is Caads Wallup?"

After my quiet muttering of 'Give me strength', I replied, "I Dunn-no."

I then said, "Anyway, as you asked me a rather awkward question the other day, I'll now ask you one".

I then asked, "As Kangaroos are already down-under, why does the male of the species go even further down-under when the air temperature rises?"

With the sound of one of the girls clearing her throat, the response was:

"Well, Cobber, sorry Mate, no, sorry, Clive or even Henry (Bingo again!), some of the menfolk back home, especially those called Bruce and others of a gymnastic or contortionist disposition are reputed to do exactly the same".

Another girl said that she happened upon her boyfriend, Randy doing the same thing while uncharacteristically wearing a frontal pouched carpenter's apron. Randy's excuse, she said, was that he thought it a brilliant idea as some marsupials do so to keep their crown jewels cool during hot weather to remain fertile, and do what your English King Henry did".

Oops! Bloody hell! The same person then told me that after her shock discovery of finding Randy emulating the intemperate habits of a kangaroo, she called him a 'Bounder' and told him to hop it. "O'Riley?" I said.

"Yes, Oh, really", came the reply.

****

While writing this book, several movements in society became prominent, highlighting the apparent inequalities within mainstream British society and elsewhere. Such activities focused on racial prejudice between black and white people, particularly to the former's detriment. Well, I have to say, during my growing-up years of the fifties and early sixties, for me at least, and as mischievous as I was, racial prejudice was a little-known factor and of no relevance to my everyday life. Of course, racial jokes abounded about Western Caribbean immigrants arriving in banana boats. Still, there were jokes about Scotsmen being as 'tight as a duck's arse' when it came to money; even Yorkshire folk were regarded as tight Scotsmen, which some would say was pretty much the case - not me. Generally speaking, Welsh people were often considered short and stubby and believed to have evolved that way to prevent them from falling off their mountains as planet earth spun on its axis. The Welsh guys were also said to be responsible for travelling east into England during the General

Strike of 1926 and nicking everyone's jobs. Men from Ireland were portrayed as thick as two short planks, probably stemming from their relatively innocent naivety and the insecurity from those who also saw Irish immigration as a threat to their jobs. It was always Paddy that wrongly became the butt of all humour, especially with vocal lines that started off with: 'There was an Englishman, Irishman, Scotsman and Welshman, all of which ended with the Irish fellow being the fall guy. Childish, I know, but after all, we were children.

As children growing up after the war years, the focus was always about going outdoors on some adventure or other, leaving adults to their own preferred way of getting on with their lives. Apart from bad jokes, racial discrimination at my level of society in my corner of the world was expressed by just a few adults, my mother being one of them, as you'll have read, blaming the only black woman at her place of work for indiscretions that were not of that person's making. The only other utterance of a racial nature I heard was from the greengrocer I worked for during the school holidays and weekends. Fed-up to the eye-teeth of customers being 'picky' about where the fruit and veg came from, especially during the apartheid days in South Africa, one customer who enquired about the origins of a bunch of grapes that were about to be placed in her grocery shopping bag got more than she bargained for. Instead of receiving the grapes, the woman was told of the fruit's South African origins in a sympathetic but snide derogatory way about the pickers' hands' colour. The customer stomped out of the shop empty-handed, much to the delight of the proprietor.

Of course, there is no excuse ignoring the plight of black immigrants or any other immigrants for that matter, but at the age of ten or twelve, such issues were in the hands of our elders and betters(?). Notting Hill in London was not too far away from where I lived; a good hike nonetheless. Still, I knew nothing about the dreadful practices of Peter Rachman, a Polish-born Jew who became infamous for buying up old houses and sub-dividing them into living quarters before cramming-in whole Caribbean immigrant families into ever-smaller rooms, intimidating the occupants and charging exorbitant levels of rent – all within the law.

Not wishing to belittle the events going on in Notting Hill and elsewhere in London at the time, my only experience was getting to a small supermarket at the top of the hill that led away from Shepherds Bush into Notting Hill. I went in search of finding a shop somewhere to save my mum housekeeping money instead of her conveniently buying her groceries at what I perceived as high prices from the Co-op in the newly-built parade of shops beneath where The White Tide Lady of many bangs lived. The Co-op used to sell three grades of margarine, Gold, Silver and Red Seal, all of them made using hydrogenated fat, the latter being full of it, so dense it could easily have been used to build pseudo-clay brick walls. The stuff was so hard, even when it came out of a fridge (although we didn't have one), it always tore the guts out of white bread when spread and probably did the same to those of us that consumed it. In truth, I'd had enough of my mum buying Friary butter for herself and Red Seal margarine for the rest of us. My mother said it was her treat, and hers alone, and for those reasons, I went in search of something different, which was how I ended up in Notting Hill.

In contrast to a minority of grown-up's racial comments, my experiences were quite different other than witnessing a new boy arriving at Secondary school wearing a Turban only for it to be pulled off his head. The unfortunate pupil wasn't seen again.

On one of many forays in and around London's streets, I happened upon a house in Sinclair Road behind the Olympia buildings in West Kensington. The building had been internally converted to a Sheikh temple of worship and still exists to this day. Somehow, my brother and I found ourselves drifting into the temple, expecting to hear, Oi! Clear off! Instead of being bawled at and told to piss off, we were met by a man wearing a turban and a big, big smile. Even though John (my younger brother) and I must have looked a pathetic sight with our arses' hanging out the back of our trousers and dirty half worn-out shoes; not to mention John wearing his customary neckless of chicken bones, we were courteously invited into the building's main rooms. What took my brother and me by surprise was the friendliness of the person that greeted us and the spectacle of seeing an array of really posh-looking carpets, although not fitted wall-to-wall, were in contrast to what we had at home (which was none) and covered the entire floor area in each room. We were asked to remove our shoes on entry before being given some unusual food as a snack, so spicy it would have blown my socks off if they hadn't had so many holes. Indeed, the Kellogg's Cornflakes cardboard inner soles of my shoes might well have become caught up in the blades of the air-cooling fan spinning above our heads if the shoes hadn't been left at the door. The experience of kindness expressed by the Sheikh temple's attendees remains with me to this day. If there had been any hint of racial discrimination in my mind, they certainly would have evaporated there and then.

अलविदा और धन्यवाद   Alvida aur dhanyavad.

Nigh-on Neighbours

When writing about Faroe Road, I've mentioned where it is in relation to others in the neighbourhood and a brief description of it, but not about those who lived there. To get an idea of some residents of the time, I thought I'd write about the few that stood out for one reason or another.

Gentrification on a grand scale must have taken place since I left Faroe Road way back in 1962, as the average price for property there, according to the British Property Website, Zoopla, stood at £1,862,521 back in August 2018, and all of them terraced houses. Wow! Based on that fact alone, it would be a pretty good assumption that most residents where I lived in the 1950s and 1960s had long-gone, either because the inflated house prices were too good to resist, the council houses among them had been demolished or else the owners of the private homes had fallen off their perches.

A journey down Faroe Road, starting from the top where it joins with Blythe Road, was (and still is) an end elevation of the two-tier flats above the shops where the White Tide Lady and her Coca-Cola hauling driver-husband lived. When our family first moved in, I clearly remember the same block of flats and shops being under construction. At the time, my father landscaped our back garden using chunks of concrete with pebble stones set within them with a cement-mortar mix to fill the gaps. I never did get to know the origins of the concrete lumps, but I knew where the cement came from that formed the mortar-mix: the building site of The White Tide Lady's flats of perpetual bangs! Bags of cement were stacked high just inside the perimeter fence, with several of them in a damaged state, their contents spread over a wide area on the ground. On my father's instructions, I had to collect the spoil by lifting the perimeter fence at ground level, helping myself to as much as I could carry in one of many single trips. I was only five years old! My dad, eh?

When the building of the flats and shops fronting them was well underway, a 'Night Watchman' appeared on the site along with a small sentry-type hut and an oil-drum brazier that glowed orange from the burning of Coke (refined coal) during cold winter nights. At the time, there were endless building sites with elderly retired men engaged in security roles to deter would-be thieves; it didn't work. Countless newspaper headlines of the time featured stories of these elderly gentlemen being subject to attack and even murdered while carrying out their nightwatchman duties, and all for the sake of supplementing their meagre state pensions.

Moving on to the first house past the flats of perpetual bangs lived a man who cross-bred Linnets with Goldfinches to produce something that would not stop twerking its stuff, day-in, day-out. All the birds used in the reproduction programme were wild-caught and, I suppose, technically illegal. I inadvertently told loads of people about the bloke with the birds and the wonders of cross-breeding, which was to earn me a world-class bollocking from birdie man himself.

A few houses down from Mr Tweeter lived a tall skinny boy of about fifteen years who always appeared somewhat aloof as he rode his state-of-the-art bicycle past our house without ever looking across. Further along on the right was the 'Farmer' family that consisted of two elderly parents and grown-up twin boys. The family weren't farmers by occupation but avid motorcycle fanatics who kept their machines in the small area fronting their house that had its railings purloined by the Government for the war effort some years earlier and never replaced. The 'Farmers' were a respectable unassuming family, one of whom gave me a lift home on his motorbike one cold, wet winter's night after spotting me getting a soaking in the pouring rain walking down King Street towards Hammersmith Broadway on my way back from Ravenscourt Park.

A few houses further along from the Bikers' family lived the Polish-Jewish lady and her Polish husband, the same lady who gave my brother chicken bones to chew. Apart from the necklace episode, we rarely saw our Polish neighbours, although we would occasionally get to know what was being prepared for dinner each time they opened their front door and released a strong smell of boiled chicken and cabbage into the air. Yummy!

Further along from the Poles lived a Mr and Mrs Irons, who had a son called Barry, just a year or two my junior. Forever watchful, Barry's parents would keep a wary eye on their son as he played with armies of lead soldiers spread out on the front step of his house. Whenever I strolled across the road to see what the boy with the toys was up to, his father would appear and sweep up the entire collection of soldiers before retreating into his house, taking his son with him, and closing the door behind them. So unnecessary.

And then there was Toby's house further down on the same side of the road, the same boy of 'Dog-poo eating' notoriety that had half of the Wehrmacht's armaments in his bedroom. Toby didn't know (or so he said) that he was destined to have what became affectionately known as a 'Bib-and-tuck' as he nonchalantly went off with his dad to what he thought was a circus outing. Adding to his woes, the next day Toby came back having been circumcised along with a newly acquired aversion about stories of 'Wee Willie Winkle', dark coloured shelled molluscs of a similar name, pork scratchings and, when the food manufacturer KP in 1973 introduced crunchy Hula-hoops that resembled small rings - them too. Our boy with the 'clip' couldn't resist showing me the 'end result' (so to speak) and told me that whenever he found the need to urinate, pee came out from holes around the blanket stitches similar to a watering can with a rose sprinkler. I neither believed him nor asked him to prove it. If ever there is an example of how not to blanket stitch - there it was; the sight was enough to bring tears to the eyes of everyone invited to look, let alone Toby himself. It was my time to say 'No fanks' although a quick glimpse at the injury looked to me as if 'Boy Go Lightly' might well have had a run-in with a Hornet's nest - or the other way around.

In 1960, the 'Keep Britain Tidy' campaign was launched to clean-up towns, cities, and the countryside, followed by a campaign in 1968 of I'm Backing Britain' fronted by the late Bruce Forsythe, the well-known and successful entertainer. The campaign led the general public to be persuaded to 'Buy British'. Simultaneously, workers volunteered to put in extra time in unpaid employment to recover the economy after Harold Wilson's Government wrecked it. At about the same time, following my friend's surprise surgery, Toby had hoped to capitalise on the public's mood by setting up a campaign of cleaning up public toilets with the slogan 'Our aim is to keep the toilets clean, your aim will help'. A good move, Toby! You can't help laughing.

Then, there was Mr Baggs, who lived next door to Toby; there's no need to bang-on about this geezer, as you'll already read about him. But, in the three-storey house that he, his wife, son of about my age, and a bloke referred to as Uncle Albert (if indeed he was an uncle), was a bachelor of maturing years that occupied the building's upper floor. My (late) younger brother John told a story that 'Uncle Albert' had been attacked and bonked on the head with a hammer during a botched burglary by two people Uncle Albert knew and who lived in very close proximity to him. Unfortunately, according to my brother, 'Uncle Albert' subsequently died of his injury.

Crossing Faroe road at the bottom where it joins Ceylon Road was where the old battle-axe of a lady lived, an expert at throwing buckets of water over copulating dogs and tandem cyclists she perceived were doing the same. She was the same 'Biddy' that successfully caused me to fall from my bicycle by throwing her long-handled broom (javelin-style) through the front wheel spokes. The troublesome lady had a raging bull's temper; so-much-so, my mum always referred to her as 'Old Muvver Riley' probably because she came from Ireland. A hint of racism showing there - perhaps. Further up the road heading towards Blythe Road lived the bus driver who died of a heart attack. His daughter, a sergeant in the territorial army, was subsequently killed in a road accident whilst driving an army truck. It was the same bus driver's wife that slapped the hot bread poultice on the side of my head when I had the boil that could be seen from the rooftops of the flats of perpetual bangs.

To approach the house where I lived meant passing Fred The Burglar's place-of-residence when he was there and not in Her Majesty's Wormwood Scrubs prison. Whether or not Fred was his real name, our furtive friend was never bothersome and seemed to be tolerated by those around him whenever he was at home. I only ever remember seeing the man a few times, who I imagined to be wearing a horizontally red or yellow striped jumper, a black eye-mask carrying a sack over his shoulder. I was only ever alerted to Fred's presence when my mother would look out of the front-room window and exclaim, "Look! There he goes, home again - for five bloody minutes". Hey-ho. Complimentary and quite forgiving was my mother.

Passing our house, number fifty-two, the next neighbour worthy of comment was a lady who knew that my mother took in just about everything people offered, saw an opportunity to be rid of her old honky-tonk clapped-out seriously out-of-tune piano, but had no easy means of doing so without incurring considerable cost. Enter my mother: £20 paid and the piano was ours. Nobody in our family was remotely musical apart from playing the radio, so the only use the Joanna was put to ended up as a shelf for our Radio Rentals wireless, a high-rise rodent tower block and a convenient landing stage for our colour-changing budgie. There were always mice lurking in and around the piano's soundboard, but they must have been as deaf-as-a-post because of it. Creating any musical sounds did nothing to dislodge them, but slamming the hinged lid covering the keys as hard as one could muster, causing earthquake-like vibrations, usually did the trick. The result of causing vibrational mayhem was to see mice fleeing at supersonic speed towards the nearest mouseholes at the bottom of the skirting board in the living room, only to appear on the other side of the wall in the kitchen underneath the 'Tall-boy' food cupboard. As the startled bunch of rodents scarpered, the braver of the scattering creatures would hesitate and gesticulate with one of their front claws or else a two-fingered 'Harvey', long before the British Showjumping Champion Harvey Smith, a blunt and broad speaking Yorkshireman, did to the judges after competing in a jump-off in 1971. Gertcha!

One-by-one, the keys of the musical piece of furniture lost most of its treads before the whole thing was bulldozed along with the house a couple of years later. In its place is a local authority complex of buildings with a tree exactly where our home and a couple of others had been. Get yourselves a chainsaw, and who knows; history just might come tumbling out?

Moving on beyond Una Winifred Atwell's (the famous Trinidadian pianist of the 1950s) protégé's home was the house my mother and my siblings frequented to watch television as I often sat outside in the rain with nowhere else to go.

And finally, the last property on the right adjacent to the bombsite that had been propped up with wooden buttresses was where the 'Dawson' lived. The family were several in number but lucky enough to have a father employed as a chauffeur and therefore financially stable.

Looking back over my time growing up in and around London, I recall having brushed with the law on at least five occasions, starting with being accused of breaking a window at the flats in Queen Caroline Street when I was four or five years old. There was also the time I was caught speeding on the Hammersmith flyover elevation on an oversized ladies-frame bicycle, bobbing up and down when peddling without realizing I was risking the sensitive lower parts of my anatomy getting tangled up in the chain mechanism. And again, there was also the occasion of unwittingly getting involved in the theft of the Irish boy's bike as well as getting caught scrumping apples near Barnes Railway Station. Last, if not least, the occasion when taking the rise out of the Diddy policeman in Paddington.

Time to reflect and consider that if I couldn't beat the Coppers, I should join them. Hmmm.

On the Up

I did not return to school after visiting the 'Careers Advisory Officer', but instead made my way to the Army Careers Information Office in Edgeware Road, Paddington, London, unwittingly signing my life away for a period of twenty-two years plus two-and-a-half years as a junior soldier. Anything was better than living at home or being violently bullied at school – anything. I guess it was my positive approach and refusal to succumb to failure that got me to this point in my life. I went home and told my mother what I had done, waving a parent consent form under her nose, but because I was a potential source of income to her, she was having none of it. My siblings might also have written that they were denied an opportunity to better themselves by staying on at school to obtain the GCE exams (GCSE). Still, the younger of my two older sisters managed to break through the barrier following relentless pressure put upon my mother from someone working for the London County Council education authorities.

At home, in an attempt to obtain my joint twin birth certificate from where I had previously known it to be, I discovered it missing. I later learned that my mother had destroyed it, either to hide the fact that my father's name did not appear on it or, most likely, an attempt to stop me from going anywhere. It didn't work. I obtained a 'single birth' copy birth certificate sometime later and took it along with a signed consent form back to the Army Careers office. Don't ask.

Two weeks after I had called at the Careers Information Office in Edgware Road, London, I received a letter of invitation to visit the then War Department in Whitehall, London. I attended and became subject to a thorough medical examination that included someone sticking their hands down my trousers to fiddle about around my nether-regions before instructing me to cough. The medical screening was followed by a written entrance examination that included an 'Aptitude' and 'Intelligence' test to determine my suitability for a specific role in H.M. Forces.

A week or so after I had visited the War Department in Whitehall, I intercepted an envelope expecting it to contain a letter of refusal or, at the very best, acceptance as a Junior Drummer Boy; my interpretation of the appointment being the Army's equivalent of a van driver's assistant. Instead, the letter informed my mother of an offer for me to join The Royal Corps of Signals (a technical branch no-less). Me? Never! Wow! After reading the letter, my immediate reaction was to take it back to the Army Recruitment Centre in Edgware Road to tell them I had received it in error. The news went down like a lead balloon by my mother when she discovered the letter that I had read, re-sealed and placed on the kitchen table.

"You're not going, and that's that!" she said.

I don't know who encouraged her to eventually capitulate; perhaps it was the same person who tried to persuade her to put me in a children's home, a real and meaningful threat often levelled at me over the years. I could quickly have become one of those children in the late fifties shipped off to Australia or Canada and had goodness knows what done to them. I suspect it was Mr Baggs who wanted me out of his way as he was partial to going down-under himself and might well have wanted to do so in an unfettered manner. I could imagine Mr Baggs saying, 'I told thee I would have thee for thy cheek' as I stared back towards a fast-disappearing empty quayside apprehensively setting out into the sunset holding nothing more than a second-hand teddy bear and memories of my loving father.

On Sunday, 2nd September 1962, I was preparing to leave 52 Faroe Road before setting out to a less-than-certain future. As I walked away from my house and looked back over my shoulder, recounting my thoughts of those that lived in other homes in the road, the overwhelming sense of emancipation almost lifted me over the roof-tops as I carried the total of my worldly possessions within a small, well-worn suitcase donated by none other than Mr Baggs himself.

Later the same day, at the age of fifteen years and two weeks and only 5ft 2ins in height, I arrived at Newton Abbot Railway Station in South Devon. A severe mean-looking sergeant, along with a couple of his cronies greeted me, and, having ascertained my identity, ushered me onto the back of a dark green Bedford TK army truck. There were already a few other unfortunate and forlorn-looking individuals of a similar age anxiously sitting in the rear of the vehicle awaiting their fate.

After a few miles travelling along bumpy roads in the back of an army vehicle, we arrived at Denbury Camp, just a stone's throw away from Denbury village itself, small in size, somewhere in the back-end of nowhere not too far from Bovey Tracey and Ashburton in Devon. The pervading smell that greeted us was that of the back-end of a dairy farm, day-in, day-out. Mind you, I was no stranger to the smell, having experienced it for a couple of weeks every year in the London Dairy Show at the Olympia where farmers would arrive with their prize cattle for showing in the Grand Hall of the building. The stench of the stuff then was somehow different with notes of, well, cow-shit really, but posh stuff, pleasant to the nose after inhaling years of London traffic fumes. It would have been a fitting present, boxed and gift-wrapped to give to someone special at Christmas. The whiff of cow manure that could be detected over a wide area outside of the building while the Dairy Show was in town was in contrast to the eye-watering smell that pervaded over the barracks in Devon. On reflection, perhaps I should have sent the Denbury stench gift-wrapped in a bottle to Mr Baggs before offering it out to the people in Knightsbridge who would have heard us carol-singing our hearts out but hadn't the courtesy to acknowledge our presence. A merry smelly Christmas to them all!

Denbury Camp became the home of the Junior Leaders Regiment's from 1959 until disbanded in 1967. Fifteen-year-old boys from mostly working-class social backgrounds and from all parts of the British Isles would join the regiment for a period of up to two-and-a-half years. During that time, each Junior Leader would be subject to meaningful education and military training with a select number taught telecommunication skills that offered an opportunity to become outstanding tradesmen and leaders in the future. Some individuals failed to recognise or appreciate the opportunities that existed; I didn't, or rather, I did.

The barracks at Denbury was built within three months in 1939 to house soldiers of World War Two, initially called Rawlinson Barracks, later to become Her Majesty's Prison Channing's Wood that exists to this day. Within the barracks, 'spider configurations' of six wooden billets (I acknowledge spiders have eight legs) were connected by a passageway around a square-shaped area of grass. Outbuildings around the camp's periphery provided essential services and amenities conducive to a military establishment's orderly running. A few months before I arrived at the barracks, a whole complex of six barrack rooms had burned to the ground when two boy soldiers perished while trapped inside the drying room without any means of escape. When I arrived at the camp, there was no sign that such a tragedy had ever happened other than a rigorous fire practice drill that took place every single day at 6 p.m.

Denbury Camp was to become my home from September 1962 until April 1965. Getting off the army truck on the day of arrival was no mean feat, having had to jump my body height from the back of the vehicle down to the ground. Shortly after arriving at the barracks, our group of forlorn-looking boys marched off (after a fashion) to the Quartermaster's Store to collect items that included a complete set of bedding along with a foam mattress that had to be carried a considerable distance to where we were to be accommodated for our first fourteen weeks in the barracks. On arrival at the recruit wing, we were all allocated a bed-space with a metal-framed bed and a large battleship-grey painted steel locker containing our military kit - nothing more. Worldly belongings such as they were, including the clothes we wore on arrival, had to be placed in a suitcase under the bed and not disturbed for the whole duration of the fourteen weeks recruit training. Along with the moribund group of travel-weary individuals, I was then marched off to the cookhouse for our first ever army meal.

As new arrivals, we spent the rest of the evening settling in and getting to know each other if only we could understand each other's various regional accents. Like me, individuals from different parts of the country came straight out of school with little prospect of meaningful employment or else destined to go down the coal mines as their forebears had gone before. Boys from Scotland arrived at Newton Abbot Railway Station accompanied by their parents, having travelled via London on the 'Flying Scotsman' steam locomotive. Many of the folk from north of the border were dressed in their best tartan finery, looking not unlike a consignment of posh-wrapped packets of shortbread on their way to supermarkets everywhere. These people were no-doubt canny enough to close the train carriage windows to avoid their kilts inverting which might otherwise have put-paid to the perennial question, 'Do they, don't they?'

Names that cropped up with these fine fearsome-looking folks from Scotland included Neal Down and Phil McCrevice, not to mention Penny Owen, N.O. McBrain, Jock Strapp, Ben Doon and Phil McCavity. I suspect the real motive for their menfolk attending was to ascertain how far south they managed to toss their cabers, having competed in their highland games earlier in the season. The sight of row-upon-row of telegraph poles viewed from the train carriage windows of The Flying Scotsman as the canny folks headed south must have driven them insane. I like the Scots and hope they will remain part of our great nation forever, especially as a recent DNA test revealed that I am 10% Scottish. Och-Aye, mate. It's all so confusing. My mother certainly didn't tell me about that, but then she probably didn't have a clue about it either.

I do not recall hearing of anyone referred to as Taffy (a diminutive of David, or someone living near the River Taff), so I assumed no-one in our intake came from the Principality of Wales – no surprises there. The Welsh lads probably found the Royal Signals too tame, choosing instead to join the Welsh Guards where rugby was an almost daily treat both before and after breakfast, day-in and day-out. The playing of such games with a wonky ball provided an opportunity for the potential stars of the future to acquire matching cauliflower ears and a flat nose in anticipation of attracting their women-folk back home in the land of their fathers, but, with an almost seamless border and just a couple of mountains separating Wales from England, a little research wouldn't go amiss. Perhaps the lyrics of 'Hen Wlad Fy Nhadau' (Land of my Fathers) might need a second look by some? So, Rhys Dillon Huw Gethin Cai Llywelyn Morgan-Jones (anyone of the same name combination is purely coincidental); 'Mae'n daclus'. I am proud to say that my delightful grandson is half-Welsh (I'm 3% Welsh according to my DNA), and if he was ever inclined to sing Hen Wlad Fy Nhadau, he'd do well to bang on about Taplow in Berkshire. There's lovely.

Although names of recruits were as varied as the country's regions they came from, almost all of us referred to each other with fore-names not given at birth. There was Alan from Newcastle, always referred to as 'Geordie', Malcolm from Grimsby (Kipper – Kip for short), Glover (Mitts), Woods (Chippy), White (Chalky), Miller (Dusty), Toye (Dinky), someone from Cornwall (Bod) and 'Titch' which needs no explanation. All the boys from regions north of the Scottish border became known as 'Jock'. A boy named Clarke from Liverpool had a penchant for ironing his uniform while naked, but through carelessness, he often caught himself on a steam iron he was using when his attention wandered. He became known as 'Knobby'. I was just Henry.

Tuesday morning, the day after arriving at the barracks in Devon and having had a good night's sleep after lugging Mr Baggs's old suitcase from home all the way from Hammersmith, I was to experience a rude awakening. A particular Junior Lance Corporal 'Fruit' Berry entered the barrack room at 6 a.m. on the first morning banging a wooden pick-axe handle on the nearest metal bed-end shouting, "Hands off cocks and put-on socks. You're in the Army now!". I half expected to hear a collective chorus of 'Wurthefukarwe?' from the new foundlings, but instead – silence. I deduced that my contemporaries could never have been in the London Underground train network - or Borneo.

As our mentor, Fruit was tasked to guide us through the first fourteen weeks' induction process, ensuring we all understood military discipline principles. Every time 'Fruit' appeared in the barrack room where we had been confined, we had to stand up to attention, regardless of whatever we happened to be doing. Always on tender-hooks during any given period of twenty-four hours, we were up and down more times than the elbows of the entire ensemble of fiddlers at the Last Night of The Proms in London's Royal Albert Hall. The slinging of highly polished boots out of windows, followed by anything else deemed not up to standard, was Fruit's pastime. Teachings also included doing as one was told, instantly and without comment, making a bed army-style, ironing, toilet cleaning, keeping one's mouth shut at all times, etc. Our mentors' task was to ensure military and self-discipline principles and get us to wherever we had to be.

The following morning, after putting on our grey-coloured thickly knitted army-issue socks, the day started with a trip to the cookhouse for an authentic English fry-up breakfast followed by a march to the barber's shop to receive a short-back-and-sides haircut, cruelly leaving a 'bob' of hair on the top to remind us of our past.

An army number of eight digits, the haircut and cloned uniforms from a pattern worn during and after World War One was all part of an indoctrination process, stripping us all of our former identities and civilian ways.

Junior Lance Corporal Fruit's remit did not extend beyond having to look after his allocated number of recruits, but his approach was nonetheless relentless. Bed-space inspections were an everyday occurrence during my time of fourteen weeks in the recruit training wing. The inspecting officer or sergeant-in-charge, along with 'Fruit', would peer into every nook and cranny looking for and spotting the slightest smears on the window behind each bed. If there were any indiscretions, the result would be a bellowing down one's ear resulting in ear-wax shooting out the other with such force to rebound off the window and end up on the grass next to the boots. Woe-betide any of us if inspections happened on sunny days. The slightest speck of dust or pencil-line smear on the windows would become glaringly obvious, ensuring the whole weekend was taken up re-cleaning the windows while at the same time staring into the distance at Haytor on Dartmoor.

Bed-packs, a term used to describe three precisely folded blankets with two middle layers of bedsheets, all wrapped in yet another blanket (headscarf fashion) and placed at each bed's head on top of a stretched tight as a drum blanket. The slightest ripple or an out-of-line blanket resulted in the whole lot ending up going through the nearest window along with the boots, ear-wax and whatever else had gone before.

Despite the intensity of imposed discipline, the recruit wing occupants were cossetted and carefully looked after, having no contact with those who had previously gone through the process before settling in the regiment. I had no issues of any kind and enjoyed being with other boys who were of no threat to me.

There was a real possibility of my life tumbling down again with talk of the regiment closing due to the Cuban Missile Crisis in October of 1962. Plans were being drawn up by the Ministry of Defence to repatriate all regimental members under seventeen-and-a-half years of age, sending them back to their families as they were deemed too young to go to war. I was at a low ebb; I didn't want to go home, but I didn't want to fight either. Ironically, it wouldn't have mattered if the Ministry of Defence ordered all under-aged boys to go home, because if a nuclear war had broken out, as was widely believed would happen at the time, people everywhere would be 'nuked' whether on a train, the front line of battle or anywhere for that matter. My only hope was that if a nuclear war had broken out, it happened before I got back to Faroe Road. I didn't relish the prospect of being blown to smithereens in the garden of our house amongst marauding dogs only to end up throwing bricks and shouting Gertcha! in perpetuity.

The first six weeks in the Junior Leaders Regiment in Denbury was a time of assessment to determine who stayed and who went home. Boys who found discipline too much to bear or unable to co-ordinate their bodies while marching found themselves on the next train home. An academic examination of core subjects was to be undertaken by those who were not exempt from a recognised qualification for future promotion in adult service. In non-technical branches of the Army, I understood that the requirement to obtain an Army Certificate of Education Class III was unnecessary, although a minimum required before one could hold the rank of corporal. As a Junior Leader in the Royal Corps of Signals, all members were required to obtain the certificate within six weeks of joining; else, it was back on the next train to Timbuktu - or Paddington.

Despite the 'Boot-camp' portrayal, the regiment was a much sought-after establishment with a long waiting list for children of serving British soldiers around the world competing to join. How I managed to be selected remained a mystery. That bright star in the sky might have had something to do with it. Thank you, Dad. The Junior Leaders Regiment was first and foremost a military training centre for young men, structured along the lines of a boarding school of further education with similar term times and holidays, albeit without half-term breaks which were themselves taken up with outward bound activities on Dartmoor. At the end of the term, Denbury Camp would fall silent, closed until the start of the following semester, with all boys having been sent home with free travel on the railways.

During term times at Denbury, daily routines continued unabated with meaningful academic education sessions being taught, interspersed with trade training and military training. Drill or 'square bashing' was honed to an extraordinary degree with boys as young as fifteen handling self-loading rifles that had lethal bayonets as long as their forearms fixed at the end of the rifle barrel wavering just millimetres from their ears. Because of the instilled discipline and being bellowed at with the words 'Stand up, stand straight, but, above all else, stand still', if anyone happened to slice off one of their ears, just like an irritating itch, the experience had to be totally ignored until the end of each parade-ground session. 'Square-bashing' sessions were practices that almost everyone disliked, but, perversely, I liked it once I mastered the movements to the exact uncompromising standard required.

The first six weeks of training were up. The impending examination to obtain an Army Certificate of Education Class III was looming, and I was going to have to face one of the hardest things in my life other than trying to board a trolley bus at 35mph. I was about to meet my nemesis, as my secondary school time did not serve me well. Mathematics was a subject I found difficult to grasp, with teachers at school completely ignoring the issues I had with the matter. A self-diagnosis of dyscalculia (mathematics dyslexia) was not readily recognised by anyone during the time I was at school, as far as I knew, but it was unlikely that I had the condition as my maths started to markedly improve, attracting written remarks of 'good work – silly mistakes.' I would often write figures the wrong way around in the final totals, although mathematical problem solving and mental arithmetic was not an issue.

Almost the whole of the first six weeks as a recruit, I concentrated on learning algebra and other forms of mathematics during evenings and weekends, with coaching and encouragement from a fellow recruit who double-checked my work and re-arranged the figures into the correct order. As far as I could make out at the time, coming from an all-boys school, 'girls' was just a word cast in a stone block above the entrance of a school gate, and, for all I knew, algebra was an item of a lady's upper-worn lingerie bought from an Algerian Bazaar in North Africa used to keep one's ears warm during the winter months in cold, draughty, non-centrally heated houses. Come on - I was only fifteen years of age.

Six weeks after sitting the first of many examinations, the results were in. Our gaggle of forty-something recruits had assembled on the tarmac surfaced parade square for the results to be announced. Out came a sergeant-major somebody or other who proceeded to bawl out names in alphabetical order, broadcasting the results.

"Darling?" "Yes, sir," I replied.

I could have said 'Yes, dear', but that would have resulted in eight laps of the parade ground in a complete military kit with a rifle held high above my head, or else feeling the draught of the cell door at the guardroom – I kid you not!

"Pass," said the man making the announcements, "Well done!"

Pass? I thought. Well done? I'd never passed anything worthy of note, except for the skilful dodge of an iron poker and copious amounts of flatulence that almost sent my friend's Brooke Bond Tea van into orbit and his mother towards a behavioural management course. While others were hearing of their results, my mind drifted into an imaginary world where I found myself running down an Austrian mountainside singing to the tune of,

♫ 'The hills are alive with the sound of music, la, la, la-la'. ♪

Those thoughts quickly evaporated when someone shouted, "Oi, Plonker! Get moving."

After everyone else had galloped off for their mug of tea and lump of bread-pudding served from the back door of the cookhouse way off in the distance, I too set off running at super-fast speed to catch up with my contemporaneous colleagues who were in a wild free-for-all, racing to be the first to grab the customary mid-morning treat. With added carnation evaporated milk served up in large aluminium urns, the hot brew was rumoured to have also included bromide that inhibited male sex hormone production and, when poured into a standard-issue pint-sized plastic mug, everything else along with it also became floppy.

Alcohol was non-existent anywhere in the camp other than at the Sergeants' or Officers' Mess, although a group of boy soldiers accommodated within the barracks were partial to a drop of the mighty stuff themselves, evident by the discovery of a considerable amount of it stashed in the loft above their beds. The hoard of illicit beverages only came to light following an impromptu inspection from an over-inquisitive confused sergeant who had detected an unexpected whiff of alcohol over and above the usual smell of 'Kiwi' boot polish and 'Brasso' metal polish. By coincidence or otherwise, before discovering the booze, 'The Jolly Sailor' pub in the nearby village of East Ogwell became subject to a break-in when large quantities of bottled beers disappeared.

In an attempt to expose the culprit or culprits' identities of those involved in the theft of alcohol, the whole troop of forty-something individuals became the subject of extreme collective punishment. Every day, the rest of the camp awoke to the sound of double-quick marching and other hyper-active goings-on with all those taking part dressed in their finest, polished up to the nines. The same activities continued every morning and evening for a whole month, but those responsible for the burglary remained unknown. If the names of those responsible for the theft had been revealed, the consequences for everyone would have been too severe to contemplate. I suspect those administering the punishment had a quiet respect for the camaraderie shown; after all, that is what would have been essential in a theatre of war.

As growing teenagers within the Army, my colleagues and I were always hungry, eagerly awaiting every mealtime where contrary to popular belief, good wholesome traditional food was available. In the evenings, a few of the lads would nip over to the Church Army canteen situated within the barracks for subsidised bacon sandwiches and toasted teacakes, paid for out of our meagre weekly pay of £2.2s 0d (£2.10p) before deductions. The average remuneration for someone of the same age in civilian life was thrice that amount, although, of course, we were housed, clothed, fed - and cloned. Here's where the weekly spends went: -

1. Five shillings (25p) compulsory contribution automatically went to the regimental sports fund. There was no free kit of any kind,

2. £1 mandatory saving, reimbursed before going on leave to show the world it was worth joining the Army. Most of the total amount I took home I handed to my mother for housekeeping, which was always eagerly received.

3. Two shillings (10p) Canoe Club fees. I opted for the club to avoid being forced into the regimental band drumming or bugling around the parade ground in the evenings during what would otherwise have been free time.

There were several choices of compulsory evening activities to keep idle hands free from trouble, but all had to be paid for by way of a deduction from our pay to the 'Regimental Sports Fund'. I do not recall seeing rugby or football boots anywhere, although the barracks did have sports playing fields. Most of our remaining pay went towards buying metal polish, yellow polishing dusters, Blanco for cleaning webbing, Kiwi boot polish, soap, toothpaste and 'Windolene' window cleaner. Oh, and bacon rolls – of course. That was it. The only cleaning material spared from purchasing out of our meagre wages was copious amounts of linoleum wax floor polish. The thick, smelly petroleum-based stuff had to be applied to the centre strip of brown linoleum that stretched from one end of the barrack-room to the other to ensure it remained polished to perfection - every single day. Walking on the floor covering was to be avoided at all costs, which somewhat negated the purpose of having the lino strip there in the first place. Some boys of affluent parents would receive food parcels containing their mums' home-baked fruit cake allowing the recipients to stretch their pay to cover the cost of a couple of packets of fags even though many of the lads were underage to buy such things. There was a term 'Two's-up' which meant that whoever was the first to utter the phrase had first-call of the dog-end before it was flicked out of the nearest window.

Occasionally, when items of uniform wore out or outgrown (including boots), the unfortunate custodian would have to pay for them to be replaced, the cost of which entered into pay-books with a steady amount deducted each week until settled. Clothing burnt while ironing or boots damaged when applying a hot spoon to smooth out the dimples, as we were required to do, usually resulted in the individual responsible being held to account. The punishment for damaging army property usually involved extreme physical activity and having to pay for whatever had to be replaced.

There was a time when our troop was under the guidance and supervision of a particular sergeant; the fact two boys had perished in a fire that destroyed an entire block of six barrack rooms was totally lost on him. We were ordered to blacken the bare floorboards of our bed-spaces using Kiwi boot polish. Not only was there a potential to create a 'tinderbox' ready to ignite at almost any moment, but it also meant us luckless individuals having to buy the polish ourselves in multitudes of small tins rendering every one of us penniless, except, of course, the sergeant.

'Shreddies', the name given to the two or three pairs of standard-issue underpants, came about because of going unnoticed as they wore out. No-one wanted to fork out yet more money to replace them, so the green cotton pants hung like shredded paper from the waist, out of sight until their very end. Detachable shirt collars had removable stud-fasteners that choked the wearer as he grew from being a 'diddy' fifteen-year-old to a strapping lad of almost eighteen years of age.

The sport of boxing has always been taken seriously by the Army, which meant having to go through a process of assessment for boxing abilities by supposedly being paired with someone of similar height and build. I was a loser from the start because of being the smallest member of the intake and couldn't possibly have knocked the skin off a rice pudding, let alone anything or anyone else. I entered into a boxing ring for the first time in my life, and, when a bell rang out signifying the start of round one, I got up to face my opponent wearing over-sized boxing gloves that were big enough to be used as covers for the yellow flashing Belisha beacons at pedestrian crossings. I approached my adversary with my spindly arms waving about that created illusionary confusing images of a troupe of Hindu dancers standing one behind the other, having launched into the Diwali 'festival of light' dance routine. I went flying in an instant. The match stopped half-way through the second round after the referee slipped on snot and slobber and declared that I was unsuitable for the sport. I was not to box again – ever. That'll do nicely, thank you! I'd had enough of violence.

'The Devil does work for idle hands' comes to mind, especially at weekends when boys of our troop had to give up Saturdays, climbing aboard an army lorry to be taken on a journey to Kingsteignton for community work, tidying up the gardens of people who, through illness or physical incapacity were unable to do themselves. All very well for the kind-heart individuals who thought up the scheme but were nowhere to be seen on the weekends of the tasks.

Sunday mornings were not our own either, having to attend mandatory church parades, not just members of the recruit wing, but all Junior Leaders in the camp. The time of 10.30 a.m. would see us all lined up in ranks of three and marched off to the Church-of-England's place of worship. We would then have to wait outside in military formation until the officers and their ladies had filed past before being allowed to enter the building ourselves. Individuals proclaiming themselves agnostic were required to attend, but instead of joining the ranks of very reluctant worshippers, they found themselves standing at attention outside the church until the end of the service, regardless of the prevailing weather conditions. Others who declared themselves as Roman Catholic marched off to the gymnasium in search of their own saviour.

One Sunday morning, there was an occasion while standing close to the church entrance when I happened to peer in through the doorway and saw a few of the officers' wives and daughters acting as if they were royalty themselves, filing in to sit on the front row of pews. One chap who stood next to me pointed towards one of the daughters and asked,

"Is that Fanny Green over there?"

"No", I replied. "It's the way the light comes in through the stained-glass windows."

'Father, forgive me, for I know not what I say is what I might have said if I had been in the gymnasium. I considered changing my religious label by joining the Catholic guys in the gym but thought better of it, knowing that their Sunday services always seemed to go on forever as the unfortunate worshippers painfully listened to all kinds of eyebrow-lifting stories. One could easily see the bored expressions on the poor souls' faces as they made their way from the gymnasium to the cookhouse for a very late limited selection of Sunday lunch. Thank you, father - but no thanks.

The first fourteen weeks in the recruits wing quickly came and went before I found myself homeward bound on my first spot of leave, carrying my all-too-obvious brand spanking new armed forces issue green suitcase, reinforced at the corners with genuine brown leather. Mr Baggs's suitcase was somewhere between Totnes and Dartmouth, bobbing along on the River Dart. When I arrived home in Faroe Road, I think Mr Baggs' enquired about the return of his suitcase; I could have told him that a good start would have been to get as far as Dartmouth Castle before the tide came in and probably sometime within the next twenty-four hours.

Returning home on my first leave at Christmas proved to be a non-event, except when I opened a tin of 'Ye Olde Oak Ham' using a pair of pliers, slicing through my thumb with the peeled-back edge of the can as I did so. The injury necessitated yet another visit to the same hospital I attended a few years earlier on the two occasions I had broken wrists, only this time to have stitches applied to the open wound on my thumb. I found myself bored witless and wanting to be back at Denbury.

Two weeks later, I was aboard a second-class railway carriage, one of many being pulled by a locomotive fitted with a snowplough at its front that huffed and puffed its way down to Newton Abbot in Devon. Somewhere between Exeter and my destination, it soon became apparent why the train had been fitted with the snowplough; snow on the tracks was so plentiful, the train frequently came to a juddering halt as the world outside remained in total darkness. At such times, a deafening silence prevailed throughout the whole of the train, broken only by the odd cough, the sound of flatulence or flushing of a toilet, the contents of which would impact directly onto the snow-covered railway tracks below. Splat!

Upon arrival at Newton Abbot railway station, I was greeted with the sight of Bedford army trucks lined up waiting to take me and others onto the relatively short trip back to Denbury Camp a few miles away within the snow-covered, icy hills of the Devon countryside.

A new year and a new term of learning were underway, but before that could happen, the parade square had to be cleared of sheet ice covering the entire surface from end to end. Several days of using pickaxes and other bits of kit passed as other members of my new troop and I formed a line to chip away at the ice. It wasn't until every trace of ice had gone and the matt-black tarmac surface returned to its pristine condition could we then resume regular activities.

Having moved out of the recruit wing into one of the established 'troops', amongst boys much older and bigger than me, I became an immediate item of curiosity, most likely because of my unfortunate surname of Darling, a name you would not want in any army. I was small in stature and probably somewhat of an enigma by having the outward appearance and demeanour of self-confidence resulting from not having a father, all of which required testing.

A short time after settling into the new 'troop', it wasn't long before one particular individual, a bully from Battersea who decided he was going to be my tormentor until he graduated into adult service eighteen months later. Some individuals within the troop positioned themselves in their own perceived hierarchy, with Battersea Boy amongst them. My tormentor often made a bee-line for me whenever we were away from the gaze of anyone in authority and became a worrying threat, especially when on cross-country runs or at weekends in the barrack room when adult members of staff were absent. Luckily, trade training for Battersea Boy was different from mine and, as he attended other classes, I was free from him for most of the time each day throughout the working week or at weekends when trudging across Dartmoor.

Within a day or so of settling in amongst a new group of individuals, the customary 'New Recruit Initiations' ceremony kicked-off in the evening when senior staff had retreated to their respective clubs or married quarters, leaving junior members within the regiment unsupervised and left to their own devices. The so-called initiations that followed allowed bullies and older more dominant individuals to re-organise the established 'pecking order' in a manner of their choosing.

At the start of each term, the initiation ceremonies involved some of the more unpleasant troop members lining up each side of the highly polished central linoleum strip in the barrack room. New arrivals from the recruitment wing were stripped naked and forced to run its length with water poured onto the surface to increase viscosity. Pillowcases stuffed with metal-studded boots and other unpleasant objects rained down, knocking me and a couple of others flying into chairs and the ends of metal bed-frames. One or two thugs amongst the perpetrators, including Battersea Boy, had a field day. The bashing led to being frog-marched to the drying-room and shackled to hot water pipes so that we were unable to move as black boot polish was applied to our genitals. It was brutal. I often wonder if the two boys that had perished in the drying-room when their billet complex caught fire shortly before I joined the regiment coincided with initiation ceremonies being carried out at the time? Hopefully not. Nothing was ever mentioned about the tragic event.

The end of each term saw the older members of the regiment graduate into adult service with a ritual of heading off into Newton Abbot to drink themselves silly for the first time in their lives before returning to barracks for their last night. The nasty guys among them would zero-in on their intended victims lying awake in their beds in anticipation of being beaten-up, feigning sleep and dreading what was to come. I was one such victim of a beating, receiving a broken nose on one occasion and a fractured jaw on another, which I only learned of many years later when attending a dentist who brought the old injuries to my attention. At the time of the beatings, no-one was willing to report the matter for fear of being marginalised or treated as an outcast - it just wasn't done. I was lucky; a boy in the bed opposite, not so. One of his tormentors was none-other than the Battersea bully who used the heel of a leather-soled metal-studded leather boot as a weapon. As a result of the beating, the recipient of that particular tirade of violence had one of his ear-drums perforated; blood was seen suppurating from deep within his ear. I don't know who struck the actual blow or if the perpetrator was held to account; what I did know was that the victim didn't make it to adult service but instead subsequently medically discharged from the service. Battersea Boy was to get partial comeuppance later after he left the Junior Leaders Regiment and posted abroad. More on him later.

During the summer of 1963, I was fortunate enough to attend a three-week duration outward bound course near Towyn, North Wales, situated on the coast in the Snowdonia National Park shadow. Before I could attend the outward-bound centre, it was necessary to undergo a physical medical examination to establish my fitness to endure the rigorous demands I would have to endure. However, it transpired that I had a groin hernia large enough to warrant urgent medical intervention. Off I went to HMS Drake, a Royal Naval Hospital in Plymouth for corrective surgery and afterwards sent home to recuperate, thankfully missing the last day of the term along with the ritual beatings that usually followed. I returned to Denbury in September 1963 for the start of the winter term and immediately re-selected for the same outward-bound adventure that I had missed out on previously.

It was early December of the same year, the outward-bound centre in North Wales was covered with a thick layer of snow. Snowdonia and the horseshoe pattern of mountains rising to the peak of Snowdonia itself, including the challenging climb of Cadre Idris that glistened a majestic ice-white in the distance. Snowdonia was the training ground for the three-week duration, including trekking, mountaineering, rock climbing and canoeing, closely monitored to ascertain an individual's ability, attitude and response to adversity. Mornings started at 6 a.m. with the commanding officer entering our dormitory along with his two black Labrador dogs, ushering us out while we were naked over to the cold showers across a snow-covered frosty concrete yard. If that wasn't bad enough, the mutts, in their own inimitable style, would follow, nudging our rear-ends with their noses as a way of helping us along and wishing us all a perfect morning. Gertcha!

After completing the course in North Wales, I returned to Denbury with a 'Badge of Achievement' proudly sewn onto my uniform, one of a few Junior Leaders qualified to do so.

At the age of seventeen years and two days, I had managed to save enough money to buy a course of driving lessons for a princely sum of fifteen-bob (75p) per session. Each Saturday, I was met at the camp gates by a driving instructor from Newton Abbot. The guy teaching me how to drive would arrive in a Triumph Herald saloon car before we both set off, relentlessly going uphill and downhill in and around Newton Abbot. After just six lessons, I underwent a driving test and, to the instructor's disappointment – passed! The vehicle I drove did not have a synchromesh gear-box for first and second gear, which meant one had to 'double-de-clutch' when changing down from third to second gear, then to first gear. Failure to engage the correct gear ratio at the right speed would have resulted in irreparable damage to the gear-box, signified by the sound of a loud metal grinding noise. The phrase, 'tap-tickle-tap', continuously repeated by the driving instructor, required putting one's foot firmly down on the clutch pedal and increasing the engine speed to match the selected gears' revolutions before then dropping the gear lever down and finally releasing the clutch pedal. 'Tap-tickle-tap' proffered by the driving instructor in modern times might well have landed him or her in the slammer. Gertcha!

Although having secured a full driving licence authorising me to drive a motor vehicle up to and including three-and-a-half imperial tons, I could not even consider purchasing the cheapest of second-hand cars, so instead opted for an old 49cc moped, which I used to race around Devon's lanes during weekends when there was nothing else to do. The late Denis Morgan, a friend and colleague, owned a proper motorbike when, on one particular occasion, lost control of it travelling at fifty miles per hour as I sat behind him as a pillion passenger. I recall cartwheeling my way through the air before coming to rest some distance away amongst some bramble bushes. I was cut, bruised, and disorientated but otherwise unharmed, but the bike took a bashing, so did Denis. Unperturbed and mindful of returning to barracks, I took it upon myself to ride the bike back to camp, passing through Newton Abbot High Street at the same time as a civil disturbance was underway. Fearful of being arrested for any number of offences, Denis and I proceeded through the middle of the trouble zone uninterrupted, despite the motorbike looking totally unroadworthy with tufts of grass sticking out from different parts of the frame. A lucky escape. Phew!

Impressed by a motorbike's power, I decided that I wanted to have a more powerful machine than my old peddle-equipped moped. Off I went to a motor-scooter shop in Newton Abbott and asked the lady on the premises if she had an 'Itchi-fani' that I could look at, believing it to be a Japanese motor scooter. After a narrowing of eyes and a cold stare that could easily have stripped wallpaper, the lady replied,

"No, we only have Italian Vespas and Lambrettas, you silly bastard."

She was right there. After my monumental blunder, I felt obliged to put a £1 deposit on an Italian Lambretta motor scooter priced at £40 to ward off any possibility of retribution from the only other male person in the shop. I never did return to complete the purchase despite knowing that I had wasted the equivalent of three-and-a-half day's wages.

Term times at Denbury Camp came and went, during which a spectrum of continued studying and trade-training was underway. Subjects undertaken included all things military, trade skills, fitness, and outward-bound activities with endless trekking over Dartmoor, from the top of one Tor to the top of another over many miles, in all terrains in all weather conditions.

Health and Safety issues were non-existent during the 1960s, which brings to mind two particular adventures. During the winter of 1964, I was part of a group required to demolish an old brick outbuilding somewhere out in the remotest part of Dartmoor without any regard for the safety of those ordered to carry out the task. All the participants were aged between fifteen and seventeen years without a clue about safety. What with the sub-zero, icy conditions at the time, anything could have happened as a hydraulic car jack was put to toppling one of the remaining external walls close to those standing nearby.

During the same winter of 1964, I happened to be leading a section of fellow junior leaders across the Moors over what was to be two nights and three days trekking in some of the most inhospitable terrains Dartmoor had to offer. Off we went with enough kit and provisions to last a pre-planned time-scale on a pre-determined route, to arrive at some distant location at the top end of Dartmoor. The first night's experience sleeping under a bivouac (defined as a temporary camp without tents or cover, often used by soldiers or mountaineers) saw the heavens open up and, in the morning, found ourselves within three to four feet (900mm or 1200mm) of deep snow. Undeterred, we continued throughout the second day before setting up our bivouacs for a second night a few hundred metres below the summit of yet another Tor. During the second night, the temperature dropped rapidly, only for us to awake the following morning to another thick covering of snow with everything around us deathly quiet. What had been running water in the stream next to where we had set up for the night was frozen solid, necessitating a trip back up the steep sides of the Tor to ascertain the source of the stream and collect enough water for a hot cuppa and face wash.

At the beginning of the third day, the snow became so deep along the top ridges of the moors caused by drifting when nature called it would have been prudent to seek out and take advantage of the just-visible tops of fenceposts poking through the snow for support. To have done otherwise would have resulted in sinking down under the surface alongside whatever was left behind. We were utterly unfazed by our circumstances.

The morning of that third-day trekking across Dartmoor saw yet more snow-storms as our patrol arrived at the top of the last of many steep climbs. Looking down through binoculars into the distance, I caught sight of the reception camp with what appeared to be several individuals training their binoculars back in our direction with all manner of activities going on behind them. Little did I or other members of our group know that the whole 'exercise' had been called-off thirty-six hours previously and everyone located and returned to base camp – except us, of course. The organisers didn't have a clue of our whereabouts at any given time – but I did. Congratulations were the order of the day from the guy who organised the event without first checking the weather forecast beforehand. Sounds of 'Well done, well done' were barked out; a common phrase uttered by some individuals within the commissioned ranks who hadn't a clue as to what had been going on, or else struggling for something constructive to say other than 'spiffing' and in a language they thought ordinary soldiers would understand.

It was the last term before Easter 1965, during which time more studying and a final push were underway to achieve the highest marks possible to reach the standards necessary in all subjects that would offer a massive advantage over recruits entering the Royal Signals who had not themselves been through the same process having enlisted as adults. No longer was I the fretful child that had jumped down off the lorry on my arrival at Denbury Camp back in September of 1962. With the absence of thugs and bullies blighting my life, preventing me from concentrating on anything other than working out escape routes, I discovered a new confidence and a determination that I or anyone else for the matter was not going to become a victim of bullying. Throughout the two-and-a-half years at Denbury Camp, I achieved a Communications Centre Operator Class III status, qualified to sufficiently operate trunk military communications systems worldwide from as far away as Hong Kong. I passed the exam with distinction, receiving an award for achieving the highest results of the examinations.

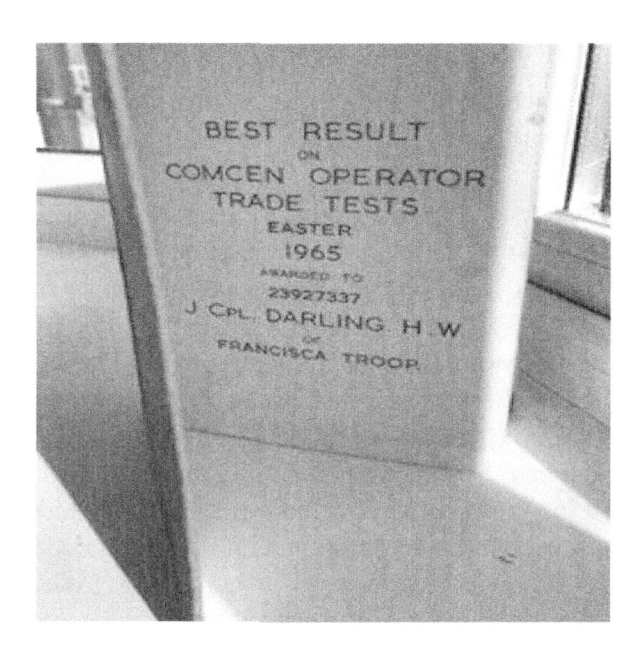

> BEST RESULT
> ON
> COMCEN OPERATOR
> TRADE TESTS
> EASTER
> 1965
> AWARDED TO
> 23927337
> J CPL DARLING H W
> OF
> FRANCISCA TROOP.

Although not essential or part of the curriculum, one particular skill acquired was being able to touch-type so fast without reading the text, the Siemens teleprinter would often malfunction. I was able to out-run the mechanism because, while other members of the class always piled out of the classrooms for an 'essential' so-called smoke break halfway through the ninety minutes of each lesson, I continued to plod on typing, determined to be as fast and accurate as I could possibly be. My determination and tenacity certainly paid off, as, during the last term of study, I ended-up marking the test papers of all the other candidates.

Reading 'ticker-tape' with a series of holes without text, although not part of the training, was a skill I developed as the tape spewed out of machines. Other exams passed while at the Junior Leaders Regiment included an Army Certificate of Education Class II and Class I with general science just one of several subjects. Although not an essential qualification for military service, the study of science did allow me to think 'outside the box' when it came to applying everyday applications such as: -

- Conserving cooking fuel when climbing mountains knowing that the higher the altitude, the lower the water's boiling point.
- Understanding the futility of subjecting one's bowels to colonic irrigation just to be trendy.
- Adding men's urea and the ureic crystals often found lurking within to a pile of rotting vegetation to accelerate the composting process. Stand back, ladies; I learned somewhere that, unfortunately, it's only the contribution from the male of our species that can make this process happen. Such actions not only obviated the need to find a loo, but the converted bio-material produced beautiful flowers to present to loved ones without even having to go anywhere near a shop. In gardening circles, some say that peeing onto a compost heap is the most helpful contribution any man has ever made for mankind, although I doubt that statement's accuracy. You decide. Mind you, 'Throwing a bucket of piss' in a Badgers run, as my late subsistence farmer neighbour eloquently once said, was enough to deter the most determined of the species running through one's garden. He didn't know if it mattered whether the donor was male or female as he lived alone. Hey-ho.

At various stages of military service, having attended courses both in the UK and abroad, I was to sit further examinations that opened the gates to all kinds of future opportunities if I were to remain in the army.

April 1965: Graduation Day. Parents dressed in all their finest arrived from all parts of the country to see their little boys becoming young men.

A 'march-past' ceremony honouring those graduating was underway attended by none other than the Colonel-in-Chief of the Royal Corps of Signals. After a protracted show of 'pomp-and-ceremony, those graduating into adult service received the order to 'slow march' from the parade ground, symbolising a move into adult service.

Junior leaders who were yet to graduate 'presented arms' with bayonets fixed to their self-loading rifles as an acknowledgement of our achievements, although their turn would come. Whatever rank we as Junior Leaders acquired counted for nothing the moment after marching off the parade ground for the last time.

Before I became Paddington-bound, an awards ceremony followed the passing-out parade, when I was presented with my award, a book titled 'German in Twenty Lessons', for being top of the course. I then went back to my room, taking my awarded book prize and mixed memories with me. The next day I was homeward bound - never to return.

Somebody at the Ministry of Defence or elsewhere in Government decided that money would have been better spent restricting entrants to establishments such as Denbury to university graduates instead of propping up the national education system's failings as it was then. The result was the closure of Denbury Camp in 1967 after only eight years in existence. Thirty-something wasted years later, a similar programme akin to the 'Junior Leaders' but of a different name was re-established after it was considered essential to recruit the type of servicemen that a modern army needed but seemed to be lacking after the closure of Junior Leaders and army apprentice regiments. Well done, somebody, well done! Did I hear 'Spiffing'?

Step-change

Catterick Garrison, Richmond, North Yorkshire; the home of just two of a few training regiments of The Royal Corps of Signals was where I found myself a couple of weeks after departing Denbury Camp. I had been selected to embark on a top-secret cipher encryption course that meant immediate promotion to the rank of corporal. A few weeks passed, but the necessary personal vetting hadn't taken place, or perhaps it had, and someone found out about my father's past naval record and my poverty-stricken upbringing, which might well have been perceived as possible exposure to blackmail. In any event, as I progressed through military service, I was able to demonstrate that those assumptions were misplaced despite coming from a less-than-desirable background by proving to be as honest and loyal as anyone else, perhaps even more so given the comments made in my army discharge testimonial as you'll read later. Interestingly, some years later, I teamed up with a cipher operator on a mission to take codes back to the U.K. to collect new data, so I must have had some sort of clearance but by which time had embarked on a different career path altogether. It was just as well that I did not enter into the top-secret world of cipher encryption; with the limited numbers of personnel engaged in the activity, further promotion would only have been into a dead man's shoes anyway.

With very little to do other than go into Darlington to sing my heart out, goaded-on by the local Geordie drinkers at 'The Hole in The Wall' public house, I became increasingly bored. During one particular visit to Darlington, I met my first ever girlfriend; we were both sweet seventeen, well, one of us was. The girl was called Helen somebody or other, who happened to live in the distant town of Bishop Auckland, County Durham. A walk along the riverbank in her home town resulted in my friend acquiring midge bites on her legs, and I receiving an unforgettable admonishment from her father. The next time the bus from Bishop Auckland arrived at Darlington bus station, it was empty. I was not to see the girl again. What!?

A flight to Germany was my first experience of being on an aircraft of any type, which happened to be a Dan-Air Britannia propeller aircraft. I was on my way to Wald Frieden Kaserne (lit trans. Forest Peace Barracks) in Herford, West Germany. At the airport, mesmerised at watching no-end of the travelling public dressed in all kinds of strange garb, I pondered about where they had come from or where they were going, except knowing that any man struggling to get through the automatic doors sideways on his way to the departure lounge was going to Bangkok!

Arriving at the barracks, it wasn't long before I spotted the Battersea bully himself, the very boy from Denbury Camp who did his best to make my life a misery a year or so previously. This guy had come to realise that I had become much taller and more grown-up than he had remembered and initially chose to ignore me; that was until I became a lance-corporal.

There was an occasion when charged with the task of ensuring discipline in the NAAFI bar. Duty completed, I was on my way to the guardroom when, in the darkness (save for a street light or two), sensed that I was being shadowed by a group of two or three individuals led by none other than my Battersea hero himself. I had been aware of some planned ill-intensions earlier from the bar by some and so on high alert. In the Corporal Guard Commander's company, I went to the most likely spot of ambush where 'low-and-behold, Battersea Boy was skulking around, minus his heroic mates who seemed to have evaporated along with his own sense of reasoning after consuming excessive amounts of alcohol. My would-be assailant was swiftly marched in double-quick time to the cells and locked up for the night only to receive seven days in the clink with intense discipline and loss of pay for the duration.

Double-quick marching, escorted by the regimental police on the journey to and from the cookhouse three times a day in full view of his mates, not to mention toiling late in the evenings polishing floors and undertaking endless other arduous chores right up until 10pm before being locked up in the cells for the night, must have been total humiliation in itself. If my adversary had actually physically attacked me, he would have ended up in the military prison back in Colchester, serving a prolonged period of internment under constant supervision of some very mean royal military police. He would then have been discharged from the service in disgrace.

Unlike Battersea Boy and his ilk, the only other ex-Junior Leader I saw in the regiment stood out like a beacon against regular soldiers who had enlisted as adults. Smartness (you could slice ham with their trouser creases), alertness and presence-of-mind to succeed in military life were common attributes. Qualifications acquired during what had been intense and concentrated two-and-a-half years of conditioning compared to several weeks of induction training for adult recruits had apparent advantages.

The unit to which I was assigned in Germany provided 'tactical' mobile communications support for the whole of the BAOR (British Army Over the Rhine), operating within a network of different command units of participating NATO armed forces. Like all others, our regiment was on twenty-four hours standby, ready to respond at any given time to any perceived threat posed by the Soviet Union and the armies of the Communist Eastern Bloc. Calls to 'action stations' were not an uncommon occurrence. One particular high-ranking officer somewhere had a 'well-done' or 'spiffing' moment; intent on spoiling everyone's fun, called an alert on a Saturday night when almost every single soldier in the land was known to be out on the town somewhere getting drunk. Sirens would sound in every German garrison town, with the military police scouring pubs and clubs ordering service personnel back to barracks for immediate deployment.

During excursions into the German countryside after being called to stations, it wasn't uncommon for military vehicles to be involved in fatal crashes due to soldiers being under the influence of alcohol when driving. I'm seen in the following picture sitting atop an army truck subject to such a collision. Like so many other victims of fatal crashes involving military vehicles, the driver of the army truck shown also died of his injuries.

One such call to stations involved our regiment being deployed to some secret location somewhere in the German countryside. The sites were almost always under forest canopies or in commandeered farm buildings, our boxed-shaped lorries packed to the gunnels with teleprinters and associated equipment hidden from land and aerial view. Linesmen would unravel mile-upon-mile of telephone cables running from one communication complex to another, climbing poles and crossing ditches to do so. Those linesmen, the equivalent of modern-day British Telecom engineers, were said to have had a life survival rate of eight minutes during active service. The wire spun out by those guys contained arsenic coated black plastic material that became a favourite snack for grazing cows that nonchalantly munched through them without ever having any side effects. Internet and satellite communications were non-existent as the Worldwide Web inventor, an English computer scientist called Berners-Lee, was only about eleven or twelve years of age when I was a serving solder in what was then West Germany.

For days on end, and with the constant expectation of receiving two hours' notice to load up and move elsewhere, regardless of whether one had had enough sleep after coming off shift, or even a chance of a meal, was always on everyone's mind. To keep up morale for lesser mortals, a large army truck loaded to its roof-top with crates of beer was always available, but not without first having to pay for it. The booze was a welcome relief from working two-way shifts without respite, especially when camped in dusty forests swarming with horseflies and mosquitoes wanting to cosy-up close at every opportunity. Catching one's rifle barrel on a soaking wet camouflage net while on the lookout for wild boar charging through our selected place of encampment was unpleasant, to say the least. Slipping and sliding on mud in the pouring rain while carrying two rectangular-shaped mess-tins half-filled with almost inedible slop, not to mention the make-shift lavatories, always oversubscribed and brimming full, added to our woes. And to think we were all volunteers!

It was 1966, and the World Cup final between the national football teams of arch-rivals West Germany and England was underway. British soldiers were undertaking tactical military exercises in and around the borders of what was then West Germany and The Netherlands, near to the residential town of Roosendaal. The Dutch residents, so enthralled with British troops' presence, opened-up their homes for us to watch the football match on their televisions, providing food along with copious amounts of Orangieboom beer (it's a lager, not a tune).

Just twenty-one years after the cessation of World War Two, feelings between Germany and its neighbours were still raw. The ecstatic happiness felt by the Dutch when England scored the winning goal was palpable. Oddly enough, during multi-excursions across the German countryside playing war-games, it was rare to find a commissioned officer anywhere. They were not present in anyone's home to watch the match either. I suspect the obligation of these 'gentlemen' having to return the salute to everyone they came across was probably just one of many reasons why officers kept a low profile.

As far as I can make out, saluting originated from earlier times when 'Knights in Armour' lifted their visors to demonstrate that they had no ill-intentions before then facing the palms of their hands outwards to show that they were not concealing a lethal weapon. The naval salute involved turning the palm of the hand downwards as a mark of respect because sailors' hands were known to be dirty. My take on the subject is that in more recent times, members of the armed forces were required to remove their hats as a mark of respect in the reigning monarch's commissioned officers' presence. I suspect that for all the pomp and fuss involved in removing and replacing caps (feathers and all in some instances), the doffing of hats became more practical before morphing into the modern-day salute. During my eight-and-a-half-years of service in the military, I saluted more times than I had hot dinners - and that was just me on a 'one-on-one' experience. I have total empathy for officers who were obliged to return the salute to everyone they came across, there being only one of them at any one time but a whole regiment of other souls' keen to acknowledge the gentleman's presence. I wouldn't be surprised to learn if every career officer suffers the condition 'Tennis Elbow' in retirement. And Gout - Cheers!

It often occurred to me that there were two armies within one; the officer class and everyone else. Officers were quite different from the rank and file in their attitude and approach to others. The demeanour and intellectual superiority displayed by some showed no sign of abatement when amongst those who knew more about what they were doing than they did. Officers of the commissioned ranks wore uniforms that were quite different from everyone else that included wearing a 'Sam Browne', a term used to describe a mid-brown broad leather belt joined by a narrow diagonal strap worn from the shoulder. The origins of the fashion accessory (that was all it was and still is) came about after Col. Samuel Browne devised a way to continue carrying a sword after losing his arm at the shoulder in battle back in the 1800s. I always viewed the wearing of such leather by able-bodied people as nonsense which served no practical purpose other than to visually elevate the wearer to a higher status when nothing more than wearing their rank insignia on their uniform served the same purpose. There Tiz.

It used to be deemed a 'rite of passage' for young men from privileged backgrounds able to become commissioned officers for their own or their family's benefit rather than for the good of the service. It was common practice for many such individuals to be engaged for a 'short term commission' of four years to attain a captain's rank if they were lucky. Apart from attending Sandhurst Military Academy, new officers had to be financially self-sufficient to pay exorbitant mess fees, which usually meant being supported by well-to-do parents, something that was entirely out-of-reach for the common man. Almost all short-term commissioned officers left the service to take up careers in civilian life, taking their ranked title with them to gain some sort of advantage in the commercial or political world. Anyone from a working-class background, especially those whose dialect was noticeably regional, and of course those without any sort of family financial backing or privilege, would not have stood a chance. However, there were some exceptions: officers that had come through the ranks. Time served within the 'Other ranks (a derogatory term for lesser mortals) would have left little time for most (not all) to achieve a captain's status before retirement. Such career officers from the lower ranks were distinctly different from their colleagues in their approach to everyday soldiers and their appointments within regiments. Most had silent empathy for those whose ranks they had left, their assignments usually non-tactical as quartermasters or in some other puerile administrative position.

In later life, I met a couple of ex-army career officers, one of whom was a Brigadier (retired) who reminisced by telling me that he started as a baby corporal (lance corporal), but his case was an exception and probably due to being conscripted before he had time to consider a commission. Another acquaintance once told me he was an ex-major promoted through the ranks but had been denied access to the Officers Mess until he removed his 'Long Service & Good Conduct' medal, only awarded to the 'Other Ranks' who had completed twenty-two years of unblemished service.

Back at the barracks in Herford, activities usually focused on keeping idle hands occupied, but without a war to be had, a lot of time was spent carrying out all kinds of everyday tedious chores. Some duties included keeping the barracks up-to-scratch or working in the cookhouse, spending the day 'tin bashing' or spud peeling by hand. It wasn't unusual to reduce twenty sacks of skin-on potatoes to two while at the same time those taking part smoking themselves to death, flicking ash into the mix to give added potash in the hope of helping their fellow compatriots to blossom. Just good science, as I'm sure you'll understand.

During the months that followed, tedium abated a little once I had been transferred to work within a British army communications centre at an American nuclear missile site somewhere near Monchengladbach. It was good to get away from everyday routines, but having a good time was almost impossible due to the low pay level for ordinary British soldiers.

Returning to the regimental in Herford, one of the most dreaded duties involved having to present oneself at 6 p.m. on designated days to form part of 'The Guard' despite having worked for a full day beforehand. The only concession offered for working through to the following morning was an early evening meal at 4.30 p.m. instead of the usual 5.30 p.m. It was then back to regular duties at 8.30am the next day without a break, polished up to parade-ground perfection for whatever was set before us.

Winters' experiences in Germany were often harsh extremes of low temperatures and penetrating frost, none more so than in the barracks' geographical location. The ammunition store was situated in isolation to the north of the main camp within nearby woods that consisted of several 'Nissan Hut' style buildings constructed of arched asbestos roofs. These buildings were confined within a high-wire compound with one point of access via the main entrance gates. It was the duty of a solitary person to be in attendance at all times overnight within the compound, armed only with a pickaxe-handle and a field telephone attached to a length of wire running back to the guardroom that didn't always seem to work.

During one particular assignment at the compound, and with nothing to do other than walk up and down during a freezing cold and bleak frosty night between deep-frozen snow-drifts; in a vain attempt to keep warm wearing a borrowed Parka coat, I huddled inside a sentry box to ward off the biting cold. While sat on a plank of wood serving as a seat, tilted forward to prevent one falling off to sleep, I would be in constant wonderment as to whether or not I was about to be 'nobbled' by those wanting whatever was in the storage huts. I wouldn't have stood a chance pitting myself against armed intruders with my seventeen years old teenage physique, naivety, and a piece of wood. The one floodlight served only to highlight my location at any one point anywhere within the high-wired enclosure, rendering one's eyes unable to see beyond the perimeter fence into the darkness.

It was on another freezing lonely night at the ammunition compound, with every extremity of my body one step away from frostbite, that I met the acquaintance of a solitary mouse that was obviously also in need of some respite. I called the mouse 'Mickey' on account of the way it stoically looked up motionless as if 'taking the mickey', conveying a message that it was not about to be going anywhere, anytime soon. We struck up a temporary friendship, Mickey, and I, with me asking if he had any English relatives that had a penchant for crapping on food stored in tall-boy cupboards, but my mousey friend remained silent despite the imminent threat of being stamped-on with a size eleven army boot. Our impromptu meeting came to an abrupt halt when the duty officer, a subaltern not long out of Sandhurst and intent on impressing his superiors, decided to test my alertness by scaling the fence at the periphery of the compound. The officer in question didn't have the gumption to realise that the high-level razor-sharp barbed-wire perimeter barrier was designed to keep intruders out of the complex. No surprise there then that the over-zealous gentleman snagged his 'bits' while scaling the fence. It was apparent that he had injured himself, evident by a noticeable crabbing gait as he strode towards me. "Evening, sir, cold enough for you?" I said; silence prevailed. Silly sod. If my unexpected visitor had turned up a couple of hours later instead of nipping back to his officers' mess for a swift half or a 'wee nip' to keep warm, he might well have achieved what he had set out to do, which was probably to wreck a twenty-two years career of a committed soldier before evaporating back into civilian life. Spiffing!

As time went on, I continued to be selected for trade upgrade studies and other subjects in readiness for future promotion. One such course was a three-week advanced outward-bound activity at a centre situated on a Norwegian Fjord shoreline. Activities involved outdoor pursuits majoring on physical fitness, mountaineering, rock climbing, sea survival, swimming, and canoeing. A journey over two days in a 'bone-rattling bus, travelling from West Germany to Denmark with an overnight stay in a Danish army barracks was part of the experience before boarding a ferry that took me and a few others to Kristiansand in Norway. It was then onwards to the Outward-Bound Centre some thirty or so miles away along compacted sand road surfaces, sat in the back of a Bedford TK British army truck, painted blue to appease the 'tetchy' Soviets who would otherwise have assumed a build-up of British military forces was underway.

 On arrival at the centre, the same group of soldiers that accompanied me from Germany were led to the sleeping accommodation under a woodland canopy that consisted of nothing more than four-persons tents on concrete slabs.

Mosquito nets suspended above individual canvas camp-beds was our only means of comfort. The first stop was the shoreline for a swimming test to ascertain, who was not a proficient swimmer in open-sea conditions. Those who failed the swimming test quickly found themselves on the next boat back to mainland Europe to their respective military units. Interestingly, no-one ever ascertained our ability to swim before setting off to Norway, but then, there were no swimming pools available to any of us back in Germany anyway.

At the outward-bound activity centre, there was to be no end of challenges, mentally and physically. One particular experience was when a few of us swam away from the shoreline and boarded a small motorboat bound for an off-shore island devoid of almost everything other than seagull guano and battering waves. Before setting off from the base camp, we had to perform ten press-ups in shallow seawater, completely submerging our torsos to ensure that anything we attempted to smuggle in our clothing or bodily crevices would be spoiled.

After the initial body checks, those of us taking part were then instructed to swim to the open boat before being taken out to sea and ordered to swim to the rock-strewn coastline of a remote outcrop of land, just out of view behind crescendo after crescendo of battering waves. The island was to be our home for the next forty-eight hours, without food or shelter - or so we were led to believe. However, sea conditions became so perilous within a very short space of time, we were ordered off the island and had to swim back to the rescue boat before being taken to a more sheltered island. Thankfully, the second location was covered in trees, but we were once again required to jump overboard and swim to shore to get to it. No food, clothing, or shelter of any kind; we were at the mercy of the elements. One enterprising individual had prior knowledge of what was to come and secreted heads of matchsticks in a condom either held between his buttocks or within his rectum. If the same bloke had been a member of the Pioneer Corps, a live chicken or two might well have been discovered lurking there too. The match-heads provided the source for a multitude of camp-fires on the island that seemed to magically appear. One lucky participant managed to catch a large fish that had been collected and dispatched back to base camp and cooked to perfection as a welcome-back gift for him - and only him. The rest of us had to be content with communally cooking our allocated British Army tinned composite rations on primus stoves sat on concrete shelves within a bricked-up enclosure.

A reminder that World War Two had not been too far in the past happened when our group of intrepid adventurers camped in woods, having navigated sea-bound lakes and rivers clogged with felled trees on their way downstream to processing plants perhaps hundreds of miles away. A stranger entered our camping area to join us around a campfire expressing his wish to communicate. Our Norwegian visitor proceeded to roll up his trousers to reveal a line of finger-nail-sized round scars that he said were a result of being shot at by occupying Nazis as he was escaping from somewhere and how pleased he was to know we were British soldiers even though we didn't have a single gun between us.

The outward-bound course concluded; I went back to Germany to experience the same monotonous everyday routine duties until selected for a trade upgrade course. That done, somebody whispered in my ear that a vacancy for a lance corporal with my qualifications had become available in Lisbon, and would I like to volunteer(?). Would I like to volunteer? Not Arf! An opportunity to get away from the boredom of subsidised drinking amongst others who had little ambition to do anything else suited me perfectly. Daily life just didn't seem right without the pleasure of seeing those of the opposite gender other than fleeting glances of wives of married soldiers, mostly hidden away in static caravan living quarters adjacent to the barracks. It must have been absolutely freezing for those guys in those aluminium-clad boxed living quarters. The thought of a nice place in the sun, working in a 'live' environment surrounded by beautiful girls in Bikinis falling at one's feet as promised in army recruitment advertisements was overwhelming, to say the least. I volunteered - of course. Within a few days, I learned that my application was successful and instructed to prepare for departure to LISBURN! A quick scurry to the library for a world atlas revealed that I should be looking at a map of Northern Ireland. Fiddle-le-dee, fiddle-le-dee, fiddle-de-bloody-dee!

A ninety-minute flight back to Gatwick Airport, I was on my way to the house I thought I had seen the back of in Faroe Road. At home, I observed Mr Baggs ducking and diving in and out of view in all sorts of circumstances while discussing the possibility of a German genetic connection with the resident mice. While I was at home on leave, I discovered that the younger of my two older sisters was about to be married, but I was neither invited to attend the wedding nor to the reception, which took place in a temporary community hall built on the derelict ground at the top end of Faroe road that had previously set the scene for stone-throwing several years earlier. My mother attended the wedding, along with my other siblings. Memories of sitting outside on wet pavements with my back against the railings of someone's house while the rest of my family were inside watching television came flooding back. This time, the rejection was of no bother to me.

A few days after my sister's wedding, I was off again, only this time definitely closing the front door of 52 Faroe Road – forever. Very soon afterwards, our house, along with a couple of others on each side and the resident bed-bugs, headlice, rats, honky-tonk piano, mice, builders' rubble that filled the basement rooms to bursting point, and memories of my father, had all been demolished.

Northern Ireland

Belfast, Oh, Belfast; part of Ireland and the United Kingdom all rolled into one, the population identifying themselves as British, Irish, or both. Northern Ireland is well documented and often in the media for various reasons, but this chapter is about my perceptions and experiences among wonderful people in a beautiful part of the world until the time I reluctantly had to leave some four years later.

I walked off the Heysham to Belfast ferry at 6.30 am. on a grey cloudy morning in the late summer of 1966 to the hustle 'n' bustle of an already busy city. Black London-type 'Hackney Carriage' taxi cabs lined the quayside picking up passengers who were happy to share journeys with strangers going in the same direction. Belfast City buses stood empty in anticipation of boarding passengers wishing to go to the city centre.

An army Land Rover with a civilian driver parked in front of other vehicles caught my eye as I walked off the ferry and was to be my means of transport to the headquarters barracks at Lisburn some twenty-one miles south-west of the city. On my way across to the waiting military vehicle, my brain in overdrive as I observed and absorbed new surroundings and experiences; I was visibly and audibly reminded of being somewhere, well, different. Passing one of the Belfast City buses, I happened to glance in and noticed a prominent poster forward of the boarding platform, which displayed the words: 'NO SPITTING'. I was unsure if the notice had been directed at the would-be passengers or feral Llamas that might happen to clamber aboard. An audible reminder that I really was somewhere quite different became apparent when I overheard the following conversation: -

"Aach, hullo thar Wullie. Are yuz feelin yurself?"
"Am indeed."
"Fancy eh paint?"

"Not atull-atull."

If pronounced phonetically, with conviction and an emphasis on the syllables, the meaning will become apparent, and you'll be a master of the Belfast dialect. The reference to 'fancy ah paint' was about going for a pint of Guinness, not about creating a mural on the end of a terraced house.

I continued to look around in complete wonderment as I made my way over to the 'wee marn' waiting by the Land Rover. The military vehicle driver promptly introduced himself as 'Wullie' and, with his enthralling Belfast accent, said, "Welcum tu Nurthern Earland Corporal." I was at the start of a deep learning curve, and I loved it, so I did, so I did. Hello Northern Ireland!

As I was being driven through Belfast city centre on my way to Lisburn, I passed several grand but austere looking grey buildings, including Belfast City Hall, fronted with statues that were visible reminders of the provinces' days of grandeur and of the individuals who help shape its political past. Two-tone red/cream-coloured trolleybuses, electrically powered from overhead cables, and diesel buses belching out black clouds of smoke filled the streets while police officers in bottle green uniforms with flat-peaked caps and armed with pistols at their sides mingled amongst everyday folk on their way to work. I was sorely tempted to ask the driver of our vehicle to stop so I could run after a trolleybus just to see if the driver was as alert as the London boys, but I thought better of it. I could imagine the response of the bus driver taking stock of the situation when glancing into the rear-view mirror as he instinctively floored the accelerator, intent on producing an arse-over-head spectacle while at the same time shouting: -

"C'mon ye fokun wee shate, luts say whut yur maad of; and uf ye munage to get an may fokun bus, thar's to be no fokun sputten - Jummie."

Sorry?

Apart from a plethora of signs advertising Guinness of single, double, or triple 'X' Porter, Harp Lager or Scottish & Newcastle's Piper Export Ale, Belfast at the time I arrived in 1966 was a city that could easily have been any British city of the 1950s (not 1960s) – including the trolleybus drivers.

A forty-minute ride in the Land Rover brought Wullie and me to Thiepval Barracks halfway up Magheralave Road in Lisburn, Co. Antrim. Thiepval Barracks was named after a strategic position on a ridge of the same name during the Battle of the Somme during World War One, noted to have been the site of the British Army's most significant loss of all time in a single day. According to an English woman named Evelyn Blücher who lived in Germany during World War One, overhead a German general called Erich Ludendorff speaking highly of British soldiers who, he said, fight like lions, but was reminded by another General who agreed but went on to say that they were led by donkeys. Those comments' relevance raises the question of why anyone should want to call a British army barracks after such a defeat? Spiffing! It's all beyond me.

The entrance to Thiepval Barracks as Wullie and I approached from the town of Lisburn was on the left-hand side of the road directly opposite a cul-de-sac of Ministry of Defence owned properties that had the appearance of a council housing estate, occupied by married soldiers of the 'other ranks' and their families. The officer's mess and quarters were secreted elsewhere out-of-sight, although an inquisitively minded person would have been able to seek them out. Such houses for officers were much more grand-like in appearance than those of the other ranks; the higher the occupant's status, the more mock-Georgian the place. It was an area totally 'out-of-bounds' for lesser military mortals where only sub-contractors or selected civilian maintenance men and gardeners employed by the Ministry of Defence were allowed access to their hallowed ground. I do not have an issue with the segregation of ranks within the armed forces, mindful that familiarity breeds contempt and that discipline, respect and instinctive obedience could only prevail while such structures exist. Corporals had their Corporals' Mess (I was instrumental in bringing one about that had not previously existed), sergeants and warrant officers had theirs too, but what struck me most was the disparity of standards between the officers' and the other ranks and in particular, the exclusivity of the former.

As I passed through the main gates of Thiepval Barracks, a soldier pointed a sub-machine gun in our direction before waving us through. The moment I crossed the entrance barrier, I became a member of 233 Signal Squadron that consisted of no more than a dozen-and-a-half like-minded souls. The squadron's purpose was to provide tactical communications in a so-called 'theatre of war', should Northern Ireland ever be one at that time, but it looked to me as being a place made in heaven - at least for a soldier.

The first three years of my time in Ulster were blissful enough, with the armed forces having no peace-keeping duties to do of any kind other than to mediate between squabbling lady soldiers at Sunday breakfast. The signal squadron also served as a staging post for Irish members of the Royal Signal and a select few from the senior ranks of other British Army branches, allowing them to gently re-integrate back into the societies they had come from north and south of the Irish Border.

The dormitories for the rank and file consisted of three or four three-storey blocks (from memory), one accommodating the single members of the squadron, another for the Women's Royal Army Corps of the Royal Signals and the third building that housed the Royal Military Police. The military police peacefully coexisted with others in the barracks but distanced themselves socially when going about their daily business, just as we all did in our different roles. The women members of the Royal Signals carried the same trade qualifications as male colleagues, often working side-by-side in communication centres worldwide, but that was not the case in Northern Ireland. These women soldiers, I suspect, operated, and managed the communications centre at the brigade headquarters, dressed in green skirted uniforms and white blouses instead of macho everyday khaki denim. Soldiers within the squadron were part of a tactical mobile unit, ready at short notice to go anywhere in the world.

The realities of daily life in the barracks at Lisburn was like no other that I had come to expect. Instead of military-style morning parades and puerile tasks, it was more of a nine-to-five job, five days a week with an easy-going, laid-back existence, at least for me and especially after being promoted from lance-corporal to corporal. One of the benefits of promotion, apart from a salary increase, was that the higher the elevation, the fewer the people there were around to tell what one should do.

The photo shown above was almost the entire Signals unit in 1966, soon after I joined and before increasing in size to meet operational requirements at a later date. The dominant cap-badge worn by most of us in the picture is that of 'Mercury', the chief messenger of the Greek Gods with the moto 'Certa-Cito' meaning: Swift and Sure – not to be confused with Hermes the parcel carrier!

The dining experience in the barracks restaurant, shared with members of the Royal Signals Women's Royal Army Corps, was always a source of entertainment, especially watching some of their interactions as they came down for breakfast at the weekends. Sometimes, the girls would be in dressing-gowns and slippers, hair curlers tightly fused to their scalps and distressed facial expressions with make-up that looked as if it had been applied before the wearer had stepped into the shower. The girls that were not interested in each other interacted freely with whosoever they chose while those perceived as being 'good-looking' were always spoken-for, leaving new arrivals such as me without a chance. I would have to look elsewhere, So, I did. So, I did. Fiddle-de-de.

I had been with the signals unit for a couple of years when approached by an army captain who asked if I would be 'Master of Ceremonies' at his forthcoming wedding, offering payment as an inducement. I agreed to do so as the extra money would help entertain a friend or two in Belfast.

Dressed in all the finery of a dark navy-blue non-commissioned officers ceremonial uniform with a coloured stripe running vertically down the outside of each trouser leg and gold chevron rank insignia on each arm, I stood alongside the bride and groom, waiting to announce each guest to the happy couple. As the wedding guests arrived, I became a focal point by being the only non-commissioned officer on sacred ground, wondering if I was showing signs of leprosy. As the guests arrived, almost all the military officers chose to completely ignore me, preferring instead to introduce themselves directly to the newly married couple. I became invisible. Introductions complete (what there was of them) and of course not being allowed to enter the Officers Mess, I returned to my room, took off the ceremonial uniform and went to the NAAFI for a beer before giving a colleague a £1 to borrow his Volkswagen Beetle before disappearing into Belfast. I went in search of a Mr Wun Hung Low, who had a former son-in-law named Lee Kum Soon who was unable to maintain long-term relationships with anyone of the opposite sex. Mr low was a chap who happened to walk with a pronounced limp and a preponderance to lean to one side. Mr Wun Hung Low was the owner of a bookshop where I had hoped to find a book about Chinese Ooomeegoulies birds, so-called because of the sound the male of the species made when coming into land. I drove into a road where I thought the shop was located only to find that it was the…

Moving on, writing an account about the privilege of rank brings to mind an occasion much later in life when I met an ex-major of the Army Intelligence Corp who had previously been promoted from the 'other ranks'. A conversation with him revealed that, as an army captain serving in India in the 1960s, he proclaimed his intention to marry a woman from the 'Anglo-Indian' caste. Moves were afoot to prevent the officer from doing so by being denied the required statutory permission from his commanding officer as his intended bride was, get this: 'Not of officer class'. The captain ended up in a mud-hut in Borneo gathering intelligence during the communist uprising of the time.

County of Angels

With little to do for the Armed Forces in Ulster while Catholics and Protestants were not yet at each other's throats, our moribund group of signallers went over to mainland Britain to brush-up on our military skills. Off we went, taking everything with us in vehicles that must have appeared to be legacies from World War Two. During my time in the army, most military vehicles were painted a semi-gloss dark-green, supposedly as camouflage, but every one of the vehicles we had stood out like sore thumbs in the sandy terrain of Norfolk. The truck initially allocated to me on arrival in Northern Ireland happened to be a one-ton Austin that had a fixed rear box compartment housing an old-fashioned telephone exchange with pull-out and plug-in cords to connect one caller to another. I do not recall the equipment being put to any use at any time apart from supporting mugs of tea, but at least the vehicle got me to Norfolk and back without a hitch other than depositing tonnes of carbon monoxide and soot that had been expelled from the exhaust pipes of clapped-out engines.

East Anglia's landscape was flat, dull, and appeared to be that way for mile after mile in all directions. The houses and cottages seemed very small, with many having thatched roofs, small windows, and doors, suggesting that the past's indigenous people were either tiny in stature or experts in limbo dancing. The police constable from Alice-in-Wonderland that caused me to have the proverbial runs back in Hammersmith all those years ago wouldn't have stood a chance getting through the doorways in hot pursuit of a fleeing suspect without inflicting severe personal injury.

While in Norfolk, members of our signal squadron were reminded that, above all else, we were soldiers first and tradesmen second and therefore had to take part in all kinds of military activities. Digging trenches in the middle of the night, throwing grenades, firing rocket launchers, machine guns and pistols, and being subjected to 'live fire' from a statically positioned machine gun while crawling under several barriers of barbed wire, was all part of the fun (not). The instruction given was to always keep our heads and bums down to avoid being shot, but that would have been little comfort for anyone whose haemorrhoids were inadvertently snagged on the barbed-wire as he or she slivered face-down beneath it. No doubt such an experience would have caused an immediate involuntary response by lifting and turning one's head. 'Ouch,' wouldn't have got a look-in. 'Bang' would most certainly have championed. Whoever would have thought haemorrhoids could be so life-threatening? The sound of a 'crack' above one's head was a sure sign a bullet had passed just millimetres above. Jeez! Get me back to peaceful Northern Ireland as soon as possible, please, even though it might well be pouring with rain.

A few days in very sunny East Anglia was refreshing enough, with our lads bronzing their lily-white skins and enjoying a respite from the constant drizzle back in Northern Ireland. Two members of our squadron had a skin bronzing session all of their own while availing themselves the use of the shared Loo. The latrine available to the lower rank-and-file consisted of a framework with two horizontal lengths of scaffolding poles joined to a 'cross' configuration of smaller bars at each end. The steel poles suspended a purpose-dug trench with one joined at the centre of each cross to serve as a seat while the other was joined low-down and forward to serve as a footrest supporting bar for those who felt they needed to strain.

Nearing departure from Norfolk at a time when the latrine trench happened to be brimming with sewerage up to ground level, a soldier hurriedly and ungainly climbed onto the contraption while another was already in situ. The result was the collapse of the entire structure, with both individuals acquiring instant fake-tans and loathing of each other, while those who witnessed the spectacle experienced life-threatening levels of endorphins coursing through their bodies.

Battleground military activities concluded, we departed Norfolk for our return journey back to Northern Ireland via Stranraer in Scotland (goodness knows why when there were nearer ports of departure at Heysham and Liverpool) with the immortal phrase ringing in our ears: "Aye-ya-gotta-ah-laite-boi?" We headed north-west out of Norfolk without so much as a single box of matches between us, not realising that the phrase actually meant, "How are you doing, mate?"

The story of the birth of Jesus that most of us will have heard from early childhood included three kings (although eleven or twelve was a more accurate figure according to ancient records), turned up in Bethlehem bearing three gifts: gold, which funnily enough didn't get a further mention, frankincense, usually used in religious ceremonies to stupefy the congregations of modern-day worshippers while causing irreparable damage to the lungs of those administering it, and Myrrh, used to embalm bodies and cure bedsores - amongst other things. Research suggests the 'Angels' were, in fact, 'Angles' from pre-Saxon Anglia (Britain) travelling the world on a 'gap-year'. People present at the perceived 'virgin' birth might well have believed the 'Angles' from Anglia could only have arrived from such a distance on camels or by the services of Ryanair, but, in the absence of both, feathered wings of a bird, it had to be. And as for the circular neon light above their heads? Who knows? When the three Anglian boys (not to be confused with someone associated with a double-glazing company) happened upon the famed stable in Bethlehem having travelled in the same direction as the streak of bright light from a comet that had entered the atmosphere and streaked across the sky in the same direction the three lads were heading, the three intrepid boys were heard to say, "Jesus Christ! Did-ya-see-tha laite Boi?"

I was on my way back from the County of Anglians to the barracks in Northern Ireland, but, having been subjected to the Norfolk accent's sound, I felt that I had to recondition my speech to once again feel comfortable boarding a Belfast trolleybus. To do so, I recited a phonetic sounding rhyme taught to me by 'Ur Wullie' the 'Wee Marn' with the Land Rover who greeted me at the dockside when I arrived in Belfast for the first time. The rhyme goes along the lines of 'Simple Simon met a Pie Man. Brace yourselves: -

"Sumple Say-marn, mut ah pay-marn
Going to tha farr,
Sud Sumple Say-marrn to the pay-marrn,
Whhhat have yew gart tharr?
Pays, Say-marn, juss fokun pays!"

No Cornish pasties, then?

I had thought of writing a Belfast phrasebook and offering it to the language experts 'Berlitz' to help British soldiers settle in after they arrived in Northern Ireland, but unfortunately, they were later to learn a different language altogether!

Warming Up

Next stop: Libya. With Northern Ireland still at peace, I was off again, only this time to a remote part of the Sahara Desert. Two weeks after our squadron's main contingent from Northern Ireland had departed to North Africa, I, along with a few others, reluctantly had to join them, although most of us would have preferred to stay back with wives and girlfriends.

Those of us who formed the rear-guard arrived at Benghazi Airport in an RAF VC10 Aircraft from Brize Norton in Oxfordshire before boarding an RAF Hercules C130 Transporter aircraft flown to a remote dustpan of an airfield somewhere in the middle of the desert. We then climbed aboard the rear of an army truck to head further south into the unknown, the final part of the journey that seemed to have taken ages. The Hercules aircraft's landing strip was of fine dusty sand that became a sandstorm every time one of them landed, causing the stuff to get into every human bodily orifice and every bolthole of the Hercules C130 – including its engines. The onward journey to the desert strip travelling in the back of the truck was both arduous and tedious, bumping and swerving over all sorts of obstructions; the monotony only paused when the vehicles forming the convoy became stuck in sand-drifts that required everyone available to get them going again.

Heading south, I recall seeing a human settlement in the distance through a shimmering haze of hot air that appeared to look like a giant low-level IKEA warehouse with a few men, a more significant number of women and children standing outside looking in our direction. The building that I had seen from a distance turned out to be a hotchpotch of wooden pallets, cardboard boxes, and canvas sheets where all the women had hurriedly retreated out of sight as we approached in our strange-looking vehicles. Much to my surprise, the indigenous men I saw were not remotely 'Arab-looking' as naively expected, but tall with jet-black ebony skin and closely-cropped curly hair - and not a camel or flying magic carpet to be seen anywhere. Unlike the Masai warriors further down the African continent who would jump fifty yards vertically to view the horizon, the men we saw were tall enough to achieve the same with losing contact with the sand. On we went, heading south into the hot desert sands. Still, it was to be another hour or so of relentless travel over the more uneven ground before we reached the top of the last remaining dune at the journey's end. Far below in the distance, I caught sight of a collection of tents spread out over a wide area.

There appeared to be very little activity other than what appeared to be refuse collectors going about their business. Indigenous enterprising individuals were enthusiastically collecting anything thought to be discarded rubbish and dumping what was not of interest to them behind a nearby dune. Where the refuse truck and its attendants had come from in such a vast wilderness remained a complete mystery.

Our sleeping accommodation at the camp amongst all the dust and sand consisted of several tents with a canvas material of a dark green shade more in keeping with the English countryside than a desert in North Africa. The result of having dark coloured canvas tents was almost unbearable heat inside during the middle of the day, in contrast to the freezing temperatures at night. Wildlife companions, such as tortoises and chameleons, would sometimes inadvertently tumble into the shade of our tents during the day with the forlorn expectation of keeping cool. Still, they were not particularly unwelcome guests and not at all bothersome, unlike the odd snake, scorpion, and so-called camel spiders that often wended their way towards us. The ritual of going to bed on a canvas camp-bed a few centimetres from the ground involved cautiously turning one's sleeping-bag inside-out to ensure nothing was going to share the night with you. Unaware of what was creeping about outside in the darkness, it was always prudent to lie on one side when sleeping to reduce the risk of opening one's mouth should one happen to snore. Early morning rituals involved tapping boots, holding them upside-down to eliminate the possibility of any unpleasant surprises. The chameleons we all befriended were very watchful and cunning creatures, continuously changed colour as they wended their way to the main cookhouse tent and positioned themselves on the overhead horizontally-stretched mains cable, mopping up a year's supply of flies in a matter of minutes. Those somewhat adorable reptiles were impervious to the human diners beneath who would shout out in unison every time a fly met its fate on the end of a very long sticky tongue. As is their nature, the chameleons doing the tight-rope performances continuously changed colour, not just because of their changing background but also because of what they were thinking and the messages given to other competing chameleons. As the adorable creatures moved slowly and deliberately along the wire, much to everyone's amusement, a squirt of slimy excrement from above landing on someone's meal with a distinctive 'ding' sound as it hit the unlucky recipient's aluminium mess-tin, would cause the whole place into an uproar.

Another moment of glorious entertainment presented itself when our squadron sergeant-major took himself off into the void of the desert on his personal mission of fitness, only to return to a world-beating bollocking from the commanding officer, Major David Randel, for having put himself and potentially others at personal at risk of death. Almost everyone in the camp heard the verbal assault through the canvas walls of the command tent. The sensory experience of hearing the sergeant-major receiving a tirade of what he usually dished out to others was so hilarious as to call for a few extra cans of Tennent's Lager to heighten the thrill. Our wishful warrant officer had, up until that time, cut a lonely figure as he embarked on his solo trips into the desert. Mind you, none of us was above reproach. 'All for one, and one for all' came to mind some years later. In 1976, Lt. Colonel David Randel (Royal Signals), the same chap laying into Ostrich boy back in the desert, was implicated in financial skulduggery involving defence contracts between the British Government and Saudi Arabia. The Colonel was arrested on charges of corruption on 15th April 1976 and appeared before magistrates at Bow Street magistrates' court. I did not know the outcome of the case. On that basis alone, 'One for all, and all for one' would have been more appropriate. It couldn't have been my former commander in the army in Northern Ireland, as mine was a kind chap permanently authorising the release of stuff from the quartermaster's stores for recreational purposes - but it was!

With all the goings-on with the sergeant-major, rumours abounded that he went looking for ostriches to satisfy his insatiable urge to have sex. I said, "Blimey, that must have been painful."

"Only for the first the first three miles", came an anonymous reply. How would he know was my thought at the time? If indeed the rumours were true, the risqué rascal must have had an appetite for long-legged females with bare thighs and fluffy tops, oblivious to the risk that even running at speeds of up to seventy kilometres an hour, his bird of choice could still snap like a crocodile and kick like a mule. The long neck of the species serves it well. Gertcha!

Although not the inventor of flushing toilets, Thomas Crapper was an English plumber who none-the-less acquired nine patents for them during the 1800s in addition to several Royal Warrants, supplying his or her Majesties with his products. I bet Mister Crapper didn't have in mind the toilets' design provided for the 'Other Ranks' of his nation's army a hundred years or so later. Who could?

Luckily, the composite rations wildly rumoured to have been held in stores in the U.K. since World War Two became our daily diet of high fat and high calorific value ensuring visits to the 'Crapper' were not too frequent. Being caught short was not a pleasant experience by any stretch of the imagination, what with the lack of privacy and hordes of flies that would busy themselves around the patron's rear-end while perched on the toilet seat. It seemed to have been a constant task keeping the flies off for as long as possible, but the gap of perhaps eight or nine inches between the seat and bucket below provided a free highway for flying insects to come and go at leisure. Waving one's arms underneath the toilet seat between bowel movements was not recommended as considerable dexterity and coordination was essential. Helicopters would often land nearby, creating a whirling sandstorm that offered some respite from the flies but at the cost of creating amusing scenes of panic for the pilots and anyone else in the vicinity, enabling them to have a bloody good laugh, except, of course, those availing themselves of the 'Khazi'.

There was an occasion when I used the toilet facilities as someone approached shouting out 'Must-apha, Must-apha, Must-apha crap and quick!' Fearing the refuse collectors were about to de-throne me in search of their fortune, I was visibly seen to be overcome with relief when joined by a fellow colleague who also wanted to use the improvised crapper contraption. The hessian privacy curtain flicked back as the new arrival rushed to get to the neighbouring bucket, having been caught short himself. Bloody hell -my nerves!

The purpose of being in the desert in the first place was to take part in what turned out to be a humongous military exercise involving all kinds of armoured tanks and infantry soldiers. Our small signals unit provided the necessary communications between the military units and Brigade Headquarters in Northern Ireland and elsewhere. A massive aerial was part of our kit installed in the desert that went so far up into the stratosphere it must have caused considerable consternation to the likes of Zeus of Greek mythology and his mates cavorting and running amok up there somewhere in search of the geezer with the wine. Dionysus, the Greek god of the grape harvest, winemaking and wine, fertility, etc., etc., was a bloke well worth going after. Mind you, Zeus and Co. would need to be careful. Dionysus had a dual nature; on the one hand, he brought joy and divine ecstasy, but on the hand would bring a brutal and blinding rage, thus reflecting the dual nature of wine, just like a Madam in a brothel perhaps? Who knows?

Despite the risks posed getting tangled up with Dionysus, our lot down amongst the sand would happily have obliged in reducing wine stocks to an acceptable level if only they knew how to get climb to the top of the gigantic ariel instead of having to make-do drinking fizzy canned lager while paddling about in chameleon excrement.

While all the mythological fuss was on-going, back in the actual dimension of physical existence, married members of our entourage in the desert were invited to talk to their wives back among the swathes of green in Northern Ireland using a field telephone we had set up. In contrast, single lads had to make do with drinking copious amounts of Scottish and Newcastle brewery's Tennent's Lager and drool over images of topless 'pin-up' models printed on the cans, each one (the model, not the can) of an enticing feminine name. Torturous!

Telecommunications involving teleprinter and 'ticker-tape' systems were not appropriate in a tactical mobile the desert setting in which we found ourselves, so my skills were of little use other than manning yet another old wartime decrepit telephone exchange that had hardly been used. I moved my bit of kit out of the communications centre into the sunshine as I found the heat inside the marquee unbearably hot.

Black plastic-coated arsenic-laden telephone wires stretched across the desert in all directions from the marquee from where I worked, connecting field telephones everywhere. However, calls through the telephone exchange were almost non-existent, suggesting that either rogue elements were at work, armoured vehicles had munched through the wires in passing, that radio communication was the preferred option, or, the indigenous fellows who collected rubbish happened upon mile upon mile of the stuff and decided they would have a better use for it. Back then, satellite communications and mobile phones were the stuff of science-fiction. I failed to understand why our Signal Squadron was there in the first place as it seemed all the troops engaged in their funny war-games had their own frontline non-Royal Signals personnel running around with radios on their backs the size of tea-chests that must have weighed more than the unfortunate fellow carrying them.

It wasn't only the absence of high-tech communications equipment during the 1960s and early 1970s available to the British Army but also everyday clothing for the frontline troops.

The following picture clearly shows me wearing an oversized desert jacket specially issued for the occasion that had to be returned to the Quartermaster's store on the completion of the exercise, ready to be re-issued to someone else at a later date. The black beret was not suitable attire either, along with black 'parade ground' leather boots. Shirts that would have been ideal for desert conditions were not available and probably non-existent. I either chose not to wear a shirt or opted for the standard-issue brown surge material with rolled-up sleeves, more suited for climatic conditions back home.

One would hope that the Armed Forces protecting the nation in modern times are better equipped than before. However, during the Iraq war of 1990-91, Sergeant Roberts handed over his protective armoured jacket to one of his subordinates going into battle, there being insufficient quantities for everyone. The sergeant paid for his compassion with his life.

The finest Virginia tobacco king-size cigarettes of worldwide renowned brands had been shipped over from the U.K. to Libya and were readily available to all-and-sundry at a fraction of the cost compared to U.K. prices. Cigarettes became a means of currency to purchase souvenirs from nomadic people who, just like the camp's refuse collectors, always seemed to appear out of nowhere.

Late one evening, a couple of lads and I scampered off into the darkness of the desert to rendezvous with a dodgy-looking indigenous person to exchange cigarettes for wall-carpets to take back home to wives and girlfriends. Having completed our clandestine goings-on, we were on our way back to camp when the sky suddenly lit up with flares that transformed the desert night into day. The great exercise, previously unbeknown to us, despite being the primary communicators, was underway with armoured tanks criss-crossing all over the place as our little band of smugglers became caught up in the middle of it all.

After a short period, the desert fell back into darkness before once again lighting up to reveal someone dressed in flowing robes hitched up to his knees, squatting directly in the path of a fast-moving armoured tank. Consumed with fear of getting caught or run-over by 'friendly' vehicles, our furtive little group might have joined him for a collective bowel-emptying experience if we hadn't had the presence-of-mind to scarper. We didn't get to know the fate of the poor chap who relieved himself amid battle or whether he got to finish what he had started, as we were too concerned about ourselves not being able to find a way back to camp undetected without the tell-tale signs of tank-tracks across our backs.

With military activities coming to an end in Libya, it was time to dismantle the gigantic aerial and return home to Northern Ireland. Five days after returning to Lisburn, news came that the very aircraft that ferried us back to Tripoli airport had crashed in the desert, killing the entire crew. No surprise there then. Luckily, there were no passengers. As far as I am aware, military aircraft operate outside of aviation rules that govern civilian aircraft and therefore, by their very nature, pilots take extraordinary risks that expose them and their aircraft to all kinds of danger. Perhaps continuously taking off and landing in a dust-bowl with sand being sucked into the engines was a risk too many - it had to be.

It was a cold, wet and miserable evening towards the end of April 1967. Our squadron of desert-weary individuals arrived back in Belfast's Aldergrove Airport from Libya via Brize Norton in Oxfordshire carrying nothing more than our army kit bulging with carpets and dirty linen, as well as small live tortoises and chameleons brought back as souvenirs by some of the thoughtless individuals amongst us. The creatures were to perish over the days that followed, either through neglect, being forced-fed Guinness Triple XXX stout, the effects of the cold, or perhaps all three.

The Orkney Bomber

Another foray out of Ulster took a few members of our squadron to the Isles of Orkney, taking up residence in a little-used military camp consisting of wooden billet huts (a legacy of World War Two) high up on a rocky coastline not far from Stromness. It was September 1967. The views out to sea were breath-taking, and so too was the cold. It was the beginning of Autumn, and with a cold north-easterly wind blowing, causing a constant rattling of loose-fitting windows, the place we had to call home was bloody freezing. A small centrally placed solid cast-iron wood stove at the centre of each hut was the only source of heat keeping us and any marauding rodents from dying of hyperthermia.

The main party from Northern Ireland arrived a week or so later, but before then, it seemed natural to go to the local hotel for a beer or two and admire the local scenery. And that is precisely what we did. While looking out to sea, I was mindful of where the German Navy scuttled fifty-two of their seventy-four fleet of warships in Scapa Flow during World War One. Ships that were not sent to the bottom remained adrift or run-aground onto the beaches by their German Kapitän. Interesting, but at the age of twenty-one, those thoughts did little to gird my loins; the local hotel's non-residential public bar most certainly did.

Graced with the presence of a soldier from the Pioneer Corps (a disingenuous term used to be army navvies), affectionately called Pioneer Pete, or Pee-Pee for reasons that will become obvious later, ensured that we were always in for a treat. Pee-Pee was not a member of the Royal Signals and so engaged in other activities such as digging holes, moving ordinance from one point to another, then back again. Pee-pee was a great character to have around and a sight to behold – never ever letting anyone down. I nearly tempted fate by ordering our pioneer to hack off the back wall of a nearby hut for firewood, something he would have instinctively done. Forever obliging and so adept at applying himself to anything physical, I wouldn't have been surprised if Pee-Pee's bodily movements had been copied by NASA when they had in mind the design of their Lunar Module that was capable of doing all things practical in extreme conditions.

When out quenching our thirsts at the nearby hotel bar, Pioneer Pete placed a partly drunk glass of beer on the ground, freeing his hands to relieve himself of pee when, at the same time, an Alsatian dog turned up on the scene and promptly did the same – in our pioneer's beer. I suspect it must have been a police dog whose handler was fed-up chasing us out of the hotel grounds after closing time, choosing instead to avail himself of the generosity at the bar and setting the dog to the task of getting rid of us instead. Unperturbed, another chum and I continued to enjoy our alcoholic beverage, which fuelled a bout of uncontrollable laughter as Pioneer Pete picked up his glass of hybrid beer with a newly-acquired award-winning head of froth and 'downed' it in one. Wallop! Getting pissed seemed to have taken on a new meaning – at least as far as Pee-Pee was concerned. The spectacle witnessed by those of us present proved that the Pioneer Corps members were manlier than those of the Royal Signals. Neither my other chum nor I dared to have any issues with that. Forty years on, some enterprising person might well have replicated the brew and marketed it as Cock-a-leekie Pale Ale and made a fortune in the process.

Lance-corporal Donald Angus Gordon Hamish McTavish-Periwinkle, usually referred to as 'Wee Winkle' on account of his size, giving his account of the pee-swilling event in his own colloquial manner, said: -

"Uf thur stuff was marketed as 'Pioneer Pus', there's no doubt it'll gai-doon well where aye come from, but it would huff to be aa thee rate price un cum with a free jurr of fokun puckled onions, fush 'n' chups or a deep-frayed fokin Marrrs Bar.

Donald A.G.H McTavish-Periwinkle then stood up, squeezed his nostrils together and gently karate-chopped the protrusion in his neck formed by the angle of the thyroid cartilage surrounding the larynx (alright, Adams-apple), while at the same time wailed in varying tones. The effect was a sound so similar to bagpipes, those of us that heard it was blown away. Wee Winkle then treated all those present to a rousing rendition of 'Danny Boy' before performing a highland fling or Celtic jig that appeared more like St. Vitus' Dance, a neurologic condition causing, among other things, a gait disturbance. After four or five large measures of 'Isle of Islay' single malt whisky later and a 'wee nip' from Pee-pee's glass of froth, our entertainer promptly fell asleep. It was a shame my dog-poo hating friend Toby from Faroe Road wasn't with us as he and Pioneer Pete would have had a field day woofing down so many doggie delights.

A few days later, our squadron's main party arrived on the islands along with our sergeant-major, a mean-looking git who set the scene for a couple of weeks of military training. The arrival of the squadron, eagerly awaited by the locals and billed as something similar to 'Irish soldiers coming to Orkney', as published in the 'Orcadian' local newspaper at the time, created much trepidation and excitement amongst single ladies and wives of fishermen who were away crabbing. H'mm. Irish soldiers? Unlikely. Not me, Guvn'r - goud luv-a-duck!

Celebrations were underway by the locals who were holding a dance event in the Stromness village hall to celebrate and engage with who they thought were Irish soldiers. A minibus had been organised to bring in ladies from outlying areas and further afield in Kirkwall for an evening of frivolous fraternisation. A local band strutted its stuff so loud it could be heard across the water as far away as Thurso on the Scottish mainland. A chap we all knew as 'Cautious Colin' on account of his predilection for being at the stern of boats in anticipation of them colliding with the dockside, joined Pioneer Pete and me at the bar of the local hotel expecting a repeat of the hybrid beer trick.

Unaware of the festivities going on back in town other than hearing the din way-off in the distance, we were finally ejected from the hotel gardens' premises by two not too friendly constables for drinking on the premises after closing time. Not to have complied with the officers' demands would have risked another Cock-a-leekie experience.

Finding ourselves out in the cold in total darkness after being ejected from the local hotel, Careful Colin, Pioneer Pete, and I set off towards the lights and sounds emanating from the nearby town of Stromness way off in the distance, only to happen upon the village hall at the point of closing. Other chaps from our camp were streaming down the stairs clutching anyone reeking of perfume or wearing female attire before disappearing into the darkness. The all-male kilted members of the band, having been warned of what to expect at closing time, exited the rear of the building at lightning speed, leaving the fire doors swinging on their hinges in their wake. The search to find the answer to the perennial question of 'Do they or don't they'…continues.

Back at the village hall's exit stairwell, the scene became comparable to feeding time at a penguin enclosure with a mad scramble by too many individuals chasing too little of what was on offer. The village hall was almost empty by the time my other two luckless individuals and I arrived. But there was a lady left behind, an ugly looking ma'am, called two-ton Tess from Tankerness who could take on any man. You might wish to look on the map of Orkney; Tankerness really is a real place. I'm not sure if the area was named because of passing sea-going oil tankers or the mere presence of the Orkney person herself. The lady in question was on a desperate mission to grab any man she could but whose options were fast disappearing. Our new-found friend was short, stubby, aged about forty, and looked as if she could well have been the custodian of a tiny genetic pool going back thousands of years with an appearance not dissimilar to the Isle of Man (Manx) flag. It looked too as if hair from other parts of her anatomy had started to migrate northwards. Tanker Tess came to be known as 'The Orkney Bomber' by the lads back at the camp and believed to have been the last woman standing (just) after waving off her two late-teen beautiful twin daughters into the company of new-found soldier boyfriends before turning her attention to our pioneer. My only remaining companion, 'Careful Colin' and I were left to turn off the last remaining light. Click! Now then, where's our Pioneer?

The following day, the squadron sergeant-major had us all up and out of bed at sunrise. Before any of us could even consider breakfast, we set off on a military-style jog in file order and military timing, intentionally passing through the streets of Stromness. Either the geezer wanted to show off his prowess or else allow any aggrieved or distraught maidens (if there were any) an opportunity to identify the person or persons that needed to be brought to account. The streets of Stromness remained eloquently silent, except for the appearance of the Orkney Bomber herself from an upper storey window of a townhouse, arms crossed in front of strutted breasts fervently looking for Pee-Pee. The person of interest to her remained back at the camp, moving ordinance from one place to another and back again, or else getting into a hole which he was very adept at doing. Internet tracking devices were not around when Pioneer Pete (shown holding the map) attempted to ascertain the whereabouts of 'The Orkney Bomber', hoping to avoid her at all cost – or so he told us. I'm in the background, having distanced myself from the whole debacle.

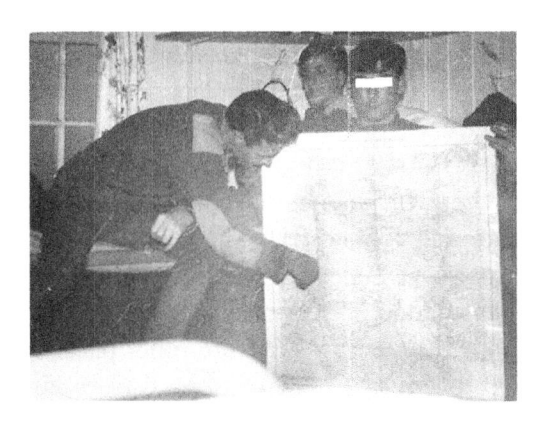

Easy times were over. Our squadron embarked on an exercise that involved being cast out in groups of four across the boggy landscape of one of the little-inhabited and most inhospitable islands of Orkney. It was a three-day mission when participants, masquerading as so-called 'prisoner-of-war escapees', had the specific task of avoiding detection, seeking to reach a final destination at some far-off remote location. Rendezvous points were set up with a 'sympathiser' camped out in the wilderness who would be approached at a set time in the middle of the night after contact had been established by using a flashlight signal to a pre-determined sequence. The reward for arriving at the rendezvous point in the middle of the night at the correct time using the proper approach was to receive two raw herring. Failure to make contact at the exact time or not following the pre-determined flashlight procedure resulted in no connection and starvation unless, of course, the weakest of us was selected to be eaten. The Army Catering Corps member with us would have been the only survivor as he rustled up a gourmet's delight for himself from what was left of us. Spare ribs, anyone?

Three nights followed of walking in the rain and sleeping during the day under nothing more than a poncho worn around the shoulders to help keep the rain penetrating through to the bones. The shoulder covering doubled-up as a bivouac, stretched out behind grass hillocks low enough so as not to break the horizon, allowing those of us seeking refuge from the weather to be as inconspicuous as possible and avoid detection by helicopters flying overhead or those scanning the skyline through high-powered binoculars. It was enough to test anyone's mettle. Less than a third of all the soldiers who set out on the task to avoid capture managed to complete the mission, either because of voluntary capitulation or inadvertently crossing a road bridge where the supposed 'enemy' happened to be lying in wait.

Out of our group of four, two completed the task, me (centre) and a Northern Irish boy (on the right) who was just months away from being de-mobbed and for whom I was to be 'best man' at his wedding a short time after he left the service. The chap on the left, a lance corporal in the Army Catering Corps, a trained chef, usually cooked up meals back in Lisburn but, like us, had to be reminded that we were soldiers first and whatever else we wanted to call ourselves second. I bet he hated the whole experience of being away from his meat and two vegs. Cheffie capitulated soon after the photo was taken, along with the fourth team member who had taken a photograph.

As part of survival training, the squadron received a visit from an army captain, drafted in from the SAS Headquarters in Hereford. The sole purpose of the visit by the captain was to teach lesser mortals like us survival techniques. Gone were the army-issue shiny gold-coloured tinned composite rations that could be detected by the enemy from as far away as the moon on a sunny day, loaded with fat, calories and, curiously, matches, sweets, chocolate, and toilet paper. What we got instead was a live chicken and instructions of what to do with it. Steady on! Fortunately, Pee-pee was otherwise engaged in digging holes and moving ordinance, so wasn't part of what was to come - one lucky chicken! We had to kill our assigned birdie by grasping the head and using its body's weight to sever the spinal column at the neck. My exuberance in wanting to get the deed done resulted in Chuckie's head coming off in my hand, the torso (my dinner) legging-it into the distance. Luckily, the escapee was seen by other soldiers further into the woods, one of whom managed a would-be award-winning rugby tackle, bringing my 'din-dins' to heel. My saviour had to have been Welsh to have accomplished such a feat. 'There's tidy' is what he might well have said as an acknowledgement of satisfaction. 'There's lovely' is what he might also have said as he cuddled the headless bundle of fluff and feather. There's lovely.

Before setting out on our epic task, members of our squadron were taught how to trap rabbits and soft talk seagulls into submission, grabbing them by their legs or else purloining their eggs while they were looking out to sea while dreaming of their next mouthful of sprats or whatever else they ate. In any event, we did not go anywhere near cliff-tops or nesting birds on our mammoth trek at all. It was September anyway, long after any sound-minded bird had departed, so there didn't seem to be any point knowing about seagulls. And as for rabbits? No trace of them either.

On the agenda was learning how to construct a 'Shackleton fire' (named after Lord Shackleton, the great British Antarctic explorer) that involved digging two twelve-inch square excavations at the same depth adjacent to each other, joined by a sub-terrain tunnel. Lighting a fire at the bottom of one of the holes with a draught fed through from the other ensured a sufficient airflow to fan the flames and ensure we could boil water or cook food in a container placed at ground level and avoid detection by an enemy. Clever eh? All very well, but the only food we had available to be cooked happened to be the remnants of my headless battery-farmed, former egg-laying chicken that was all skin and bones before the carcass was thrown in the flames of a fire to 'char', a process that ensured the meat didn't rot. The Shackleton fire idea was brilliant, except we didn't find any trees or hedges anywhere proffering twigs or kindling wood that could have been used as fuel other than at the base camp where the training took place.

At the end of the exercise, my Northern Irish friend and I found ourselves at the water's edge, waiting for a boat back to the main island, but by which time, through hunger and lack of sleep, both of us promptly fell asleep on top of a pile of coal.

Back at the base camp in Stromness, having endured considerable hardship battling through the inhospitable terrain where it never stopped raining, I took off my outer rain-sodden garments to reveal a thick layer of white fungal hairs; no surprise there as I had not removed any item of clothing for four days, except to attend to calls of nature. With very little to eat, there wasn't too much of that going on anyway.

It wasn't very long afterwards that we were back on the ferry returning to mainland Scotland on our return journey home to Northern Ireland. The all-male kilted band back in Stromness prayed thankfulness in absentia.

Home Again

Northern Ireland was where I wanted to be, not Norfolk, Orkney, or Libya, for that matter. I had absorbed myself into civilian life in Northern Ireland, and having to leave it for any period for whatever reason became an encumbrance. I enjoyed being part-soldier, part-civilian while reaping the benefits of both. Someone, though, must have been tracking progress through my career as I seemed to be going from one course to another without touching the ground. Unfortunately for me, that meant periods of absence from Northern Ireland for one, two, or three months at a time, which did not always suit my social activities.

Meeting girls usually happened at a dance event somewhere, often at The Floral Hall situated somewhere on Belfast's periphery. The purpose of attending dancehalls was not necessarily about dancing but more to do with speed-dating and getting to know one's chosen dance partner during each the three minutes of every dance session. Nightclubs were rare, and dating agencies non-existent, so dancehalls it had to be. It was not easy to entice a girl sitting on the side-lines if you were a local lad, as I had observed countless times when prospective dance partners would, unless desperate, short-shrift any man demonstrating a modicum of machoism. Instead of copying the Northern Irish male approach of walking up to a girl and flicking one's head towards the dance floor, I gracefully presented myself and asked if they would give me the pleasure of the dance. It worked almost every time.

Although I found asking a girl to dance easy to do, I suspect it was more to do with wearing an under-arm deodorant spray that contained sex pheromones collected from the undersides of male antelopes. The product was later to become unavailable, either because of its carcinogenic properties or because bouncers at dancehalls couldn't control the herds of female antelopes congregating at the main entrance. Such gatherings of herbivores were made worse by some at the back of the herd hastily pushing their way through to the front wearing the most delightful of Tutus donated by the Maasai tribes of Northern Kenya and Tanzania to 'look their best' when abroad. The cause of the panic among the glamour-girls was said to have been caused by someone fresh out of the North African desert closely resembling our wildlife-fancying sergeant-major closing in from behind. Gertcha!

Richard Branson, a well-known business magnet, as well as being extraordinarily successful of so much, once said, "Life is a helluva lot more fun if you say yes rather than no". Giddy-up!

Within the confines of The Floral Hall, dance floor conversation with one's chosen dance-partner, other than antelope, usually started with: "You're not from these parts, are you?" H'mm.

There was a particular occasion while visiting the Floral Hall when I was lucky enough to meet a girl whose surname suggested she might well have been one of many descendants from the Scottish Protestant immigrants of the late 1660s. Such people arrived in Northern Ireland as part of the cobbled-together bunch of murderers and rapists, set free from Scottish prisons after agreeing to join William of Orange's fighting forces to quell the Catholic uprising, else go to the gallows. Non-combatant Scottish settlers arrived after the military when things settled down following the Catholics' bloody defeat at 'The Battle of the Boyne', the symbol of victory depicted as a blood-red hand on the flag of St. George; that was my take on it. I could be wrong. Whatever the intended purpose for the purge of Irish Catholics, the legacy after four-hundred years or so ensured an abundance of debutantes at dancehalls that were there for the dating.

Dancing was certainly not my forte as I pranced around looking like Pinocchio on steroids while moving about to the tunes of 'Lily-the-Pink', a song originally sung by 'The Scaffold'. While dancing, the same Scottish decent girl said she had lost one of her contact lenses, and would I find it for her? Would I? Of course, I would. Unfortunately, my ego took a dent because I didn't manage to do so. There I was, on all fours frantically searching to impress, when it dawned on me that I was probably sent to the floor to avoid the possibility of her having to endure a close-up smooch. I experienced a semi-platonic relationship with this girl with one contact lens that lasted for almost four years (on and off), even after leaving Northern Ireland.

I recall travelling on an Ulster Bus from Belfast to Portaferry to meet the one-lens girl's farmer parents, asking the bus driver to let me know when to alight, as names of some places in Northern Ireland, for me were mind-boggling, to say the least. The bus driver did just that, stopping at a non-designated bus stop at the end of a private gravel driveway leading to my friend's parents' house. The bus remained stationary for a considerable amount of time, with everyone in the bus tracking my progress along the path, the passenger-carrying vehicle only moving off once I had reached the front door some considerable distance away. The relatively few British soldiers that were in Northern Ireland at that time were a welcome curiosity, and I indeed had to be one of them, what with my London accent, appearance, bearing, hairstyle, and apparent naivety.

It was 1968, and the film Paint Your Wagon was showing for the first time in Belfast. Not having anywhere to take a girl for quiet times, the cinema it had to be. We were periodically watching the film from the very back row in the stalls (where else?) when the film whirled to a stop. The lights in the auditorium suddenly came on to reveal a man sat further forward, entirely enveloped in a 'ballooned' cape, leaving only his head exposed. During the film, grunts and other weird sounds could be heard coming from the cape's vicinity when a scene depicted provokingly dressed ladies trussed 'up-to-the-nines' in tight-fitting liberty bodices and very little else as they arrived in town inside and on top of several horse-drawn stagecoaches. Members of the Royal Ulster Constabulary were quickly on the scene to confront the grunting cape-wearing man, and, when asked to give his name, he replied. "Jummie", and then when asked where he came from, he replied, "Thrrr fokun bulcony!!!". Whooooomph! The unfortunate soul then went on to tell the officers that he 'wasn't feelin himself', implying that he was indeed unwell. Fiddle-dee-dee, fiddle-dee-dee, fiddle-de-fokin-dee.

There was an occasion accompanying my farmer's daughter back to her parent's farm just outside Portaferry in an old Volkswagen Beetle car that I had yet again borrowed in exchange for the payment of one pound to a colleague when one of the vehicle's tyres punctured. There was no means to remedy the situation that night, especially at 2am. The father of the girl who happened to be just a friend, rather than risk his neighbours and everyone else in the nearby town of Portaferry knowing of his daughter sharing the night with a British Soldier in the family home, insisted that I take his Black Humber Super-Snipe prestige car to get back to Lisburn, an hour or so driving distance. It wasn't the outcome I was hoping for, but I felt [like] the 'Dog's Bollocks' turning up at the barracks just as dawn was breaking, passing through the entry barrier. A soldier trained a sub-machine gun towards the gate before waving me through, mindful that my comrades-in-arms were fast asleep, having spent their previous evening boringly downing pints of booze in the N.A.A.F.I. The news of my arrival in such style spread like wildfire, with the Humber car becoming an object of curiosity. Boy, did I swoon? You bet I did!

Regarding the term 'Bollocks'; before anyone baulks at that written or spoken word, consider this: Professor James Kinsley, former head of English at Nottingham University and Anglican Priest, stood witness to a case involving the 1970s rock band The Sex Pistols who widely used the word often referred to as an animal's testes, to promote their music products. The court became convinced that 'Bollocks' actually meant a small ball, an Orchi (as in Orchiectomy - removal of one or both testicles), or a nickname for a clergyman. Odd, is that. From the Middle Ages onwards, it was widely accepted that the clergy often spoke nonsense or what was then termed 'A load of Bollocks' when addressing their respective congregations - apparently.

At the courthouse hearing the case against the Sex Pistols, Richard Branson went along – probably just for a laugh. I wouldn't mind betting that if the 'B' word causing so much unnecessary fuss to this day had been about in Tudor times when King Henry VIII went off on his walkabouts, no-one would have turned their heads. I'm pretty sure the offensive word to some was the least of their worries at a time the kings 'Subjects' everywhere were more concerned about avoiding decapitated heads rolling about all over the place. If anyone wants to impress by using the past's English language, consider the 'B' word instead of describing something as nonsense. Your local Vicar will be immensely impressed and, unlike the usual response of 'I couldn't possibly', he or she might happily accept that offer of a third cup of tea and another slice of Victoria Sandwich. Gertcha!

****

Times had been enjoyable in Northern Ireland, with recreational events at weekends, hiring cars and spending nights on Tyrella Beach near Downpatrick, County Down, in the shadow of the Mourne Mountains, barbequing, and generally having a good time until the daylight hours. I had carte-blanche permission to do almost anything I wanted to do with the blessing of the squadron's Commanding Officer, Major David Randel. I even had the authorisation to use a so-called 'pallet generator' that provided light and power on the beach and other military ordinance while the NAAFI's manageress provided credit facilities enabling me to take as much booze as required on a sale or return basis. There was an unwritten rule of 'No Gooseberries', which implied that not having a partner meant you were not welcome. That wasn't difficult; a quick trip back to the Floral Hall Dance Hall while being entertained by the showbands of the 'Royal Brothers' and the 'Miami Showband' (the latter murdered by the Ulster Volunteer Force in 1975) provided an opportunity to invite any potential girl companion to join the parties on the beach.

My charmed life had to be put in abeyance once again when I attended courses in different parts of mainland Britain, some lasting several months at a time in Catterick, North Yorkshire, but more interestingly, a nuclear, chemical, and biological course near Porton Down, Salisbury. I returned to Northern Ireland as a qualified Nuclear, Chemical and Biological Defence instructor, skilled in the art of calculating and predicting areas liable to radio-active fall-out in the event of an atomic war and training soldiers how to protect themselves in a contaminated nuclear or chemical environment.

Being one of only two qualified instructors in Northern Ireland Brigade headquarters authorised to have exclusive access to the storage bunker housing radioactive isotopes meant frequent visits to Belfast City Hospital for blood tests. Such tests enabled doctors to monitor levels of any damage to my white corpuscles through the build-up of radioactivity - Gamma rays in particular. There was no mention about the possibility of a reduced sperm count, but that would have been of little consequence to the Army as we were not on active service and therefore could only fire blanks anyway. I didn't know what I was letting myself in for when attending the NBC course, but then, it wasn't my choice.

A Butcher's Hook (Colloq.)

May 1968; I was on my way to a temporary posting back to mainland U.K., this time to RAF Greenham Common in Newbury Berkshire for a six-month stint with the American Air-force on 'Exercise First Look'. Selected U.S. Force officers paired with a handful of British Army and RAF non-commissioned officers, of which I was one, were tasked with touring a wide area of Southern England in Army Land Rovers to seek out British military units wheresoever they happened to be. Throughout the whole summer, the activity covered areas from Salisbury Plain in the south to Oxford in the north, Wiltshire in the West, and Berkshire in the East.

The purpose of 'Exercise First Look' was to demonstrate to the Soviets the possibility of a foreign army (the Americans) being able to monitor the movement of another sovereign state's armed forces (the British) as a pre-requisite for unilateral disarmament talks. What struck me most of all when teaming up with the guys from across the big pond was how their equipment seemed to be far superior in quality and purpose than British service-issue equipment. Everything about the U.S. stuff was purpose-made while ours was rudimentary and often 'make-do'. British soldiers kit included what was listed as a 'Housewife', essentially a sewing and darning kit to repair worn-out items of uniform, obviating the requirement to purchase replacements that most soldiers could ill afford to do. The sewing-kit included a sizeable mushroom-shaped piece of wood used for stretching army issue grey woollen socks to facilitate a darning repair. I remember back in Denbury camp being told that the 'Housewife' would be with us throughout our time in the army, and most likely the nearest most of us would ever get to the real thing. British 'field rations' were still only available in gold-coloured tins compared to U.S. rations of lightweight dehydrated equivalents in camouflaged green-painted aluminium cans or aluminium foiled bags a tenth of the size and weight compared to our canned food. Purpose-made short-sleeved shirts for wearing in summer were sported by U.S. service personnel compared to our serge-cotton long-sleeved shirts rolled up for the same effect. The list was endless.

Back at RAF Greenham Common, the food served up was American style with green leaf salads as a starter, something unheard of in British Army culinary circles at the time, at least in the main cookhouses that served the lower ranks. I was in food heaven. The P.X., the American armed forces equivalent of the NAAFI, offered all kinds of American groceries, but those items were only available to U.S. personnel. The handful of British military guys were the poor relations and barred from purchasing P.X. duty-free items, and in any event, almost everything at the store was beyond financial reach.

Throughout the summer of 1968, U.S. Air Force Captain Martin Leeman and I toured England's designated area in our allocated Land Rover, collecting intelligence information on unsuspecting military units, recording identities and movements while taking endless photographs. What the captain hadn't bargained for when teaming up with me was my 'carefree' attitude away from the constraints of British military discipline - he was to know soon enough.

Here's the captain (note the short-sleeved shirt), silently expressing his feelings as I took a photograph, unable to hold back from laughing. I could never imagine a British officer ever allowing him or herself to be in similar circumstances – at least not then.

When out and about with my assigned partner, I would often remove the canvas canopy of our Land Rover and inflate the tyres until rock-hard in an attempt to minimise contact with the road surface, thereby increasing the ability to drive at super-fast speed (at least for a Land Rover). My minor tweaks must have worked because they earned me my one and only lifetime speeding penalty of £6. Holy cow! Keh?

While testing the limits of the vehicle's capabilities and the captain's patience, I devilishly drove over small humped bridges at considerable speed to induce the spectacle of my front-seat passenger being jettisoned skywards while at the same time, and with a fiendish expression, kept a tight grip on the steering wheel to avoid a double-act. My American friend had no prior experience travelling through narrow rural lanes in the English countryside with surprises around almost every bend not to mention small hump-back bridges over small rivers and streams. We had no-end of short conversations between ourselves of "Oooops" and the captain responding by saying, "Holy Cow" that echoed across the English countryside throughout the whole summer of 1968.

Despite my significant indiscretions, Captain Martin Leeman and I became terrific friends, with him, his wife, and an officer friend of his joining me in Northern Ireland for a few days of history learning and merriment. I was later to join Martin in Germany to stay with him and his family and dine in their American Air Force Officers Mess. I had temporarily crossed the 'class' barrier, although, of course, there is no such thing in American society - is there? My goodness! The British commanding officer back at barracks would most likely have gone into a series of uncontrollable fits had he known, together with a life-long affliction of spontaneously shouting expletives wherever he went.

Returning to the airbase time in Greenham Common, Newbury, it was business as usual. Dressed in a uniform that might appear as a hybrid of an American/British soldier, almost always caused panic and confusion.

Added to that, accompanied by a U.S. Airforce provost officer always caused heightened anxiety levels amongst the British troops we came across as we popped-up in their perceived hallowed ground as if from nowhere. My partner and I would arrive in our Land Rover wherever and whenever we detected the presence of British troops going about their businesses, observing their activities through powerful binoculars while at the same time brandishing cameras. No-one seemed to have any idea of what we were about, which, of course, was the object of 'Exercise First Look' in the first place.

During one of many excursions somewhere in the south of England (probably Pirbright), the Captain and I happened upon a Grenadier or Coldstream Guards barracks at the same time as a passing-out parade was in full swing. We mingled amongst well-heeled dignitaries with an air of impunity; Martin in awe of the pomp and ceremony as I counted troop numbers. A few minutes into our foray, I felt a tap on the shoulder. Two lance-sergeants (a rank given to a corporal in the regiments of foot guards to carry out a sergeant's duties on the cheap) had their faces all but hidden behind peaked caps to look like guardsmen on boxes of old-fashioned confectionery.

So confusing. I willingly accompanied them to their regimental sergeant-major (RSM), who happened to be waiting for me in his guardroom, looking as if he was about to have a seizure. Had my escorts been of lesser rank, I could have told them to clear off, but had they been proper sergeants, I might well have been arrested and quick-marched to the 'clink'.

I had been in the army some considerable time, but the events that unfolded in front of me beggared belief. The two guys who escorted me to their guardroom marched alongside as I casually sauntered up to the RSM's desk and straddled a white painted line on the polished linoleum floor, unaware that I should have lined myself up one side of it. The big guy turned scarlet with rage, steam noticeably coming out of every one of his body's orifices, unable to comprehend my appearance, demeanour, and apparent lack of ability to be guardsman-like.

At considerable risk of being thrown in the slammer for silent insubordination, I refused to answer any questions (as was my remit), other than to say I shouldn't even have allowed myself to enter into a military building in the first place - Sir! I was left waiting while the big boy departed to make a phone call as he found it unbearable to sit and watch me. Oh, how good it would have been if I had had some well-stretched bubble-gum in my mouth to create a substantial pink bubble to pop. Before my adversary returned, I was to witness guardsmen coming and going to the sound of foot-stamping, screaming, and bellowing everywhere with ear-wax and fundamental extraneous cranial matter ricocheting off all four walls. I looked on in disbelief. Five minutes later, I was out of the door and back with my American provost captain on our way to a roadside café for a bacon sandwich. Gertcha!

September 1968, and 'Exercise First Look' was drawing to a close. Russian generals of the Soviet Army were invited to observe our findings, with a couple of them joining a 'Land Rover team' on a final mission to see how we gathered the information that would eventually lead to an 'Arms limitation agreement'. Alas, I was not chosen to accompany any of the Russian guys, perhaps for fear of being able to tell them about the 'banger' fireworks in milk-bottles that had upset their fellow citizens way back in the 1950s. Hey-ho

Between the Lines

In 1967, I had the privilege of spending a weekend or two at an Irish colleague's house with him and his family, pending his Army discharge. His home was somewhere near the Irish Border, not too far from Newry, in the midst of Irish Republic Army country. During one such visit, my friend's brother warned that the IRA were re-emerging, and it was probably not a good idea to share company with an English soldier. There was a real threat of putting the family and everyone else's safety at risk. As a wide-eyed London boy with no concept of the Northern Irish situation, the warning was wasted on me, although I was savvy enough not to make any further visits. Still, given the circumstances, it was more likely that I hadn't been re-invited.

In 1969, I took to believe, actual or otherwise, as the start of hostilities in Northern Ireland when the IRA blew up a dam in the Mourne Mountains. At the precise time of the explosion, my one-lens girl companion and I were some distance away enjoying a drink in a pub when news of a blast that had taken place way off in the distance many miles away. My immediate reaction was to utter a few Russian eye-watering expletives that started with "что это за хрень?!".

A few weeks later, a mass rally in Londonderry (referred to as 'Derry' by Republican minded people) brought about the British Army marching into the midst of it all with fixed bayonets at the end of rifle barrels. Silence descended. I was in the barracks in Lisburn, watching events unfold when the announcement came that all British soldiers not involved in Londonderry had been ordered to remain in their barracks. The event happened on the weekend, but I had a date and needed to get to Belfast.

Most weekends, and at other times during the week, I would cycle down to Lisburn Railway Station and board a train to Belfast with the train's guard always on the look-out to take my bike and place it elsewhere in the carriages for a nominal fee of one shilling (5p). The day of the first military confrontation in Londonderry was no exception as far as I was concerned. Despite the confinement to barracks order, I carried on as usual. A contingent of the Royal Military Police was stationed at strategic points throughout Northern Ireland to enforce the curfew imposed on military personnel. At Lisburn Railway Station, the military police officers I got to know were in abundance but looked the other way as I boarded the train.

After the bombing at the reservoir in the Mourne Mountains, things were never quite going to be the same again. British soldiers were piling into the province, upsetting the status quo. Our signal squadron increased in size to create an active operational communications unit, and, at last, I was able to apply just some of the skills I was trained to do.

Within a 'pop-up' cobbled-together operational Signal Centre, it was my task, amongst other things, to arrange and coordinate the Signals Despatch Service of Land Rovers travelling between active units in Belfast. The lads sent out in those vehicles would often come back quivering wrecks, having passed through riots, unarmed and unable to protect themselves in the then unlikely event of an attack. They probably considered themselves lucky they were not serving soldiers during the Cypriot hostilities a decade or so before when signals despatch riders set out on motorcycles only to end up decapitated by cheese-wires tensioned across roads.

Back at the signal centre, one unfortunate soul called Sam turned up late for duty on my watch and promptly put on a charge for doing so. As a punishment, the individual concerned had to run around the parade square's outer perimeter carrying a complete set of military battle-kit while holding a rifle over his head, each day and for seven days, first thing in the morning and last light in the evenings. It nearly killed him. He was never late again; summary justice at its best – or worst. I felt terrible. Very soon afterwards, events in Northern Ireland took a further downward turn. I was transferred to the

Royal Ulster Constabulary's police headquarters in Belfast, operating a communications link between the Army and the police. They were interesting times.

Notwithstanding the circumstances, I was determined to carry on my life as before. The 'Peace Line' was a physical barrier set up in adjoining roads between the Shankill Road and the Falls Road with Protestants on the one side and Catholics on the other side. The walls extended from Belfast city centre northwards for a considerable distance to what I believed to be Silverstream. The 'Peace Line' provided temporary protection for both communities, although missiles and petrol bombs would often be lobbed over both sides' barrier, further alienating the two communities. By then, I had a new girlfriend whose first name could well have come from the television sit-com, Only Fools and Horses. Unlike her namesake in the comedy series, Marlene was an intelligent and articulate comptometer operator employed in a Belfast courthouse recording each day's events. My girlfriend lived with her parents in Silverstream Road, a hefty walk from Belfast city centre, up and beyond the predominately Protestant Shankill Road. I would often have to travel back down almost the entire length of Shankhill Road to get to Belfast's city centre for my return journey back to barracks in Lisburn twenty-one miles away. The trek involved crossing the 'Peace Line' into the Falls Road during the hours of darkness long after midnight, using my army identity card as a legitimate pass. Foolish, to say the least.

During my travels south down through the Protestant area, often in the middle of the night, I would encounter groups of 'B Specials' huddled together on street corners, dressed in bottle-green police uniforms and armed to the teeth. Those so-called 'Officers of the Law' were made up almost entirely from the Protestant community and virtually indistinguishable from members of the Royal Ulster Constabulary except that their bearing and unkempt appearance told a different story. Those boys in green were part-time volunteer police officers and regarded by the Catholics as licenced government thugs.

While traversing the dividing barrier between the two communities, I often wore a badge on the lapel of my jacket that displayed the red cross of St. George with a blood-red hand at its centre. The badge was the object of choice usually worn by strong-minded Protestants, but I came into possession of it from a canteen worker back at barracks without really knowing its significance. After a cursory nod of recognition and approval from the gatherings in green, I would turn into one of the adjoining streets separating the two communities that led onto the Falls Road, removing the offending badge as I did so. I then headed down to the city centre and across to the start of the Lisburn Road to rendezvous with an Ormeau Road Bakery articulated heavy goods vehicle each morning at 3 a.m., the driver willingly going out of his way to drop me off directly outside the main entrance to the barracks. I took risks, and in hindsight, concede that I was one lucky boy.

Seventeen years after I departed Northern Ireland, two 'Under-cover' corporals of the Royal Signals inadvertently happened upon an IRA funeral procession, and for doing so, were savagely beaten before being shot dead. The two soldiers' bodies were then bundled into the back of a black taxicab and taken elsewhere before being unceremoniously tossed over a wall. But of course, times had moved on from my time in Northern Ireland; back then, there was no animosity shown towards the British military to the point that residents of the Catholic Falls Road community welcomed soldiers' presence, even providing cups of tea and a friendly chat. Flirting with their daughters was something the soldiers looked forward to but doing so carried risks. Some years later, when the relationship between the Catholic community and the British Army turned nasty, three soldiers collectively dated girls from the Falls road only to be met by members of the IRA with dire consequences. They, too, had an unhappy ending.

It was on one particular journey down the Falls Road at the exact time a riot was in full swing with flares, noise, and tear-gas just about everywhere, when I was almost overcome by the effects of the tear-gas as I passed a cigarette vending machine attached to a wall. A car stopped alongside as a girl got out to use the device. I expected her to succumb to the effects of the gas – no hope. The young lady was unaffected and unfazed by the whole event, even to the point of telling me how to get into the thick of things by going down a particular road, speaking in 'Sumple Say-marn' parlance with a few choice expletives put into the mix. I was tempted to respond in a like manner by saying: "Gat an y'rrr fokun wee bake" literal translation: "Get on your little bicycle and toodle off ", but, fearful of letting my dialect slip and unsure of the outcome if that was to happen, I decided to remain silent except to exhort a grunt or two. To have responded in any other way, knowing that there were three male occupants in the car, would have been tantamount to a dalliance with the devil. Every moist part of my body, including my important little places, stung like buggary from the effects of tear-gas. I wanted to be gone. I can image the national newspaper headline worldwide: 'BRITISH SOLDIER ARRESTED FOR RIOTING IN THE CATHOLIC FALLS ROAD OF BELFAST'. Holy Jeez!

Several months passed with a deteriorating political and civil situation when, in December of 1969, I appeared before the squadron's commanding officer, Major David Randel, and told that I had been in Northern Ireland longer than almost any other serving soldier and it was time I moved on. I cannot help think that my close association with the local population at the time might have had something to do with it. In hindsight, I guess I must have been 'clocked' travelling in and around Belfast using my army identity card to get me to wherever I wanted to go, and probably noted as becoming far too cosy with the locals.

During my time in Northern Ireland, no-one in the military or the civilian population had been killed or injured; all that changed following the Bloody Sunday riots of January 1972, when twenty-eight unarmed civilians were shot dead by British soldiers.

I had left Northern Ireland with a heavy heart and headed to Catterick Camp in Yorkshire in transit to what was destined to be a prime posting to Singapore, but alas, it was not to be. While at Catterick, Prime Minister Harold Wilson's government announced the withdrawal of all British military presence in former colonies, notably Singapore and Malaysia. I found myself in limbo with nowhere to go. Several weeks later, after no-end of visits to the Church Army Canteen and The Hole in The Wall pub in Darlington awaiting my fate, I learned that I was to join the NATO forces in Krefeld, Germany back among the monotonous alcohol-consuming culture I had turned my back on a few years earlier. And I didn't like it.

Back Again

The 28th Signal Regiment in Krefeld consisted of a couple of hundred or so men in the company of a small section of Flemish-speaking conscript soldiers of the Belgium Army. The chaps from Belgium had their agenda for being in a British Army barracks at part of NATO forces, their presence welcomed although little social interaction existed between them and the British soldiers. I arrived at the regiment in the early spring of 1970, later joined by my younger brother, who had transferred from the Royal Engineers, an equally technical branch of the Army. Whatever John, my brother, achieved as an engineer counted for very little in the Royal Signals and had to undergo a trade training course in operating telecommunications to stay within the regiment, starting from the bottom. Unfortunately, sibling rivalry showed its head. John always saw me as the more dominant, which didn't help, especially as I held rank over him. The final ignominy for my brother came at a time when he attended a trade upgrade course. I was one of the instructors on the course and treated him in the same way as I did with others, showing no bias from the outset, even to the point of giving him a bollocking in front of his mates whenever he stepped out of line. I'm unsure if he passed or failed the final examinations, although being brighter than me, I expect he did.

Shortly after my younger brother joined the regiment, the stone-built billets that housed the junior ranks underwent a significant renovation. The toilets situated at the far end of the bungalow-type buildings had W.C. basins designed to catch excrement onto an integral shelf, presumably to be inspected before flushing. The putrid smell of human bodily waste permeated through the corridor and into every room, day in and day out. It was hoped that this issue was going to be addressed - but it wasn't. Typically, those charged with keeping costs down had little regard for the occupants' comfort during what turned out to be nothing more than a protracted period of painting the internal walls. Instead of being housed elsewhere, everyone from the barrack blocks had to live in tents alongside the buildings undergoing renovation while maintaining tip-top military standards; not easy whenever it poured with rain. Luckily, I had the privilege of having a tent to myself, but less fortunate individuals had to live in groups of four or six.

Before too long, I was off again to Norway, only this time to train as an army canoe instructor, spending a month at the same army outward bound centre I had attended in 1966. Unlike the previous experience of having to rough it, this time, along with a few others, including a couple from the commissioned ranks (two from Canada), we were treated with a degree of reverence. Status became irrelevant for the one and only time I was in the army. The centre's accommodation was a warm cosy wooden billet hut with proper beds instead of camp beds in tents on a concrete slab. Meals served up by others included real bread, an expensive commodity in Norway at the time - and maybe still is.

The canoe instructors' course included endless forays at sea, including a ten-day expedition that started out way up in the mountains, travelling downstream amongst felled trees that had probably started their journey months or years previously, before our small group of canoeists headed out to sea. The expedition's final three days involved going from one outcrop of islands to another, setting up camp among rocks to protect ourselves from the relentless crashing waves. The so-called tent used to protect us from the elements consisted of two single-person up-turned kayaks laid parallel with a plastic sheet stretched between them.

Skills taught during the course included how to survive at sea in adverse conditions by being able to 'Eskimo Roll'; a manoeuvre to 'right' oneself after capsizing without having to bail out from a kayak. An additional requirement was to survive in water by removing one's trousers, tying the ends, and inflating the garment by hauling it over one's head to trap air. The effect was to create a temporary float that lasted for several minutes before needing to be continually reinflated. By the end of the course, I qualified as an instructor and able to take groups of soldiers on canoeing expeditions when back in Germany or wherever I happened to go.

Back at the barracks in Krefeld, free time at weekends was a problem for many single men with nothing else to do other than drift back to the bar to drink themselves silly on low-priced alcohol, while at the same time smoking subsidised king-sized cigarettes, coughing their guts out as they did so. These guys, without any form of entertainment to occupy their minds, took to creating their own fun. Such joy came in the form of applying a condom over a half-filled wine glass containing tonic water and an Alker Seltzer, just to see how far it rose into the air before crashing down to the ground to a rapturous roar from all those taking part. As novel as it was, I soon tired of seeing the same trick being performed night after night.

Weekends for me often involved having the option of using a NATO army truck, taking willing individuals away canoeing, traversing down rivers to a freshwater lake and setting up home in accommodation provided by a local German recreational club.

Evenings at the club involved strolling over to the nearby Gasthof, whacking back a few beers, and interacting with the locals. There was a particular weekend when I happened to be lazing about with a 'humdinger' of a hangover. A small girl of about four years of age passed by nursing an injured foot. I called the toddler over and applied a dressing to the wound, who then promptly returned to her parents to tell them of her experience. Her mother and father, Anna and Fitche Roemer were to become good friends. The little girl's name was Gisella, and she came to stay with my family and me years later in England, long after I left the Army. Giesella's parents came too at a different time, and our family stayed with the Roemers in their house in Germany.

It was approaching the end of 1970 when I returned to the U.K. for some leave. Unbeknown to me, Fitche and Anna Roemer arrived at the army barracks back in Germany on the eve of Christmas, intending to take me back to their home to share their family celebrations. When I later learned of their visit, I felt terrible and full of remorse for not having been there.

I yearned to be back in Northern Ireland, and the only way I could see that happening was to join the Royal Ulster Constabulary. I had arranged a visit to Belfast for an interview but, as I was expected to finance my travel arrangements to get there on a soldier's salary - hesitated.

I happened to be in Slough in Buckinghamshire a week or so before Christmas when my attention was drawn to an upstanding and intelligent police constable about my age doing what police officers did at that time. Impressed, I telephoned the Thames Valley Constabulary's recruitment office in Aylesbury and immediately invited to attend the department the following day, even though a batch of new recruits had already been processed and were on their way to training colleges across the country.

The day after I contacted the police headquarters in Aylesbury, I caught a bus from Slough to Aylesbury and met up with the same police inspector I had spoken with on the phone the previous day. After a lengthy interview, followed by a multi-subject academic entrance examination, I was invited to return the very next day for a medical check-up. I did, and, subject to a vetting process and checks against criminal records, was offered a place at the No.1 Police Training College in Warrington, Cheshire, to undergo a fourteen-week intensive training course. There was a hitch: I was, of course, a serving soldier of the armed forces, contracted to serve for a period of twenty-two years. Oops! Being bossy by nature, partly because of my military experience of telling others what to do, I remember saying to the recruitment inspector,

"If you furnish a letter offering me a place at the police college, I will take it back to my regiment and see what comes of it."

The letter arrived within two days.

Back in Germany, I returned tendering my resignation, firmly clutching the letter of acceptance from The Thames Valley Constabulary. It wasn't long before I was summoned to the regiment's commanding officer colonel-in-charge, who told me that I did not have the right to leave as the service had invested heavily in my future. And was I aware that further promotion was imminent? "Yes, sir," I replied, "But I have a right to determine my future." It worked. I didn't have to give six months' notice either.

Having paid the then princely sum of £200 to sever the service contract, I was homeward-bound taking a glowing (unabridged) employment reference. And here it is: -

Cpl Darling is an intelligent, loyal, and trustworthy NCO. He has attained Class One rating as a Communications Centre Operator and holds the first class's Army Certificate of Education. He is articulate with a nicely developed sense of humour and has earned the respect of all who have worked with him. His personal turnout and bearing have always been above reproach. He is an excellent tradesman with a complete grasp of his Army Trade. He has been employed during the past year as an Instructor at his trade and as a Supervisor in a Tape Relay Centre. He has shown himself to be completely competent in both capacities.

I had turned my back on what was probably a blossoming career, qualified in all sorts of things that would take me to the higher ranks. Still, it counted for nothing the day I handed back my uniforms and military equipment and walked out of the gates of Catterick Camp in Yorkshire - never to return.

Three months after joining the Police, I received a letter from the Ministry of Defence inviting me to join the Territorial Army (later known as Army Reserve) with Sergeant's rank. The Royal Signals Record Office must have been looking for me on a notional completion of three years holding corporal's substantive rank but found me gone. I didn't end there. Although discharged from the regular army, I was contractually committed to the army reserves and liable to call-up in the event of hostilities up until I was forty years of age. While serving as a police officer, I was exempt from such conscription, although I became eligible again when the Falklands War kicked-off in 1982.

It has to be said that the Army had been my saviour, in that people within it, without pre-judgement or knowing of my upbringing, recognised that as an individual, I was capable of much more than anyone outside of it ever did. I gained a meaningful education and confidence that has stayed with me until this day. I've travelled extensively and had many experiences that others could only have dreamed of, and for all of that, I shall be eternally grateful. Was I envious of the 'Officer Class'? Of course, I was. I, too, would have liked to have been a person of privilege in the armed forces, but having arrived in this world on 'starting blocks' of life set way back on the track compared to almost everyone else, I guess it wasn't to be. That's life.

Allo, Allo, Allo

On 1st February 1971, I arrived at the Thames Valley Police Headquarters in Aylesbury to be sworn-in as a police officer, pledging an oath to the Queen, fitted out with a police constable's uniform, wooden truncheon, whistle, and handcuffs. After a week's induction, I was off to a police training college in Warrington, Cheshire, to undergo a fourteen-week intense training course. The studying of 'Moriarty's Police Law' was part of the process of becoming a proficient police officer, upholding 'Law and Order', protecting life and property, and prosecuting offenders against the peace, which was all part of the order. Boom! Boom!

Having been subservient to the Army's commissioned ranks for so long, I was in wonderment at being treated with respect as an individual. My room at the college had appointments that would not have been out of keeping in a quality hotel of the time and was to be my home and place of study for the entire fourteen weeks duration.

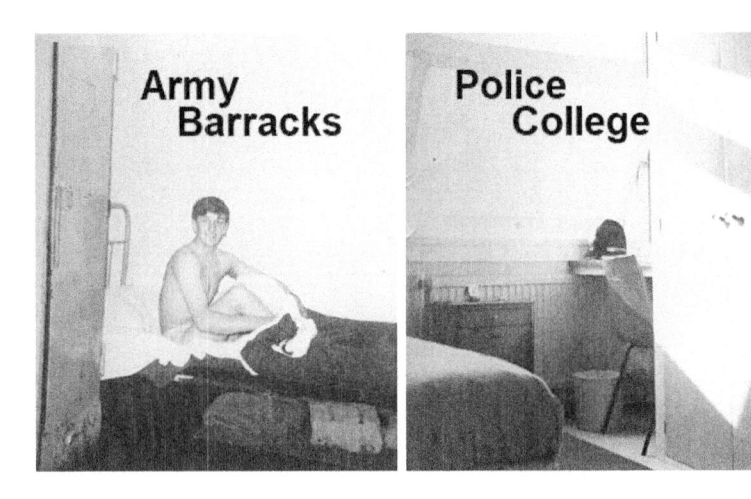

Army Barracks | Police College

From the outset, I became the class-leader for military-style parades, almost putting the drill-sergeant to shame. My experience bellowing at soldiers on the drill-square while in the Army served me well, so-much-so that our class won a drill competition set up between other groups in the college.

The reward for winning the square-bashing competition was to get the drill-sergeant pissed at the class's expense despite all of us being on a police constables' starting salary.

I was also the captain of the volleyball team - we won that too. The reward for winning the competition was temporary custody of a plaque while all the glory went to the class instructor, who never left the bloody classroom. Coppers, eh?

Studying Moriarty's Police Law, saving someone from drowning, physical offender-apprehension techniques, and higher first-aid, including delivering babies using rudimentary non-medical aids, was all part of the course. Dealing with the death of individuals at all levels was always high on the list of subjects, so too was recovering escaped budgies, returning them to their elderly owners and sitting down to share a cup of tea, offering the reassurance that the world really was a safe place.

Powers of observation at the police college were honed to a high degree before being tested by watching flashing images on a screen while seated in the college cinema. A film shown featured a London Metropolitan police constable going about his daily duties chasing and attempting to apprehend an offender that ultimately led to the officer filmed being murdered. Showing the film was designed to filter out those of a weak constitution, regardless of their academic achievements.

My first experience of coming into close contact with a corpse was attending a post mortem of a deceased female. All those present witnessed every aspect of dissection as the coroner sought to ascertain the cause of death. Opening up the chest cavity and cranium, the contents put on display for all to see were a step too far for some. The smell was overpowering and an experience I'll never be able to forget. Several members of our group found the experience too much to bear and hurried outside, retching as they went. It was another intended filtering process to weed out those of a weak constitution. Two members of the class that I was part of quit the service the following day.

Back at the police training college, studying and intensive police training went on as before. Mealtimes in the communal restaurant always provided a respite, providing delicious food, often waiter/waitress served. As the fourteen week's course concluded, a gala dinner had been arranged that required all those attending to wear dinner jackets, something most of us had never had to do before. Entertainment was provided by members of each class in the form of stand-up comedy or choral singing.

At the Gala Dinner, I had been appointed the master of ceremonies for the event, tasked with having to rap a gavel to announce whatever was about to take place - much like an Old Time Music Hall. It was great fun. We were all made to feel special, an experience that was a far cry from that in the Army, even though I then had certain privileges. At the police college, all students were treated with respect by the college staff, expecting that we would do the same when serving the community.

I left the training centre at Warrington, having secured twenty-first place out of eighty-two. It was a final class photo opportunity for those who completed the course before we were all off back to our respective constabularies, fully trained and brimming with confidence, ready to take on the world.

The police station in Maidenhead in Berkshire was expecting me, but first, I had to attend the Thames Valley Constabulary

Police College in Sulhamstead, Berkshire, for two weeks further induction into the force to learn the ways of the constabulary that I was to serve. Some national police authorities such as the Metropolitan Police, British Transport Police, constabularies of the Channel Islands and Gibraltar all worked to their own sometimes different rules.

After the course at Sulhamstead, the entire contingent of newly qualified officers of the Thames Valley Constabulary headed out in all directions to wreak havoc among the unsuspecting population with new-found confidence and keenness to zealously enforce the law. I pitied the public.

Maidenhead Calling

I arrived at Maidenhead Police Station in May 1971 and, as the only recruit to join the station for some considerable time, became an object of curiosity for some of the other officers. The only single woman police officer (WPC) at the station was teased to form some kind of relationship with me, but I was having none of it, and I'm not sure she was either. The first month or two quickly passed, during which time I was to meet someone who would change my life forever. It was a girl called Rosie.

Although I had made Rosie's acquaintance on a previous occasion, I did not 'date' this beautiful girl until the day I was on duty in Maidenhead High Street. One sunny Saturday, I happened to spot Rosie with a female friend, both of whom were approaching a pedestrian crossing. Both girls were wearing the then fashionable ultra-short hot-pants that brought every salivating young man to heightened levels of excitement! Drawn to the spectacle of the two sexy looking girls walking towards me, I immediately stepped into the busy High Street, bringing all traffic to a halt so that both could safely cross the road. They did, giggling as they crossed the road before disappearing into Woolworths. Several minutes later, both girls re-emerged and presented themselves at the pedestrian crossing's kerb-edge, accurately predicting that I would once again stop the traffic. For all I knew, the two flirtatious ladies could well have been shoplifting in Woolworths and giggling at their own audacity. As they stepped down onto the black and white painted pedestrian crossing, I once again brought all traffic to a standstill, using classic hand-signals for two-way traffic to a stop, even though Maidenhead High Street was part of a one-way system. I asked both of the not-so-coy ladies if one of them would like to join me for lunch at the pub adjacent to the Police Station, just off the Broadway in Queens Street after I came off duty at

2 p.m. It was Rosie who said she would - and did. I bought her a round of salad sandwiches which cost me an absolute fortune relative to my police salary, which she later admitted she did not like. I fell in love with this beautiful, sexy, and happy person, the liaison of which has lasted almost fifty years at the time of writing ...and we're still counting, despite murmurs that our marriage would not last more than six months. Oh, and how she liked a man in uniform; and, oh, how I wanted a girl that wasn't.

Before I left Northern Ireland, the farmer's daughter with one lens had moved to London. I met up with her later and took her to meet my mother - big mistake. My mother demonstrated total indifference and completely ignored her. Any relationship I might have had with my friend, not that I was seeking a closer one, was at an end. Mind you, just as my mother successfully wrecked my friendship with the girl from Northern Ireland, she was at it again with Rosie. Before my wife and I were married, she and I returned one evening to my mother's house, Rosie dropping me off after a delightful evening out. As my beautiful and charming girlfriend and I sat in her car arranging our next meeting, my mother appeared and repeatedly thumped her clenched fist onto the roof of the vehicle while at the same time shouted, "Hasn't that girl got a home to go to?" and, "What does her mother think?".

I couldn't have possibly known what her mum was thinking, but, sadly, what I did know was that I wanted to distance myself from my very jealous mother. Without hesitation, I went indoors and collected my worldly possessions as Rosie kept the engine running before both of us disappeared into the night. Hurried arrangements followed between Rosie and her aunt for me to become a temporary lodger in Windsor before moving across to accommodation in Maidenhead. Job completed - almost.

Not being content with the events of her making, my mother would regularly visit a pub that she knew Rosie I occasionally frequented, although she knew that I worked out of Maidenhead Police Station and could have contacted me at any time. She hadn't given up.

****

Forever romantic, I invited my girlfriend out on a trip to a shopping centre in the middle of High Wycombe in her Triumph Herald motor car and, after arrival, pulled up and parked inside a multi-story car-park. Without any appropriate surface to kneel on, I swivelled in the driver's seat to face Rosie and asked her if she would marry me. The answer necessitated a trip to one of the jewellers' shops inside the shopping complex (no, not Ratner's Jewellers), where I bought the most expensive engagement ring imaginable relevant to my dismal constable's salary, although I don't think Rosie was too impressed. It was to be a whirlwind romance, culminating in our marriage on 13th November the same year, five months after Rosie and her mate safely crossed the road to enter Woolworths for some Pick 'n' Mix. Our wedding was planned for the following January but brought forward on account of having an impatient little boy waiting to arrive into the world. In any event, nothing was going to stop me from marrying a girl the likes of which I had never previously encountered. I had fallen head-over-heels in love with this beautiful, kind, and caring person.

Although always short of money, it was time for my intended bride to choose her wedding dress. A quick scan in the second-hand 'For Sale' columns of the Maidenhead Advertiser local paper, and it was job done. A few weeks after our wedding, Rosie's bridal dress featured in the 'For Sale 'columns of the Slough Observer and sold very quickly. No room for sentiments; we needed the cash to supplement my Constable's salary.

A week before our wedding, Rosie and I were to receive the keys to a police authority three-bedroomed house and, as a bonus, received an income-tax rebate for the whole amount of tax paid backdated to the beginning of the tax year. And I got the girl of my dreams, later to become the mother of our two children and grandmother to our three grandchildren. That'll do nicely. Thank you.

The 24th January 1972 saw the arrival of our son Justin, three months earlier than expected. Justin weighed little more than a bag of sugar at birth and not expected to survive after being taken away in a stainless-steel kidney-shaped surgical bowl covered with a white cloth. We were later to learn that someone had detected a slight cry from under the material covering the container on its way to the incinerator, which was to signify the start of Justin's battle for life. The following morning, unbeknown to me, a Church of England vicar was summoned to our new-born son's incubator to administer Church of England religious 'Last Rights'. Gertcha!

Two and a half months later, Justin was at home having gained almost three pounds in weight thanks not just to the hospital staff, who were outstanding in every respect, but also the chief of police at Maidenhead Police Station, Superintendent Peterson. It was the same guy who had arranged for a policewoman the exclusive use of a police car to collect Rosie every single morning the whole two-and-a-half months Justin was in The Canadian Red Cross Memorial Hospital at Taplow in Buckinghamshire. The arrangement ensured that Rosie was able to be with and hold Justin's hand through the side of an intensive care incubator and, just as importantly, provide him with essential breast milk after it had been stored overnight in the refrigerator at home. Aged forty-nine at the time of writing, Justin continues to maintain his aversion to anything dairy!

****

After the post-mortem experience during initial training, my second experience of seeing a corpse was attending the sudden death of an elderly gentleman who had collapsed and died at the roadside garden gate leading to his property. There it was, the corpse, lying prostrate across the pathway with his wife wailing hysterically in the background. A steep learning curve for me - that was for sure. Arrangements were made to remove the body to a mortuary before sitting down with the widow to share a pot of tea, expressing as much empathy as a relatively young inexperienced police officer could muster. Statements were obtained recording the events leading up to the time of death, especially from the last person to have seen the deceased before he died.

Back at the mortuary, and in the absence of a mortuary attendant, and with only one small lightbulb hanging from the ceiling that created a spooky atmosphere, it was my duty to undress the corpse and remove all jewellery items and clothing for return to the widow. I then followed the usual procedure of tying a label to the right wrist and left big toe of the body, clearly showing the name of the deceased, along with my name and police number, before popping the body onto a horizontal pull-out metal stretcher of a body-fridge. The experience was unnerving, but one that became a matter of routine over the years that followed.

In my quest to gain the experience of dealing with a wide variety of offences, as actively encouraged at the Police Training College, I would pick a subject out of the latest edition of Moriarty's Police Law and robustly seek out specific offences that related to it.

The law concerning Vagrancy required law enforcers to move on homeless individuals considered Vagrants, instructing them to go and 'Tramp' the streets elsewhere, else lock them up. Eager as I was to get on with the job, I had my first lesson in humility while walking the streets of Maidenhead with an experienced sergeant who later became a good family friend. One cold Christmas day, my colleague and I happened upon a scruffily dressed homeless man of middle years sat on a low-height wall in the middle of town. He was reading a copy of The Times newspaper, oblivious to everyday goings-on around him, his worldly belongings contained in plastic sacks scattered at his feet. My instinct was to move this guy on, but after entering into conversation with him, the fluency and knowledge expressed of topical subjects and politics took me aback. The experience was an early lesson about not stereotyping somebody just because of their looks or behaviour. The sergeant accompanying me nipped back to the police station and returned with his packed-lunch full of Christmas goodies along with a bottle of something alcoholic that he promptly handed over to the homeless chap, wishing him a merry Christmas as he did so. I was never quite sure if this bloke referred to as 'Jock' was a Scot, but I detected a slight lilt in his voice when he spoke, which suggested he might well have been Scottish. Sadly, I never did get to know about Jock's journey through life; he died a lonely soul amongst a pile of disused bricks at a quarry near Winter Hill on Cookham Common. I was humbled. After all the years that have passed, I still think of him. It seems that the good guys always seem to meet their maker before anyone else.

'Run to a fire, walk to a fight' is an adage instilled in every constable's brain during training, the theory being that running to a fire could possibly save lives while walking to a fight allowed sufficient time for opponents to knock the living daylights out of each other. All one had to do after turning up was to pick up the pieces. Simple.

   After just a few months into the two-year obligatory probationary period, there was an occasion when, on a summer's evening just after dusk, I was walking the length of the new partially completed ring road linking the east and west of Maidenhead, semi-circumventing the town centre at its north. A call came for all available officers to attend the nearby youth club situated at the bottom of Castle Hill, where it was reported a rival gang of youths from a club elsewhere were at the scene brandishing knives and machetes. Mindful of the adage 'Run to a fire - walk to a fight', the call was exceptional due to the risk of life. It was dark as I headed off towards the disturbance, but in the absence of street-lighting, I failed to notice that covers had been removed from newly installed drains along the entire length of the road. I promptly stepped into one of the open shafts, seriously jarring my back as I did so. By the time I got to the youth club, the perpetrators had scarpered, thankfully before anyone had been injured.

The next day, following the previous evening events, I signed off duty for six weeks on sick leave. Fearful of being asked to leave the police service under the terms of the two-year probationary period, I returned to work three weeks early, feigning health, sneakily nipping into the local medical centre for infra-red-light treatment during a break when pounding the beat. The legacy of falling into the drain remains with me to this day.

After several months walking the streets in and around Maidenhead Town Centre, I was sent off on a driving course to learn police driving skills. I had to undergo another necessary Ministry of Transport driving test before embarking on an extended two-week intensive period to learn progressive police driving techniques. The course culminated in a comprehensive driving test going from Aylesbury to the Wye Valley in Herefordshire with a police instructor motorcyclist outrider watching my every manoeuvre. Upon reaching the planned destination, the driving instructor accompanying me within the vehicle and a police motorcycle outrider had a 'conflab to discuss the merits of my 'progressive' driving skills. Thankfully, I passed and was authorised to drive…a panda car! Driving such a vehicle (I'm in the driving seat) meant that I didn't have to 'plod' the streets and hold up traffic for good-looking girls to cross the road ever again - risky business.

As far as I can make out, many of the original panda cars of the 1960s in some constabularies were Black Ford Anglia cars with white doors (hence the name 'Panda'). By the time I joined the Thames Valley Constabulary in 1971, the vehicle of choice was the Mark I Ford Escort, some of which were 'duck-egg blue' with white doors as shown above, while others were white with duck-egg blue doors with the contrasting colour painted across the roof giving a visual link to each side of the vehicle. The reason? Cost, I guessed. The panda cars were purchased as separate lots and then subject to door swapping, the white doors put onto duck-egg blue cars and vice-versa. There had to have been a Scot or Yorkshireman in charge of purchasing somewhere.

As with all public service bodies, the armed forces and the then forty-five police authorities across the country were all bereft of sufficient funds to function effectively. Unlike police officers of today, who, from my observations, appear to be kitted out with all kinds of stuff, including state-of-the-art batons, CS Gas, taser guns, radios, body armour, body cameras, etc. etc., on display. The standard-issue items of my time consisted of a solid oak wooden truncheon discreetly hidden from view within a long slim pocket running down the inside trouser leg, a pair of handcuffs and a whistle on a chain, the likes of which had probably never seen the light of day since the time of Jack-the-Ripper. Two plastic-encased radios, one for sending and the other for receiving, were later additions, although more than a hundred metres from the police station, both became totally useless and not worth the effort of carrying them.

Back on the beat policing Maidenhead, I experienced every facet of human life and behaviour, usually at its worst. The pervading theory of the time was that most law-abiding members of the public would rarely come into contact with the police unless they were providing cups of tea, asking for the time of day or directions, experiencing trauma, reporting, or claiming lost property, or generally undesirable individuals. Almost all of the times I responded to calls of help or despair, I would be alone, armed with nothing more than the wooden truncheon and acquired skills to approach and assess people and situations in an instant. During my time in the service, I was never violently attacked other than receiving a bodily 'baulking' by one individual I caught removing parking tickets from vehicles outside of his taxi business premises. The business owner was arrested and slammed up in the cells overnight before being brought before the Magistrates Court. The offender was subsequently convicted of assaulting a police officer (me), a heinous crime in those days. The sentenced man received a hefty fine and a suspended six months custodial sentence.

It has always been said that the best form of defence is to attack, so, with that in mind, if I thought a situation showed any signs of escalating, reluctant as I was to get involved in violence, I always went in first using the tactic of surprise that always worked, as any military strategist will testify.

There was an occasion when, during the middle of the night, sometime around 2 am, I attempted to arrest an individual following a motor-car chase that terminated in a cul-de-sac. I got out of the police car and grabbed hold of the driver I suspected of driving a stolen vehicle, only for us both to end up tumbling over a low-level wall into someone's prized flower garden. As we both stood up, the suspect sparred as a professional boxer with an invitation to respond similarly, but instead of doing so, I took a step back and pulled out my solid oak wooden truncheon from the inside sleeve of my trouser leg, intending to bonk the geezer on the head. Realising that I was becoming serious, the suspect quickly did a 'runner' but was later apprehended by other officers in Maidenhead. It transpired the suspect was an ex-police officer who decided he could earn more money engaging in multiple thefts of vehicles than serving the general public.

During my six years with the Thames Valley Constabulary, police officers in uniform almost always earned the general public's respect and whose mere presence symbolised order and unquestionable authority. The highest ethical standards, morals, honesty, and integrity were always taken for granted. Several cases in point arose when arresting drivers of motor vehicles for being above the alcohol drink-drive limit. I would store the blood samples of those I arrested in our domestic fridge alongside everyday groceries. It was always the following morning that I sent phials containing an accused's blood off to the Forensic Laboratory at Aldermaston for analysis. Evidence of continuity never questioned - not even by defence barristers.

   The presence of a police officer in a dark uniform with shiny silver buttons and a silver badge glistening at the front of a very tall, intimidating police helmet was usually enough to defuse potentially dangerous situations, but how things have changed. In these modern times, a police officer's mere presence, wearing high-visibility jackets festooned with all kinds of protective equipment and menacing-looking weapons, not to mention glaringly obvious looking vehicles, is often the catalyst for violence.

   Several verbs can be used to describe someone being arrested, such as; nicked, pinched, nobbled, and collared, but, more commonly, the term 'feeling a collar' was often used to describe a police officer's actions in the process of apprehending someone by grabbing their shirt collar from behind as an individual attempted to escape.

It was on a hot early summer's evening while on patrol in a panda car in around Maidenhead when I received a report of a naked man running amok on Blackmoor, a piece of common scrub-land a couple of roads away from where I happened to be, just off the Bath Road in Maidenhead. As I turned into the lane, the common on one side and a row of houses on the other, I saw several of the residents hanging out of top windows directing me to where they had last seen the streaking stripper flitting between shrubs and hedgerows. Off I went on foot in hot-pursuit, bent on bringing the naked man to heel, but at the same time wondering how I was going to physically apprehend him in his birthday suit.

In the absence of the fleeing gentleman wearing any clothing, let alone a collar, the only other way of feeling him was something I was not prepared to consider. Gertcha! Oh, if only Taser Guns had been available. A physical apprehension method I thought of using involved grasping my wooden truncheon at its centre with a clenched fist and shoving it between the flighty fast runner's legs to stop him from going any further. By pushing the person forward with the baton held firmly in place, he would be unable to do anything other than stumble along in perpetual motion. It worked every time, although in this case, such a method of apprehension would have resulted in direct contact with the offender's 'Bits', something I was not prepared to risk. My last remaining option was an award-winning rugby tackle at knee height, which finally brought my naked gentleman to the ground. The unfortunate chap was handcuffed, placed in the Panda car, and karted off to the police station without first being allowed to cover up, much to the applause of everyone watching. Fiendishly, just for the fun of it, I drove back to the station, taking the longest route possible, doubling back through the High Street as I went. The clothing of the person taken into custody was piled up in the front passenger seat, just out of reach. Always being a bit of a 'Tyke', mischief was never far from my mind, but I'm not proud of myself.

The murder of a South-Asian Pakistani man lying on the ground outside the 'Green Dragon' pub in Maidenhead was one of my first experiences witnessing the effects of extreme violence and racism. The unfortunate victim had suffered a stab wound to his abdomen, causing a proportion of his intestines to bulge out from the knife's point of entry. The death of the victim followed almost the moment I arrived on the scene. The attack appeared to be racially motivated and was my first experience of witnessing a victim of murder.

There was also fun, usually at the expense of others. A probationary constable referred to as Crystal Tips for reasons that escape me had been instructed by the section sergeant to attend Windsor Safari Park and present himself to someone called C. Lyons to investigate the theft of seals – for Christ's sake. 'Crystal Tips' was on his way to Windsor sometime after midnight before being intercepted and returned to town duties. The laughing from those of us within the police station was loud enough to rouse the entire population of Maidenhead and might well have done so for all I knew.

Another incident involving Crystal Tips involved setting-up a roadblock at 3 a.m. on the A4 major trunk road at the top of Castle Hill. Radio communications alerted a group of 'knowing' officers to a speeding car approaching from the Reading direction, hotly pursued by a 'marked' high-performance police car, sirens blaring and blue lights flashing. The vehicle sought was an unmarked police car that came to an abrupt screeching halt at the roadblock when the two occupants alighted and ran off into the darkness, pursued by none other than Crystal Tips himself. Hey-ho. While all of that was going on, John Collier's men's outfitter's shop in the High Street was being cleared of stock by burglars. John Collier's television advert ditty of the time was:

♪ 'John Collier, John Collier, the window to watch' ♪

The John Collier ditty, if heeded, would have served us well. The everyday lads about town were always able to 'suss-out' new police officers, and, as a result, the police career of Crystal Tips became a short one.

During the obligatory two-year probationary period, I was to join the local detectives (CID) for a month's investigative policing. It was a novel experience wearing civilian clothes and paid an allowance for doing so. Entering pubs almost on a nightly basis for a drink or two while surreptitiously seeking out handlers of stolen goods was an experience that provided an opportunity to demonstrate that I was capable of being more than just a P.C. Plod.

There was an occasion when being at the right place at the right time served me well. Accompanied by an experienced detective during my time with the Criminal Investigation Department (CID), we attended the Holiday Inn Hotel in Langley following a report of someone having left the building via the fire doors without settling the bill. After obtaining a description of the alleged offender, a casual search of the vicinity was underway. As the detective and I turned a corner, I spotted a man a hundred metres or so in front of us, walking in the same direction. I immediately said to my colleague, "That's him!". We then apprehended the chap and took him into custody. The detective inspector back at the station, so impressed that a reported crime had been solved within 30 minutes, couldn't stop talking about it to others, believing that I had some super-sensory perceptions and that, amazingly, I was still a trainee. He and others didn't know that two days previously, I was in the Magistrates court on a different matter when I had ample time to gawp at the back of the same person's head as he stood accused of something or other. What was striking about the fellow was that he had been a detective in the Irish Garda Síochána, which was probably why I still had him in my recollective memory.

Another secondment involved joining the traffic police department, zipping up and down motorways and main routes within the Thames Valley area. After stepping inside a souped-up high-performance police car for the first time, I had my first experience of exceedingly high-speed travel, the biological result of which would have put any trolleybus driver to shame.

Attending major traffic incidents was the primary function of traffic police and enforcing road traffic law. I returned to regular duties wiser and ready to effectively deal with road incidents. In the absence of other officers, I often had to deal with road traffic accidents single-handedly, almost always at night, in all weather conditions and almost always in the back-end of nowhere.

Apprehending speeding offenders was not known to be the remit of panda car drivers, as most motorists will have known. However, travelling along St Chad's Road in Maidenhead in such a police vehicle, I was overtaken at speed by a youthful-looking chap obviously out on a promise. It was to be my first and only case of speeding. Securing a successful prosecution meant having to prove that the speedometer in the panda car was working correctly. To confirm the accuracy of the equipment required travelling over a measured-mile, marked out by white painted squares on most road surfaces of major roads and motorways, another officer sat next to me holding a calibrated timer that too had to certified as accurate. So, if you've ever wondered what the white squares are (or were) on the road, now you know, although I suspect technology has since taken the upper hand. What I didn't know was whether or not the poor lad managed to keep his date. It was mean of me, I know, but if he hadn't blatantly overtaken my marked vehicle at speed well above the speed limit in town looking through a pink mist of love or lust, I wouldn't have known any different. Obviously, the thinking part of his anatomy, like so many young men of his age wasn't in his head but elsewhere.

I suspect the lustful lad only realised that he was overtaking a marked police car at the point of being parallel to it and saw the POLICE sign on the side. Silly sod. To be fair, though, same-coloured Ford Escort cars of the time had been a prevalent and familiar sight.

Several months had passed, and, as part of on-going training, I was required to attend a three-weeks continuation study course at a police college in Redhill, Surrey, to face more law exams and job suitability. The extended induction completed, and back in Maidenhead, I was summoned to the Superintendent's office and offered the appointment of 'Area Beat Officer', another name for a village Bobby, in Wraysbury, near Staines. I was to set a precedent of being the only probationary constable ever to be transferred to a much-coveted appointment, usually the preserve of the more worthy and experienced officers. Sorry, guys.

In the Sticks

Before too long, Rosie, Justin and I were to take up residence in The Police House, Staines Road, Wraysbury in Buckinghamshire. The building, a modest detached property built before World War Two, had the words 'COUNTY POLICE' set into the front elevation that attracted lorry drivers knocking on our front door asking for directions or else pleading to use the loo. Attached to the house, and accessible from within, happened to be a prison cell we used as a utility room. The rear garden stretched for some considerable distance to a water-filled excavated quarry that Rosie and I would access for recreational purposes. A pigsty that must have housed a solitary animal providing a protein source for law enforcers in the war years, Rosie and I used it to raise chickens. Life was idyllic, but there was a job to be done, and not all of it pleasant.

The general area I was to police bordered the London Metropolitan Police area whose officers seemed to be a force of their own, working to a different and sometimes dubious set of rules. The 'MET' officers even looked different with their white shirts, smaller streamlined uniforms, and dapper-looking helmets rather than rural constabulary officers wearing clunky headgear more in keeping with the Keystone Cops or the London fire brigade. Our rural constabulary uniforms, with blue shirts, driving Ford Escort vans loaded up with wellie boots, shovels, rubber traffic cones and the like instead of state-of-the-art police cars with all their flashy equipment, would have been a sight to behold.

London Bobbies were often seen crossing boundary lines on recreational trips of curiosity, most likely arranged by Scotland Yard to allow their officers to see what country coppers looked like and undoubtedly offering an opportunity for their guys to have a bloody good laugh. The Metropolitan Police guys always seemed to travel in twos rather than on their own, presumably to reduce their risk of exposure to harm. Wusses!

Everyday events were underway in Wraysbury, as I observed local people going about their days of business. One particular farmer appeared to have fallen in love with one of his sheep that accompanied him everywhere he went while seated in his car's front passenger seat. I wouldn't have been surprised if his dearly-beloved sheep was called B-a-a-a-a-r B-a-a-a-r-ra, either in memory of the farmer's late wife or that the animal was indeed his wife - sheep or otherwise. No point bleating. Bestiality was a criminal offence, but with a distinct lack of proof of such a crime had ever taken place, there was nothing I or anyone else could do. In any event, the sheep looked happy enough, behind closed doors and all that. I often wondered if reincarnation ever existed, and if it did, I rather fancied coming back as a sheep - not anymore! Gertcha!

Not all days were good days; there was a particular occasion when I received a report of a house fire well underway a short distance from where I lived. Upon arriving at the scene, I could see several fire-fighters in attendance doing what firefighters had to do, hosepipes crisscrossed across the pavement that led to a bungalow. I was informed of a body within the property but could not enter until safe to do so. When I finally had been allowed to enter the building, I came across the charred body of a female lying on top of a melted foam mattress. I had to examine the corpse to satisfy myself that death resulted from accidental burning rather than anything else, although a coroner would have determined the ultimate cause of death following an autopsy. That done, it was off to the mortuary to receive the body and carry out the routine of undressing the corpse, removing any jewellery, and tying identity labels to the wrist and big toe. I'll never forget the sight and stench of burnt human flesh of the victim's arms that to me resembled enormous sausages that had split from the intense heat of the fire. The deceased had been a physically handicapped bed-ridden lady who had lived alone and fell asleep while smoking a cigarette. Sadly, just another day. Unlike today, instead of a posse of officers turning up at almost all incidents involving a deceased, in my time, it was almost always down to an individual officer alone to attend and single-handedly deal with whatever befalls him or her short of homicide, serious sexual offences or injury as a result of extreme violence. Attending scenes of domestic violence between married or unmarried couples became routine that required no further action unless, of course, the altercations resulted in severe injury or death.

Tea-stops for police officers was the stuff of PC Plod in children's storybooks, depicting the caricature of a rotund police constable going about his daily business, saying good morning to the likes of Noddy and his mate Big Ears. I might well have fitted the same profile as I had a van, although I was bereft of a rotund figure and those big ears endearing to the character. The police vehicle I used was not as well-equipped as the police van P.C. Plod drove as mine only had a single blue flashing light and an audible two-tone emitting warning sound that I discovered I could make by pressing the signal indicator arm that protruded from the side of the steering column and waggle it backwards and forwards. Sometimes, to robust comments of disapproval from colleagues back in Langley Station, I would opt for a bicycle, so I could cycle around the countryside singing the lyrics to the song:

♪ 'England swings like pendulums bobbies on bicycles, two-by-two... etc." ♪

Riding a bicycle, I hoped, might well have resulted in being given a half-a-crown or even a crown coin from passing American tourists as I rode on by - some chance. I cannot imagine that any American tourists would want to go where I sometimes had to go.

Despite having to co-exist and interact with a couple of troublesome travelling itinerants, daily life, with a relatively low crime rate, life was good. I learned that the same two troublesome itinerant guys eventually passed through the pearly gates to heaven only to be told by the big guy that they could go no further until they put the gates back. Not content with the story of events, I asked one of their former accomplices about the matter, who said to me,

"On me dying farver's orse, officer, they ain't dun it".

"O'Riley," I enquired.

"No", he said, "O'Hara"

I got my answer. It was blatantly obvious the geezer hadn't visited the Australian stand at Olympia.

The Great Western Railway's level-crossing signal box at Datchet happened to be staffed by a chap of intemperate habits who always had tea on the go. The Great Western Railway building became a regular stop-off point to slurp a brew while gleaning information about everyday events. The elevated signal control box was high enough to provide a vantage point to look out onto ordinary folk going about their day-to-day affairs. The tea was absolutely putrid.

After a few months into the job at Wraysbury, I began to have concerns that, as I had a premature baby, the police house we occupied, as grand as it was, was showing signs of damp within the bedroom walls, which I thought might have impacted on our son's health and wellbeing. An opportunity arose to move house when the Duke of Gloucester moved out of his residence at Iver, negating the requirement to have the few police officers attending his place of residence. The officers that formed part of a protection squad were posted elsewhere, while at the same time, the sergeant-in-charge who lived in a very modern detached police authority house in the middle of the village next to the village police station decided to retire. I was recommended for the post and took up the residency of the retired sergeant's house and the 'Area Beat Officer' appointment that came with it. I worked opposite shifts alongside an older and more experienced colleague in policing the village and outlying areas. The association with my new colleague, Police Constable Ronald Edwards, became a friendship that still exists at the time of writing, some forty-two years on. Ronald, aged ninety-nine years, tells me that he has received far more money from his police pension than he ever did in salary for thirty years or more of service. Beat that!

One of my near neighbours, who occasionally lived just a couple of hundred metres away from the police house, always seemed to be 'Down-under' in Australia and not in his place in Iver. The neighbour was none other than Sid James, star of many world-renown Carry On films. I never did get to meet Sid, but I did deal with his boxer dog's occasion after it had been run over and killed in a road accident. The dog's body, a breed of Boxer, was unceremoniously dumped on Sid's estate's compost heap by someone associated with his affairs and who later became a person of interest to me for having failed to renew his shotgun licence while still in possession of such weapons. The person concerned lost his shotgun licence, shotguns, and credibility in exchange for a criminal record. These days, it would probably have been temporary confiscation of weapons without prosecution until a new licence had been issued?

Just a couple of miles or so away from Iver village could be found Pinewood Studios, where I would often find myself on so-called rest-days. It was an opportunity to earn some overtime and involved patrolling the film set and studios whenever firearms happened to be present or used as props in James Bond films. I had carte-blanche authority to wander wherever I chose, often walking onto film-sets when Roger Moore (as James Bond) happened to be in full flow. I spoiled no end of film-shoots and was frequently asked by the film director through a loudspeaker megaphone, "Would the police officer please remove himself from the set?".

If the director had shouted 'Gertcha!', I would have instinctively run into any available enclosed room and put my feet up against the door to stop anyone entering brandishing an iron fire-grate poker.

I happened to be on foot patrol one winter's day sporting a clunky police helmet and a super-duper posh serge cape that had a small chain joined at the collar, affixed both sides to badges, depicting the head of a lion. A lady with what I perceived as having an American accent asked me if I was 'Ray-eel'. I was tempted to say, 'Yea Ma'am, I sure cotton-picking am - ma'am' while offering to show her my truncheon secreted away in a pocket down the inside of my right trouser-leg.

I then thought of saying, 'As it's nearly Guy Fawkes night, perhaps you can spare a 'ray-eel' half-crown or any silver coins you don't know the value of?'. Instead, I just said,

"Yes, madam, I am real - and don't forget to drive on the left - madam".

I recall being at Pinewood Studios during the making of another James Bond film depicting scenes of submarines in a docking area. I was to witness the cast of 'extras' supposedly being blown up only to fall onto a stack of cardboard boxes at a lower level that was covered with large swathes of hessian, or else running amok on plywood tops of fake submarines pretending to have been shot or blown-up. My enjoyment of watching films generally had been ruined for life.

On a different film-shoot for another movie at Pinewood Studios, there was a scene involving Canadian Timber Wolves, one of which had escaped from its enclosure and was last been seen heading towards the village of Iver where I lived. There was talk of a real risk of the animal attacking someone out of fear or that it would run onto the nearby M4 motorway with the potential to cause untold carnage. Standing in front of my police van while scanning the horizon, 'Wolfie suddenly appeared a few metres in front of me. "Good dog, Good dog," I uttered in the best Canadian accent I could muster as the piercing ice-blue eyes of the quarry latched firmly onto me like laser beams, conveying a message not to get any closer. I scampered back into the van, slipping on cow-pats that went all the way up the back of my uniform. Sadly, the wolf was shot dead by a police marksman as it made its way toward the M4 motorway.

****

Five years after our son Justin's birth, the national press was once again interested in the progress of our 'miracle boy' who had survived against all the odds.

After all the media attention surrounding the 'Miracle Baby Darling', I was back on the job with another report of a death, this time at a house in Iver Heath, very close to Pinewood Studios. Within the integral garage of the property, I came across the body of a young man lying on the floor, obviously dead. There were visible hallmarks of a ligature having been around the neck that suggested a hanging. Enquiries established that the deceased had taken his own life following a history of depression. The last person to see him alive was a decorator who said that he had entered the house and later saw what he thought was the deceased standing in the garage looking up towards the rafters. Little did the contractor know he was looking at a corpse swinging from a rope. Labels tied to right wrist and left big toe, statements obtained and satisfied there was no evidence of foul play, it was yet another job done before handing the case over to a coroner's officer.

There were times when I would be emotionally drained. For me, a particularly harrowing experience was attending an address following reports of the sudden death of an infant boy, just a few months old, who died of asphyxiation by inhaling his own vomit. The usual procedure followed such events with the body removed to the local mortuary and then arrangements made to meet the deceased's estranged father at the morgue to identify the body. At the time, I suggested that the father waited outside the main entrance of the mortuary as I was about to enter the building, but he said he was a hospital porter and knew exactly what I was about to do by preparing the body for viewing, decided to enter the building at the same time as I did. What took us both aback was the sight of the infant's body covered in blood and other matter that had dripped down from the body of a road traffic accident victim placed above in the body-fridge. Despite dealing with sudden death situations, nothing could have prepared me for that experience, mainly as I was the parent of an infant of a similar age. I can only imagine what must have gone through the father's mind as he gazed down upon the body of what had been his only child.

It was by good fortune that I never did get to attend a football match during six years of service as I would have been bored rigid. What I had to endure was racing days at Royal Ascot in Berkshire. Racegoers would arrive at pre-booked exclusive parking areas in chauffeur-driven Bentleys and Rolls-Royce cars before setting out hampers of champagne and high-end edible delights. Dressed in all kinds of ridiculous outfits, the same pompous people would return to their vehicles at the end of each day, many in an inebriated state, the women amongst them wearing torn tights and wonky hats. At the same time, the so-called 'gentlemen' among them sported plump ruddy complexions, pumped up by a full day of gluttony, impatiently demanding priority to exit the car parks over and above the flow of traffic, and everyone else for that matter - no chance. The same type of people stomping about full of their own self-importance left behind less than favourable memories, along with my own memories of a vast mountain of miss-sharpened strawberries that had been rejected as being imperfect. Pride stopped me from collecting some of the fruit to take home, even though they were something my family could ill-afford. The worst and most painful part of being at the races was to witness multitudes of those strawberries being scooped up in mechanical buckets before being loaded onto trucks and taken off to landfill after each day of racing.

****

Back on the home territory after Ascot races, I received a report of yet another sudden death, this time an aged farmer who had gone into his milking shed washroom to sluice out some buckets when he happened to kick one himself. He was gone – dead. I arrived on the scene to find the deceased spread-eagled across the small concrete floor with his foot firmly jammed in one of the buckets. I carried out the usual routine to check for signs of life and then looked for possible clues of criminality.

Before the undertaker's arrival, a somewhat awkward lad of about sixteen appeared and headed straight for the same milking-shed. I recognised the boy as being the same individual who persistently rode his bicycle at night without lights despite warnings not to do so. I did not prevent him from entering the milking parlour but rather hoped he did. And he did. Within seconds I heard deep crooning noises and wailing followed by the same teenager making a swift exit out of the milking-shed.

"Morning", I said as he swiftly passed by and disappeared into the distance.

Saturday nights were nearly always quiet in the Village of Iver and the surrounding area, so much so, I often wended my way to the not-too-distant town of Slough to boost police numbers after public house licencing hours came to a close at 11pm. As part of a so-called heavy mob that comprised of a dozen or so fellow officers huddled together in a police people-carrier, we were ready to deal with any disturbances that arose. With all the excitement over and a few hapless individuals finding themselves having to spend the night in custody, it was back to the darkness of the countryside.

Brighter Eyes

The rural area bordering the London Metropolitan district of Uxbridge brought its own challenges, especially at weekends when it seemed as if the entire cast from the film 'Watership Down'; a classic story of rabbits by Richard Adams who caricatured rabbits with having human traits but continued to indulge in all things rabbit. Following a report of a young lady being seen with two male accomplices entering a wooded conservation area near the M4 motorway at Richings Park, Iver, all available officers were dispatched to the scene. What greeted us on arrival reminded me of yet another film: Pinocchio, a fictional character protagonist of a children's storybook of the same name. There was a scene where two of the main characters, a Fox and Jackal, happened upon the naïve puppet before making off with him into the distance. So many similarities. Within the wooded area of Richings Park, it became apparent what was about to occur, but with no breaches of law, the disappointed lady was instead escorted home in a police vehicle while the young bucks were sent packing, on foot, in the opposite direction. The only bright eyes that night, at least from the area of the woods, came from a multitude of flashlights reflected in three pairs of eyes. Gertcha!

Oryctolagus cuniculus' (rabbits) habits weren't confined to the species; the police station in the nearby town of Slough had a complex of offices with accommodation at ground level for single officers. There was an officers' club on the upper floor where Rosie and I would very occasionally visit for a spot of social intercourse over a pint or two of lower-priced drinks from the bar. Some club patrons would then drive home (probably over the limit) while on-duty patrolling officers turned a blind eye or made themselves scarce. A story circulated that the station's superintendent was on his way home one evening from the club when he happened to glance into a ground floor window of one of the single quarters. What the big chief saw was two males and one female officer cavorting naked in full view of patrons coming and going to the club. The merry trio's male participants were brought to account, 'cautioned' for their immorality, and told not to be naughty or else pull the curtains across before doing so again. The female officer was posted to a far-flung station in rural Oxfordshire to the delight of the station sergeant called Roger. Sergeant Roger (later referred to in conversations as Jolly Roger) who, up until the time the woman police constable joined him, had been pre-occupied removing morsels of food from his matted beard. Not anymore! Some wise-crack individual mentioned the name 'Dawn' (actual or otherwise) for the female officer, which turns the phrase 'getting up early to experience the crack of dawn' on its head, wouldn't you think?

Double Diamond Bitter Ale was a favourite beer of the time and most likely the choice of tipple for the immoral threesome as they staggard off for a bawdy session in the single quarters. The brewery that produced the stuff ran television adverts at the time that went something like this: -

♫ A Double Diamond works wonders, works wonders, works wonders. A Double Diamond works wonders, so drink some today. ♪

Who can dispute that claim? The abv. alcohol content of Double Diamond was enough to blow the hats off lightweight drinkers; trousers and under-garments coming off at the same time had to be a bonus. Doubles all round, I'd say. Gertcha!

And, not wishing to drop the topic of trousers just yet, a new face arrived at Langley police station, that of a constable unexpectedly transferred from a police station elsewhere in Berkshire. The married officer in question was 'allegedly' having an affair with a woman in the city where he worked while her husband was away working night shifts. The officer decided to keep the mystery woman cosy during cold winter nights while on night-duty; that was until the husband of the wayward lady returned to find our buddy in bed with the lady he thought he had left tucked up for the night with a mug of cocoa. Without disturbing the indulgent couple too much, the aggrieved husband scooped-up the officer's trousers that had been mindlessly draped over the back of a settee and promptly delivered them to the custody sergeant on duty at the police station with the comments, "If you want to know the whereabouts of the owner of these trousers, you would do well to look in my bedroom". The rascals – all of them!

Another Saturday night, long after pub closing time, I would often patrol the dark nook-and-crannies of outlying areas for unusual activities. There was one particular occasion when, in the darkness of a remote country lane, I came across a young lady faced-down and spread-eagled across the bonnet of a car. I thought I caught a glimpse of the crack of dawn, but I must have been mistaken as it was only a little after midnight. A vigorous youthful-looking chap, showing-off the unmistakable red label of a pair of Levi Jeans wrapped around his ankles, provided a convenient opportunity for me to park my bike; if only I'd had one. The exuberant fellow was vigorously pushing his willing accomplice forward in an attempt to get her to a hospital (memories of dogs in Faroe Road) and, by the look of things, taking the unbraked car with them. After fifteen minutes with my patience becoming a bit thin, I considered enough was enough. In the absence of a house-brick or bucket of water to send them on their way, my only option was to drive up closer with headlights blaring in an attempt to light-up their way. To help further, I switched on the blue flashing light on the top of the police van, but all that did was heighten the frenzy. Finally, satisfied that what was going on had been consensual, I sounded my van's audible warning device by waggling the indicator lever on the side of the steering column while at the same time shouting that fearful phrase: Gertcha! They were gone. At the time, my thoughts were that it always paid to be well-rounded as I reached for my sandwiches, realising that I had just finished eating them. I didn't have the heart to book the car driver for not applying the handbrake before he alighted from his vehicle. Equally, it was just as well I didn't have the luxury to issue what would have been an inappropriate on-the-spot fine as I would not have known where to put it! More tea, Vicar?

Rain in Vain.

The year nineteen seventy-three witnessed a historical event in Northern Ireland's politics in what became known as 'The Sunningdale Talks.' British Prime Minister Edward Heath, Gerry Fit, Ian Paisley, Garret Fitzgerald, John Hume, the leader of the Irish Taoisech, Liam Cosgrove and others, got together in an attempt to iron out their differences albeit with limited success. The meeting titled 'Direct Rule and Sunningdale Agreement' chaired by the late ex-prime minister Sir Edward Heath was an attempt by the British Government to bash everyone's heads together to address the appalling events in Northern Ireland. I was called in along with many other police officers to provide security for the politicians as they strolled from one building to another. The dignitaries must have felt safe seeing a British Bobby at every turn, but if they had known we had nothing more than a packet of crisps, Polo Mints in each pocket and a wooden truncheon, they might well have thought very differently and probably gone to ground.

While in Sunningdale, it didn't stop raining the whole time. Standing out in such appalling weather conditions are some of the memories I took away with me, along with having constructed a shelter out of twigs and a plastic sack to keep rainwater from running down my neck, only to be told to dismantle it the moment it was completed. I couldn't wait for the talks to end so the Northern Ireland guys could go home and take their liquid sunshine with them. Nice guys, those politicians from Ulster, always smiling and courteous to everyone they encountered. I had come across Ian Paisley before when I was back in Belfast while accompanying the farmer's daughter with one lens to a travel agent's shop. Ian was there, but he meant nothing to me and could have been selling bananas for all I knew. I do not know what Ian Paisley's holiday plans were then, but I bet it wasn't the 'Ring

'O Kerry' in the Republic of Ireland or any other ring for that matter. I was tempted to ask him in passing if he had ever been a Belfast trolleybus driver, but undoubtedly the answer would have been: 'Never, Never, NEVER!' But that'll probably have been a 'YES'. I would have chuckled along with Ian and the late Martin McGuiness, a 2nd in command Provisional Irish Republican Army leader who later became the Deputy First Minister at Stormont until his resignation in 2013.

According to one account of the two controversial politicians:

'One was a crusty Protestant firebrand from Antrim. The other was a Catholic militant from Derry and young enough to be his son. They stood on opposite sides of battle lines for decades, and both shared a mutual hatred and a history of involvement in sectarian violence. Yet, the two men eventually became close working colleagues.'

So amiable and always laughing at each other's comments, Ian and Martin became known as 'The Chuckle Brothers', after an English comedy double act of Barry David Elliott and Paul Harman Elliot. The 'Chuckle Brothers' comedy usually derived from slapstick, wordplay, and other visual gags with their catchphrase 'To me, to you!' Northern Irish politics. Keh?

Sunningdale over, I was again back in the village of Iver when boredom would once again show its hand with the absence of other officers with who I could share company. I would eavesdrop on the radio for anything going on that I could get to within a limited timescale.

The Britwell Estate in Slough, a Greater London housing development, was built to rehouse residents from areas of slum clearance and some of the most over-populated and deprived areas of London. The estate was a regular port of call for the police having to deal with unruly individuals that almost always involved locking someone up.

On another occasion, a particular call overheard on the police radio was for all available officers to attend a burglar alarm alert at Argos on Slough High Street. The premises were checked out, and officers on their way back to wherever they came when a university graduate fast-promoted police inspector decided to search each departing patrol car for stolen goods. Excellent morale booster for those officers who put their lives at risk daily; I'd say. Interestingly, the inspector wasn't seen again, probably related to the guy who snagged his 'bits' climbing the perimeter fence surrounding the ammunition store way back in Germany all those years ago, or maybe, even the same guy. Gertcha!

In September 1976, my mother was rushed to the hospital and died on a trolley in a passageway awaiting treatment. The cause of my mum's death was recorded as a 'Pulmonary Oedema', a medical term for water on the lungs. All through my childhood, I remember my mother going into fits of coughing with her face swelling up before drawing what we as children always thought was her last breath. The coughing bouts used to worry me sick with anticipation of her dying at each moment, and us all ending up in an orphanage and shipped off to a far-flung colony somewhere in the world. My mother's condition was exacerbated by smoking John Player's No.6 or Embassy cigarettes. Each packet of cigarettes came with coupons that could be saved and redeemed for household electrical items. The more she smoked, the higher the rewards; bring on our first-ever electric clothes iron!

My mother's funeral was a very low-key affair, from what I recall, with just one of my sisters, my wife Rosie and me in attendance. Although saddened, I was unmoved having to identify my mother's body to the police coroner's officer. I was no stranger to viewing the deceased, but seeing my mother's body concentrated my thoughts. Although not a wicked or usually violent person, at least in her later years, there must have been reasons why my mother chose to beat me when there would have been other options open to her, apart from sending off to Australia. My instincts tell me that I must have reminded her of my father, who was twenty-one years her senior and someone she no-doubt hated. I often wondered why my mother lived and died a sad, lonely person as she took her secrets to the grave with her. Curiously, I did not resent my mother, even to the point of supporting her whenever I could. During the latter years of army service, I sent a proportion of my wages home each time I had an increase following promotion or passing examinations in certain subjects.

My wife Rosie and our son Justin had never been warmly accepted by my mother, who found it difficult, if not impossible to communicate with each of them directly - just as my grandmother did with us. Whatever reasons my maternal grandmother and my mother's sibling had for excommunicating my mother and us children by default never became known to me. I always remember my mum wanting a low-key existence without making a fuss. The only occasions I recall her stepping out to the front of our house in Faroe Road, and only when no-one was around, was at times she fastidiously scrubbed the seven front steps with step-powder to a worn but pristine finish.

****

Six years as a police officer was drawing to a close. I had an annual salary that was always below the national average at the time. Other people not employed as police officers and much younger than me were earning twice or three times as much, even though I worked five out of my eight rest days a month as overtime.

As a family, we could ill-afford a car, so we had to rely on the local bus service once a week to get to Slough for the weekly shop, seeking out and buying groceries as cheaply as possible. There was one particular occasion when Rosie and I, along with baby Justin in a second-hand pushchair, happened to be waiting at the village bus stop to travel into town on yet another of our weekly shopping trips when I noticed our son wearing a Mothercare brand red coloured cardigan that had just one gold button remaining out of what should have been three or four. I asked Rosie if our son could wear something different as it seemed to me that he was always in the same cardigan; the reply I got was: "He hasn't got anything else!!". Another reminder that my family was living on low wages came when we purchased a can of rhubarb from the local grocery store but returned it after discovering mould, only for the shop's proprietor who said, "That's what you get when you buy cheap". The final ignominy came when police authority houses became available for purchase by the occupants. I applied for a mortgage, declaring my salary and Rosie's part-time earnings, only to be told by the would-be loan provider that between us, we did not earn money enough to justify being offered a mortgage. I had 'moonlighted' by repairing Volkswagen Beetle cars to earn extra cash, with Rosie assisting me late into the night handing tools over to me and operating a trolley-jack as I removed and replaced engine blocks, but it wasn't enough.

Throughout my six years in the police force, Rosie undertook an assortment of different jobs to supplement our family income. Six days after losing a six-month developed unborn baby boy foetus by miscarriage, Rosie took employment on Faberge's factory line, a luxury brand cosmetics manufacturer, but as a local police officer's wife, was made to feel unwelcome by other employees. Rosie left after two days and took up a piece-time job at home making Christmas crackers in return for a pittance. I helped out when I could, but the time put into making the things amounted to nothing more than wages generally associated with Asian sweat-shops. We gave up almost as soon as we started.

It was time for me to leave the police force or serve a minimum of twenty-five years on a relatively low salary. If I had decided to stay, I would have had to continually 'moonlight' to supplement my income and no-doubt end up in a council house, just as the police sergeant that had previously occupied our house had done. I tendered my resignation letter, expecting to be called into the Superintendent's office (not Supt. Peterson) to air any grievances. All I received in acknowledgement was a letter from the Police Authority Housing Department instructing me to vacate the house I occupied within four weeks or else an application for a court order to evict my family would be submitted. I was not alone; my resignation was just one of many officers leaving in droves purely because of the low pay and conditions imposed by the dying Labour government led by James Callaghan.

Bendy Bobbies

During the 1970s, adverts appeared in newspapers, offering contracts to serving constables the appointment of becoming a police inspector in the Hong Kong Police Service. The generous remuneration package carried a life-style and tax-free salary most British constables could only have dreamed of, along with an added bonus of free membership to Hong Kong's exclusive Royal Yacht club. The appointments were available to serving British constables of two years minimum service who were of non-marital status. The offer was overwhelmingly tempting for many, but of course, being a probationary constable when I was single, the opportunity for me was not available – and it was just as well.

Just to digress a little: I did manage to go to Hong Kong in later years with my wife Rosie three years before the colony returned to the Peoples Republic of China in 1997 after the one-hundred-and-fifty years lease held by the British Government had expired. At the time of my visit, I spent two weeks observing the everyday goings-on noticing that several men walked with a pronounced one-sided stoop. It suggested that they might well have a genetic connection with Mr Wun-Hung-Low, the owner of the 'Wong Fokin Book Store' back in Belfast. Perhaps not. I noticed too that many of the city's streets had English names while others were in Cantonese. There were names such as Natham Road, the longest and most commercial of all, Coronation Road, Stanley Market, where a pair of made-to-measure jeans could be produced in minutes. Curiously, a road led to a so-called live animal 'Wet' market named 'Hu Flung Dung', probably on account of the stench that permeated the air.

Trams that constantly weaved their way along the main streets displayed advertisements of 'Double Happiness' brand cigarettes between the twin-decks both sides of the vehicle, together with a 'Fortune Cookies' advert at the rear. I did wonder if such adverts equally referred to the morose-looking tightly-packed passengers inside the trams during evening rush hours on rainy days. Sensing that someone might have been spying on them, the occupants would often swivel their heads in a perfectly choreographed fashion and pose the question: 你想要乜嘢, which, above the din of the traffic sounded more like 'Wah-U-Wahn'? that I took as meaning: what do you want?

The passengers in Hong Kong's trams, dressed in everyday garb, looked uncannily like citizens of the Peoples Republic of China of the 1960s as they made their way to a Mass Transit Railway station (MTR) for a return journey northward through the New Territories. I wondered why people needed to take short trips on public transport to the nearest underground train station, especially on rainy days, even though there were MTR access points on almost every street corner. Still, I mused, perhaps those guys didn't like getting wet, even though some of their older relatives might well have gleefully plodded about up to their knees in floodwater planting rice crops in Paddy fields. At the time of the Cultural Revolution in 1966, almost everyone in The Peoples Republic of China, including bank managers and business owners alike were forced to work in the countryside. But then, you knew that. It was probably working in and around water that brought about Chinese citizens aversion to the stuff; their dislike of it genetically passed on through generations. Topics discussed during such times probably included questions like, 'Wot wen wong Mao Zedong, and while we're at it; wot's that pong?... as they bent forward to plant yet another stem of rice as the oxen in front of them nonchalantly deposited streams of nutrient-rich plant food in their wake.

Several years later, I met a bloke whose task was to carry out investigations into allegations of corruption within the Hong Kong Police. What was of particular interest to him, he said, involved some of those holding the rank of Inspector, who, through naivety, would inadvertently be drawn into situations that were not of their making.

On arrival into the colony, newly appointed inspectors from the United Kingdom, some as young as twenty-two, would be assigned several Chinese constables headed by a sergeant, also of Chinese origin. Following police raids on illegal traffickers and gambling dens, the group's sergeant would appear with a bundle of Hong Kong Dollars and offer it to the Inspector in charge of the operation. Initially refused, the sergeant would explain that, in Chinese culture, it was an insult of the highest order to turn down such offerings. Money accepted - job done! More advertisements appeared in British national newspapers.

Back home, attempts to bribe police officers or to gain favours were much more low-key and subtle. Some motor vehicle drivers' classic trick would be to hand over their driver's licence at the roadside that sometimes contained a neatly folded £20 or £50 note (depending on the severity of the offence) within its pages.

One cold, wet winter's day, I happened to pull over a driver that I suspected of committing various road traffic offences. I asked the occupant of the vehicle for his vehicles' documents when lo-and-behold, out of the window, a hand appeared bearing a driver's licence with a neatly folded £20 note protruding from its pages. As nothing was said by the driver, there was no proof of attempted bribery. I allowed the £20 to fall to the ground and proceeded to carry out a comprehensive inspection of the vehicle. That done and at the point of leaving, I pointed out that I had inadvertently trampled on a monetary note in a puddle beneath my feet, suggesting it might well have fallen out of the vehicle. Gertcha!

There was another trick some individuals got up to when faced with being arrested for non-payment of court fines; the person subject of the summons would sometimes hand over denominational notes far above the amount required with the comment 'Keep the change' creating a dilemma of not giving change or being able to make an arrest as payment had been offered. The solution was a brief entry into one's pocket-book recording a donation to the Police Benevolent Fund.

In an attempt to gain favours, approval or just wanting to gain familiarity, some public members would go out of their way by providing cups of tea or, if a business, small gifts. Faberge, the factory where Rosie lasted just two days, was an upmarket manufacturer of toiletries with a factory in the village of Iver. The intruder alarms would go off every now and again, causing all available officers to rush to the scene. The alerts were always false-alarms, and we all knew it, but that didn't stop the rush to get to the premises, as all those that attended went home clutching bags of luxury products given by the security staff as a token gesture of gratitude. My wife, Rosie, happened to be one of the poorest wives in the village but exuded the same fragrances as the Russian queen, Volga Olga Constantinovna or maybe, Queen Olga without being Vulgar.

A fish and chip shop back in Maidenhead opposite the ABC cinema dished out free chips to any passing Bobby on the beat;

I didn't mind that. During cold winter nights waiting for the pubs to turn out, wearing the same impressive serge cape around my shoulders that I had later worn in Iver, I would nip into the 'Chippy', pick up my free offering and retreat to a quiet spot in front of the cinema in Bridge Street. With a hot snack secreted away under my cape, I would feed myself by bringing my arm out from underneath while nonchalantly popping a chip into my mouth while at the same time look in both directions acting as if nothing happened. Anyone seeing what was going on might well have thought I was performing a puppet show with an Emu as a prop – or worse! Evening all!

Also, while in Maidenhead, I willingly exposed myself to the possibility of compromise. During night-shifts, I would nip into a local bakery where all kinds of pastries and cakes were being created for the next day's offerings. Six jam doughnuts were always on offer - and I accepted them. Arriving home at about 6.30am each morning, I would wake my slumbering Rosie with a hot cup of tea, at which point would both devour the bounty whilst still warm – all six of them. Thankfully, the doughnuts were only available seven out of twenty-eight nights; had it been every night, there would have come a time we would not have been able to get out of the front door. Free doughnuts went on for more than a year, and the nearest I came to being a 'Bendy' or 'Blobby Bobby'. I'm sure I wasn't alone as there always seemed to be traces of sugar in police cars after night-shifts. Who'd be a copper, eh?

Many of us will have heard the term, 'Once a copper - always a copper', and I suppose to some extent that is probably true. Although I was just a growing teenager at the time, I still often think about the fire in Denbury Camp that happened all those years ago on 10th March 1962, only five months before I joined the regiment. With the experience of being a former police officer, I often wondered why the two fifteen-year-old boys perished inside the drying-room of their billet complex when everyone else managed to escape. Had anyone given thought to the possibility of so-called initiation ceremonies going on at the time? I hope so.

Some of the traits inherited from working in the police force, like so many other of my life's experiences, continues to serve me well. Although never actively looking for anything awry, I cannot help but notice when something is not quite right; step-up George Bernard Shaw. Instinctively standing against a wall or building whenever out-and-about, waiting for Rosie to re-appear from a shop, meant that everybody and everything had to pass in front of me and not behind; a wise tactic as many a sailor will vouch, and especially handy when in crowded areas where pickpockets could well be lurking. Another trait is working out situations and people in nano-seconds by being aware and watchful of others' body language, completely sub-consciously knowing that what is often said appears different from what the speakers' body is saying. After reading this, I'm not sure if anyone I know would wish to talk to me again.

Looking after family and property safety has always been uppermost in my mind regarding deterring house burglars. I try to think like a burglar to avoid becoming a victim. I knew an ex-police superintendent who always needing to be aware if he had had unwanted visitors while away from his house, positioned his mailbox at the gate and strung a length of cotton across his driveway as he left. How sad is that?

Although we humans, genetically speaking, split from Chimpanzees more than seven million years ago, some of the same traits remain in both species; aggression, violence, coercion, subterfuge, dominance, etc. I often wonder if, as a species, we'll continue to be like Chimpanzees for the next seven million years or perhaps evolve to behave more like the Bonobo ape, a more closely related species with a similar-sized head to us relative to its body mass. The Bonobo are only found in a relatively small area within the Democratic Republic of Congo on the African continent. Such cousins of ours usually settle dominance and other domestic issues by engaging in consensual sex at every turn (in a manner of speaking) regardless of gender, to maintain harmony. Why then are they endangered, I ask myself? Metaphorically speaking, if anybody reading this book thinks their genetics will continue Infinitum, they will do well to remind future generations to keep their backs to the wall, especially if the Bonobo gang make a come-back. Old Mother Riley of Faroe Road fame would have had the time of her life chucking buckets of water over anything and everything that moved. Gertcha! Evening all.

Moving On

One thousand-and-thirty-four-pounds annual salary, including working five out of eight so-called rest-days, is what I left behind. A family-owned company was my next employer on my life's journey that offered a starting salary twenty-five per cent higher than that of a police constable, even though I had given six years of unblemished service. I also benefited from a company car, motoring expenses, free lunches and working hours of just thirty-five hours a week with every weekend free. What could have been better? Well, no longer cossetted living in a rent-free police house with the equivalent of council tax and water rates that were the concerns of others, times would continue to become financially challenging. Rosie and I had our first ever mortgage that exposed us to all the risks associated with it. The commitment of repaying a two-year interest-free loan to my employer that enabled me to lay down a deposit on our first house, and a mortgage interest rate of fifteen per cent, was a constant worry.

There was some respite during our times of continued hardship: I received £15 in cash each week to cover the petrol cost for my company's car. Every day, driving to and from work, cruising at a speed to maximise fuel economy ensured there was enough money left over to buy family treats. At the end of each working week, I would fill up the petrol tank of the car at a total cost of £12.50 with the remaining £2.50 spent on a bottle of Martini, a quart bottle of beer, a bottle of lemonade for our children and a massive slab of Cadbury's Milk chocolate for us all to share over the following two days of each weekend. The chocolate became known as 'Saturday Night Chokkie', something we all looked forward to enjoying. To keep within the parameters of what our small family could afford to spend, Rosie kept a large hardback notebook listing all our outgoing commitments, neatly listed on the inside front cover. Each week, the total spends were totted up and spending plans modified to ensure we remained debt-free whenever possible.

I joined a company that marketed Butane gas cigarette lighter fuel and aerosol products with a worldwide distribution. The total head-count of staff was eight, which included the two business partners. I carried the title of Warehouse Manager after initially being an Assistant Warehouse Manager, although, in truth, there was no-one else to manage. I was part of the combined effort that ensured the success of the business. I loaded and unloaded lorries driving a forklift truck, handled and despatched stock as well as occasionally arranging to ship goods in the absence of the chap whose job it was to do. I was also tasked with visiting different suppliers as part of a liaison process, including a trip to a factory in The Netherlands, providing feedback to the Managing Director. Flexibility was the key to success without the boundaries of demarcation. I didn't particularly like my work, but it suited my purpose to provide for my family. I was to remain with the company for six years as year-on-year profits continued to rise. Annual bonuses were paid, equivalent to a month's salary, but that was until the end of the fourth year, when such payments decreased, despite the business's continued growth. It was a family-owned business, but four other employees and I were not part of the family. By coincidence, or otherwise, two sons of the joint owners had joined the company, suggesting that changes were afoot. I was called into the office of the two partners after it became apparent that my allocated company car was knackered and needed to be replaced, only to be told, 'These cars are proving to be costly luxuries for the boys.' Funnily enough, I do not recall such comments being made when the job was initially offered. I suggested motorbikes (I couldn't help myself), although I did indeed get a new car of my choice, the comment went down like a lead balloon. Periodic sneak peeks of the payroll revealed that while employees' bonuses went down, rewards for the two sons were going in the opposite direction, not to mention trips to the Royal Ballet and Opera houses in London.

After six years, it was time to leave the family company despite the generous salary and loan to pay a new house deposit. If there is a moral to all this, it would be: Think very carefully before entering into a family-run company if you are not part of that family, as the likelihood is one's prospects could be limited, unless, of course, one was to become part of the family.

From my perspective, I felt that I should have been approaching the peak of my chosen working career, whatever that happened to be, but here I was stuck in a job that I perceived as having no further prospects. But then, my only concern was earning enough money to buy our food and keep our home.

****

During my time with the worldwide marketing company, Rosie and I had become proud parents of a new arrival: our daughter Victoria Anne on 26th June 1979. No sooner had Victoria arrived in this world, I went home to collect her brother Justin so that he could meet and bond with his new sister. A few weeks later, Justin, in his quest to carefully look after and protect Victoria, accidentally tipped her out of her pram as she landed head-first onto a concrete path. 'Bonk!' Our son was beside himself with grief and remorse, forever after keeping a watchful eye on his sister until she was old enough to express her own opinions. And she did.

The picture shown is of my son and daughter, map in hand, with Justin doing what he does best: teaching the basics of Geography, which he says is all around us. In more recent times, Justin has also been known to say that there is no such thing as bad weather, only the wrong clothing, but if he's telling that to people in other parts of the world that experience extremes of temperature, he would do well to keep the engine of his car running!

At this point in our lives, Rosie took on various part-time jobs to supplement our family income. One such adventure involved becoming a Tupperware Dealer, holding product demonstrations in peoples' homes before becoming a manager and recruiting others to work towards doing the same. Rosie was so successful at what she did, it wasn't long before she was invited to become a self-employed distributor of Tupperware products, and I expected to join her as a full-time business partner. Within two days of presenting ourselves at the Tupperware headquarters in Harrow, London, we moved lock stock-and-barrel to South Wales after giving my employer just forty-eight hours' notice of my resignation, even though I was contracted to serve three months' notice before I could leave. Our house in Buckinghamshire sold very soon afterwards.

With secure employment gone, a new beginning was before us, but so too the risks associated with running a self-employed business for the first time. The first three months in South Wales as a family was spent in a local hotel (since demolished) that appeared to be the hub for all kinds of sexual skulduggery. Every weekend, a coach would arrive from Scotland with guests taking up every available room in the hotel. Our two children were in a place of their own opposite to us, but unfortunately, we were next door to the bridal suite that always seemed to be occupied despite no signs of any wedding. As parents, Rosie and I managed to shield our children from all the goings-on despite the perpetual sound of giggling and loud thumping noises coming from adjacent rooms. Bonkers seemed to have taken on a new meaning other than just being mad, a term I would use wisely in later years.

Much of the three months spent in residence at the hotel in Cwmbran was spent setting up a 'normal' pattern of life, getting our children into school, purchasing a house, and building on our newly acquired retail business. Those were stressful times as we waited for the completion of our new home. Rosie and I took our newly acquired enterprise from strength-to-strength in terms of sales and the financial rewards that allowed us to enjoy the fruits of our efforts. However, from the outset, we felt ill-at-ease living in a bubble of 'make-believe', but we had an opportunity to better ourselves and so took the challenge head-on. We travelled the world in style and treated as V.I.P's on the White House lawns in Washington D.C. when the then German Chancellor, Helmut Kohl, met with President Reagan.

As one of several distributors of Tupperware products, our success took us to the most exclusive of places, a benefit that was far removed from those available to our managers and the dealers we had recruited. The theme we portrayed to all recruits was that anyone who recognised the opportunity to succeed could be as successful as we presented ourselves. And it was true. To be successful in the Tupperware business required a full-time twenty-four hours commitment of hard work, without which one could easily have 'Gone-to-the-wall'.

Every Monday morning, Rosie and I hosted a dealer and manager assembly meeting that always started with loud music, including a ditty that will be etched in our children's minds forever: -

♪ 'We will show you the way, show you the way to happiness, and you can see it ev-er-y day, every day a friend and new success, etc.'. ♪

I'll spare the reader (and our children) the verse espousing the virtues of being given a new car when achieving manager status. The formula worked every time, with ordinary wives and mothers improving their lives in a way that they might never have thought possible. After all, Tupperware products, a generic term for all food containers in modern times, were and might well be the best of what there is in the culinary world of plastic food containers.

Successfully managing a profitable Tupperware business involved acquiring warehouse premises, ordering, and paying for stock on a non-return basis before distributing it to our sales-team of demonstrators. To create a sales-force capable of shifting large amounts of merchandise involved managers with a determination to succeed who would, in turn, recruit 'dealers' as part of an on-going process. Rosie and I would elevate the best-performing dealers to manager status by providing a free company car and an override commission structure based on their own recruited dealers' sales.

The advice given by anyone who knows anything about human behaviour will probably tell you that if you are the only male in a female gathering, especially in a party setting, be prepared to accept being the subject of their ridicule; it's only natural, but why did it have to be me? The picture shown below is of me looking like a rabbit caught in the headlights of a car. Being the only man present at what should have been a routine meeting of managers, a partially-clad lady arrived masquerading as a police officer before singling me out for attention, tantalisingly dropping her overcoat to the floor. What was I to do?

I was always on my best behaviour, especially in the presence of so many respectable married women, including my wife (the beautiful smiling lady second from left in the back row). Somehow, although I was as stiff-as-a-board, I had the presence of mind to prevent this extraordinary visitor from slipping off my lap and hurting herself. 'There's tidy', as they say in Wales. As a former police officer, those times spent saw women officers (WPCs) of all shapes and sizes kitted out in uniforms with bowl-shaped hats more suited to the original traffic wardens at a time when lady wardens had a reputation being as hard as a ship's rivet.

The WPCs I ever came across looked nothing like my visitor except for Dawn back in my police days. My introduction to the pseudo police lady was undoubtedly a ship-riveting experience for me, that was for sure, evident by the delight shown on the faces of all those present who had collectively paid for the event. And not a snake charmer with a flute or basket in sight!

The year of nineteen-hundred-and-eighty-four was when Rosie and I 'technically' bought a Tupperware Distributorship in England's West Country, or at least became financially liable for it. The Tupperware business was ranked as the fifth most successful Tupperware retail outlet in the United Kingdom but in slow terminal decline before we arrived. Although living in Cwmbran at the time, we travelled each day over the Severn Bridge to our workplace, but it was to take a further three years to sell our house in Wales before moving back over to England.

At the height of our Tupperware business, Rosie and I worked alongside twenty-three managers and two-hundred part-time dealers, most of whom were mothers and housewives who, like us, wanted to better their own and their family's lives.

The Tupperware business had to come first, often spending time away at national and international conferences, which might well have impacted our children if we hadn't made every effort for that not to happen. Rosie is in the front row, seventh from the left in the following picture, wearing a beautiful smile and stunning dress: -

In 1988, after four-and-a-half years of total commitment to our business, my wife and I decided enough was enough of the extremes of stress, mainly on Rosie's part, despite all the benefits and lifestyle it offered. The 'highlife' was something we no-longer-wanted. All we did want was to have an everyday family existence, a desire that inspired us to take another of life's gambles and finally turn our backs on the Tupperware world of beautiful experiences. It was to be a breath of fresh air and a real opportunity to re-engage with our children and the 'normal' world, whatever that was – or is. Rosie and I stepped out of the bubble financially better off. However, we were to learn of at least one other Tupperware distributor not so fortunate who succumbed to bankruptcy, losing everything into the bargain - including their home.

Before letting Tupperware go, I secured employment as the Branch Manager for a wholesale tool company based in Croydon, Surrey, with several branches around the country, each supplying hand tools and power tools to independent retailers and major D.I.Y superstore outlets alike. I was to manage one of the company's branches for eighteen months before external market forces, and a mini-recession brought about its closure and redundancy for all employed within it.

A few weeks after a period of unemployment, I became a wholesale food company's branch manager supplying up-market food products to the catering industry. After successfully haggling for what I thought was a fair salary, I embarked on a week's induction course somewhere in the back-end of Norfolk. I stayed in the home of a director of the company, which seemed odd to me, sharing time with his wife and young son. I was ill-at-ease during my time with them, especially when the chap that recruited me decided to go out for the entire evening on at least two occasions, leaving me in the company of his wife who sneakily presented herself dressed as a nurse – except that I didn't think she was one. Gertcha!

After a week in Norfolk, I arrived at the company's branch I was to manage. No sooner had I walked through the door for the first time and introduced myself to the staff, one senior employee announced that the branch was earmarked for closure within six months and that [she] was seeking new employment elsewhere.

After six months, the branch in Avonmouth did indeed close with all those working within it made redundant. I was out of work - again. I did so enjoy the experience of ordering foodstuffs from European suppliers, salmon from Scotland, fresh fish from Cornwall, crabs, lobsters, etc., from the east coast, encouraging the telesales team to clear the delivered stock by the end of each day by whatever means necessary. The branch's closure was cast in stone, so it was goodbye to all that good food. I loved the job; I loved meeting chefs' challenges by providing them with high-quality products to their exact requirements. It could have been so different had I not been (so to speak) sent up the river without a paddle.

Having attended the Department of Health and Social Security to claim unemployment benefit, which I thought was the correct path to follow, as so many others had done, I observed that many claimants were on first name terms with the staff, readily and cheerfully receiving benefit money. After an intensive session of what appeared to be an inquisition, I left with nothing more than an apology, having been told that I did not qualify for benefits because of having been self-employed within the previous two years. Effectively, I was told to look to my wife for financial support – not the State. Thank you, the Department of Employment and Social Security. Thank you.

During the second time of being out-of-work, the realisation of having very little money to spend struck home. Although Rosie worked full-time supporting our family, we still had to watch every single penny. There was a time during this period of unemployment when my son Justin, home from university, decided to join me as we both went to the local supermarket to buy something to eat. The only money I had at the time was just enough to buy a French baguette - nothing more. Justin sat with me as we both sat with our backs against the outside wall of a Sainsbury's supermarket, sharing the bread, as we watched shoppers entering and leaving the store with baskets and shopping trolleys loaded up with all kinds of foodstuffs; foods that I had previously bought without ever having to think about. But suddenly, there I was, unable to afford what I saw being taken to and loaded into cars. Oddly, I did not feel disenfranchised or marginalised from mainstream society as I'd had those same experiences during my childhood and somehow felt content at being humble. I was thankful that sitting outside of a supermarket sharing a baguette with my son was just a fleeting experience, but one that made me think how lucky we had a home to go to, mindful that countless others would not have had the same luxury. It was also the only time I had ever defaulted on my mortgage payments and continued to do so for three months, another three months and we'd have been looking for somewhere to live. It was a timely reminder of what I had been through earlier in life and something that needed doing. Here's what I got up to: -

- Worked for a local farmer who became a life-long friend, helping him manage his stock of animals, receiving a minimum agricultural wage of just four pounds an hour when most wage levels were at least double that amount. Curiously, while cajoling sheep from one place to another, one of the animals kept bawling out, 'B-a-a-a-r-b-a-r-a' which, from my time in Wraysbury, led me to believe it wanted to offer some sort of favour. Not with me, you don't, Luvvy – wrong guy, I thought. Gertcha! I did wonder why one or two of the flock were sporting false eyelashes and winking, something I didn't know sheep could do. I wondered too if perhaps some Somerset farmers were literal in their execution of 'Sheep Dipping', which led to the practice being banned years later. Gertcha!

- I worked with the same sheep farmer cutting down trees, but instead of receiving cash payments, I opted to accept 3ft lengths of tree-trunks instead. I used a borrowed chainsaw to hollow out the sections of tree-trunks into what my friends called 'Pot-logs, before planting them up with flowers from my garden and elsewhere, delivering them to all sorts of outlets, care homes, service stations, etc. I couldn't produce enough. Using cut timber lengths from felled trees, I also embarked on creating trellis and other garden features, marketing them as 'Larch Arches'. Alas, all that I made and sold was just a seasonal product with meant I had to look for new opportunities when the summer sun went down and took the demand for my products with it.

I joined a legitimate and well-known money-lending company as a 'self-employed' agent, offering sub-prime high-risk loans to many people who could ill-afford to take on debt. I dished out cash to low-income borrowers, a perfectly legal practise that lasted for eighteen months until I became bored and voluntarily moved on to other things. The amount of commission received covered our mortgage repayments but very little else.

An advert appeared in a local newspaper inviting applications to become a 'Self-employed Agent' of a garden-related product, prepared to invest £25,000 by furnishing a show-site and all the associated costs that went with it. I applied for the position and convinced the interviewer that I was the right man for the job - except I didn't have £25,000. It mattered not as it seemed that the person interviewing me concluded that I was the right man for the job. However, just a few months into the enterprise, the company that I had become an agent for went into liquidation, taking with it £2,500 owed to me in sales commission that I could ill-afford to lose. Despite the setback, I found ways to continue to trade with other manufacturers' products that became a saving grace. Changing to marketing different manufacturers' products proved to be a success, but although defaulting on mortgage payments for the first few months after starting up, our family set off along the path of financial security.

Although applying myself full-time to my new-found enterprise, orders were very short in coming. Having previously served as a police officer, I was offered and accepted a Somerset County Council's appointment Sherriff's Officer. One particular occasion was charged with removing protesters from Whatley Quarry in Somerset to facilitate the development of a bypass road for lorries to gain access. Along with a couple of others, I had the law courts' power to eject from the site all trespassing demonstrators using all reasonable force as necessary to do so. The police arrested those protesters that offered or displayed any form of physical violence and put them before a Magistrates' Court.

Environmentally concerned people, many of whom were disingenuously referred to as 'tree-huggers', did their very best to fraught efforts to be ejected by climbing trees and refusing to come down, even to the point of having to relieve themselves in situ. There was one particular moment of note: two police officers positioned themselves at the base of a tree in anticipation of a protester, having suffered the effects of the bitterly cold January weather, hunger, or the need to use a loo, was about to capitulate – but there was no such luck. After uttering eye-watering expletives that would have embarrassed the most-rounded police constables, the female protester promptly adjusted the crotch of her knickers and urinated on the unfortunate constables below. Obviously, the police officers who voluntarily decided to carry out sentry duty at the base of the tree should have paid more attention at school when talked about Sir Isaac Newton, an English mathematic of the mid-1700s, who, while pondering gravity, received a bonk on the head from a falling apple and deduced that whatever went up, had to come down. Those of us that could foresee this happening as the two constables chatted away, standing in direct line of fire, became a sight to behold. The spectacle happened to be a once-in-a-lifetime experience for almost all of us that witnessed the spectacle and one I shall never be able to forget, thankful that it wasn't me.

Out and About

While living in the beautiful county of Somerset, I had ample opportunities to observe and enjoy the pleasures of living among local subsistence farmers whose forebears might well have lived in hovels on the side of country lanes. One such local, a neighbour, never did hold a driver's licence, but that didn't stop him driving an old clapped-out grey Ferguson tractor with a hessian sack over his shoulders in an attempt to keep the rain from penetrating through to his bones. He was the same chap that advised me about throwing a bucket of urine into badger runs.

Like many other West Country boys, our neighbour never did find love; the nearest he got to do so was being shot-at by an over-protective father of a girl that moved over from Ireland.

Our loveless neighbour once told me about one of his Batchelor friends of advancing years who said he taught two of his cats a lesson by blasting them to Kingdom-come with his shotgun, along with his dinner and half of the kitchen table. And that was before I ventured out onto the Mendip Hills.

After many years of viewing the distant Mendip Hills in Somerset, I had ample opportunities to visit the area and admire the locals' scenery and novel ways. I recall a story of a farmer named John (pronounced 'Jaaarn') who had a 34-year-old son of the same name. The duo lived alongside a lady called Myrtle in a damp stone-built converted farmhouse called Myrtle Cottage, nestled in amongst those hills in the middle of nowhere. The building was covered in various lichens of various colours growing on the roof, suggesting that there was nothing in the atmosphere other than clean, pure air. John junior, whose thoughts were anything but, had never experienced a relationship with someone or something of the opposite sex - as far as was known. The effect of seeing females, human in particular, a young strutting maiden called Myrtle caused our Mendip boy to be in a state of total confusion and bewilderment, which bothered him. Unable to account for his feelings, Jaaarn junior sought the advice of his father. Daddy said that whenever his son had an uncontrollable urge, he was to go into the cowshed and scoop up a large dollop of steaming cow-muck, the fresher and hotter the better, and put it on to the end of whatever it was troubling him.

A few days after receiving his father's advice, Jaaarn Junior saw the start of their first employee, a dairy-maid called Gertrude. A busy little soul was our Gertie, always doing as she was told while at the same time keeping a watchful eye on our could be Mendip Stud. At the sight of our girl, also known as 'Gurt-Great Gertie', and overcome with urges, 'Jaaarn Junior' quickly ran toward the cowshed, scooped up copious amounts of the fresh stuff as instructed, and retreated into the milking parlour. Jaaarn Junior then proceeded to apply the panacea to what was indeed troubling him when in walked Dirty-Gertie, who said in a feigned tone of astonishment, "Ere, Jaaarn, wot's doing?" and "Watz gart thur then, Jaaarn?". J, J, overcome with embarrassment, quickly explained the advice given by his Mendippy father. Without further ado, Gertie said through pouted lips, while at the same time allowing her undergarments to drop to the floor, "Yuuz dooosn't wanna dooooos that, Jaaarn, yuuz wanna be putten it ere"…, and he did – two gert-great blummin handfuls! Hah, ha-ha!

Forget soft floppy pointed hats, lattice-patterned smocks, check-patterned shirts, and baggy trousers held up with broad-strapped braces or baler-twine; some boys from the hills were almost always dressed in oil muck-stained coveralls that matched the colour of their tractors. Each coverall had a corporate logo emblazoned in a prominent position that was always worn with pride. A few portly wearers of the garments had matching scarlet-coloured cheeks suggesting that many-an-hour had been spent in front of an AGA cuddled up with orphaned lambs during cold, wet lonely nights while at the same time getting stuck into anything dairy – or pork!

Extended abdomens resulting from a lifetime of drinking rough home-made Scrumpy cider was often a pastime for some people living in the Mendips' hills. The benefit of walloping down so much liquid sawdust contaminated with suspended remnants of rodents resulted in arteries that were as clean as a whistle but livers shot-to-pieces.

I often wondered if there was a genetic mutation resulting in a few of those indigenous menfolk up in them-thar hills having larger-than-normal hands with one manus spanner-like in shape as a result of fiddling about with outdated farm machinery. The other more dexterous manus probably evolved with a vice-like grip to keep lady companions from straying as the custodian temporarily lost line-of-sight when lifting a pewter mug full of Scrumpy to their lips at village hall dance events.

Bank Holiday weekends for some Somerset hill farmers wanting to be away from their womenfolk usually involved driving along country lanes straddled across old decrepit tractors painted up-to-the-nines in colours thought to be trendy at the time. Encounters with other tractor drivers usually resulted in shouting out above the din and smoked-filled air: "Alright, Jaaaaaarn?!". The usual response was a gleeful expression of double chins instantly morphing into a multitude of folds along with a thumbs-up gesture as they reached the pinnacle of mental and physical sensations. Such observations suggested they were indeed having a good time. The durty, durty, durty rascals – all of them!

In more recent times in Yorkshire (here we go), much of the same thing would be going on with Yorkshire farmers that would gather in remote parts of the Yorkshire Moors straddling yellow bicycles left behind after the 'Tour de Yorkshire', greeting each other with sounds of "Aye-up Malcolm, ow du?" These guys, many of whom had the name Earnest Everard (not Malcolm, Stanley, or Kevin), only ever reached their peak of inebriated stupidity after consuming more John Smiths Yorkshire Bitter than was good for them. Not a single utterance would be heard until the very last drop of ale was gone, and then the whole giggling gaggle would cry out in unison, 'Bye-eck, did I need that!' followed on with 'If it ain't from blooudy Yorkshire, it ain't 'blooudy worth having'. Anyone turning up offering a ride on a bicycle made for two, asking, 'Can thee ride tut Tandem?' only served to heighten their experiences. Cosying-up to any number of veritable pies packed to the gunnels with pork while also indulging in anything Haddock created the same effect. Returning home from the moors, the same lads would get stuck into Yorkshire Puddings the size of dinner-plates, filled with onion gravy followed by yet another Yorkshire pudding topped with Yorkshire jam that served as a pudding, finished off with a nice brew of Yorkshire Tea from what was believed to be a world-famous tea plantation in Harrogate. Any uneaten edible dinner-plate-sized Yorkshire puddings would then be turned upside-down, vigorously stamped on at one end to form a peak before being dried and worn as caps, saving having to buy the customary tweed patterned ones worn by their elders, or else having to wait to receive one as part of an inheritance.

The Tour-de-Yorkshire, an annual event, draws in world-class cyclists from around the globe to compete in a cycle race around the county on a route marked out by the same old re-instated yellow-painted bicycles acquired by some of the Yorkshire lads. More used to training on smooth-tarmac surfaces funded by the E.U., our continental friends often came to grief negotiating bends on rain-sodden cobbled streets in Scarborough after falling arse-over-head and landing in a heap of twisted metal and groaning bodies. Local Yorkshiremen spectating from the sidelines while enjoying the pleasures of a local tart from the Patisserie or 'Ceak Shoppe' would, in their inimitable manner, pause just long enough to say, 'Blooudy-eck, Eric, did you see that? I bet that blooudy-well urt - did thatt! Anyway, ow's thee missus, is she all-reet, or are err piles still playing oup?' At the same time, these guys would be casually looking over their shoulders in the hope of seeing competitors from Lancashire narrowly miss the tangled mass and end up crashing through the front door of Betty Entwhistle's drapery shop that continued to sell wool by the yard, or better still, Arkwright's butchers shop displaying a sign: 'Purveyors of the finest Yorkshire Pork Pies'. Aye-Oup!

During the bicycle race's annual event in Yorkshire, television viewers worldwide would watch the race on ginormous screens, baulking at the sight of distressing scenes of lycra-clad riders piling into each other, reminiscent of shoals of Herring being tipped onto the decks of fishing trawlers. Some of those witnessing the sickening spectacle on those television screens, especially in France, would no-doubt have pulled facial expressions of squeezed lemons while sucking in air through pursed lips to the sound of: 'Oooooooooooooh!' or 'Oh là la' as they checked out the latest fashion designs of Lycra suits amongst the slivering pile of injured bodies and bent bicycles.

Following the calamitous debacle in Scarborough, knowing that the French have a predilection for visiting pharmacies more times than they go to the toilet, it was noted that one such Gaelic individual, having freed himself from the tangled heap of other cyclists, limped across to an ice cream shop in the mistaken belief of it being a Pharmacie. Once inside, the same chap was heard to say, "Veuillez m'excuser, av vou arse crème?". The proprietor, a stoutly built Yorkshireman of a well-rounded character named Kevin (yes, Kevin), replied,

"Aye, but all we av left is Raspberry Ripple; tek it or blooudy well leave it!"

"Oh, mon dieu Monsieur, vous Anglais sont si grossiers!" replied the cyclist as he clenched his buttocks and stomped out of the shop. Having been told by some clever-clogs a day or two earlier that French words make up twenty-nine per cent of the English language (fifty-something per cent if you include Latin), the proprietor of the shop shook his head in disbelief. Moments after the unfortunate cyclist had 'minced' out of view, the shopkeeper's assistant, a small skinny chap fresh out of university, also called Kevin (yes Kevin), reminded our Kev that in times gone by, French was the language of choice for the so-called aristocracy and those of wealth, while German was the spoken language of peasants. Enraged by the whole experience, our ice cream proprietor ran to the shop door, opened it, and shouted out,

"And there can take yer blooudy fancy talk outa 'Yurrkshur with thee", along with mutterings of, "I'll give im blooudy arse creme…Mon Dieu!"

With the Tour-de-Yorkshire at an end, some of the yellow-painted bicycles chained to lampposts as before would disappear into the hills at the same time as our foreign visitors limped home, many of them reflecting on their Yorkshire experience and wishing they'd never heard of the 'blooudy place'.

Now here's a little bit of information that'll titillate your tonsils: Once a year, usually the first Tuesday in February, there's always a big celebration called: 'The British Yorkshire Pudding Day'. Can you believe it? I blooudy-well can - Eric! Not content with scoffing heaps of the things that could easily enlarge the consumer to the size of the moon, 'Yurrksur folk' would, at the drop of a hat, cook-up no-end of the fluffy things for immediate consumption. That Ariel motorbike back in Hammersmith with the saddle large enough to accommodate anyone with an arse the size of an African Bull Elephant, and side panniers sufficient to accommodate enormous left-over puddings, would serve the Yorkshire community well. And, 'On tut way ome' from a Yurrkshur Pudding event, Stanley Arkwright 'n' friends would go home via 'Brid' (Bridlington) to pick up tut' bundle of 'addock' un chips to gu wid their world-famous left-over treat. Just for the sheer hell of it, some of the motorcycling home-goers would then race along the quayside in Brid just for the thrill of skidding on grease-sodden cobblestones fronting fast-food outlets, half-expecting to topple into the dockside at low tide. And it was always regarded as being 'Reet blooudy fun'.

If you are still in doubt about the authenticity of traditional Yorkshire ways, a visit to the Goodmanham Arms in the village of Goodman Near Market Weighton, East Yorkshire, will put you right. A traditional pub with its bare floorboards and a dark interior requires a degree of caution when entering for fear of tripping over a black Labrador dog that might be lying across the walkway to the bar. Still, once inside, the place is always lit up with its honesty, sensible prices, and down-to-earth friendliness, so much so the local bar-flies would happily allow you to sip from their half-filled glass of beer before you make your mind up what to order. Be careful before sharing a drink with anyone sporting a beard and moustache; you might well end up with a morsel or two of the previous days' pork scratchings. The Goodmanham Arms also features a so-called 'Gypsy-pot' suspended over an open fire containing an ever-changing meat recipe served within a 'Blooudy greete Yurrksurr pudding' - with gravy. Don't worry about any connections to Sweeny Todd, the barber-cum-purveyor of meat pies filled with the flesh of his customers – he was fictional. Enjoy!

A trip to Millington, not too far from the quaint village of Goodmanham, is where you will find a pub called the Gait Inn pub where a trip to the gents' toilet (it doesn't matter if you're male or female) is a must. If you were to avail yourself of the only available W.C. in the 'Gents', be careful to keep the outward-opening wooden door tightly closed by holding onto the length of baler-twine attached to the door for that purpose. Goodness knows how one avoids becoming vulnerable to an unexpected visitor during the final stages of completing whatever you were in there to do, effective as the arrangement was when I was there, I can imagine anyone complaining might be well have been told, 'I've already replaced the bolt once, and if you think I'm going to waste more blooudy money forking out for another blooudy one, you've got another blooudy think coming - Beryl."

Not wishing to let our northern folk off the hook just yet; sight-seeing around the entire county of Yorkshire can still reveal hordes of old AA motoring signs, chipped enamelled Oxo signs, 1930's petrol pumps in situ., old cars and red single-decker buses parked up in private gardens with daffodils growing out of windows and Convolvulus (bindweed) wrapped around the wheels. I wouldn't have been surprised if I came across ex-army Ariel motorbikes with rotting Yorkshire puddings inside panniers, hidden away in old run-down corrugated sheds that sported 'Union Jacks' and flags depicting Yorkshire's White Rose. With their pride-and-joy machines painted to perfection with army-green paint, reinforced huge coil-springs under the saddle suitably lubricated, the owners of such contraptions, always mindful their bikes were capable of bearing the combined weight of both rider and puddings, would be all set to go off to one of many Great British Yorkshire Pudding events somewhere - anywhere. Aye-oup, Stanley, 'Aye bloody oup'.

Back on the Mendip Hills, some of the single men, fed-up to the back teeth driving tractors and having to call everyone 'Jaaarn', would arrange a B-B-Q on or near a pig-farm somewhere in the middle of nowhere amongst craters formed by Lead mining and exploded ordinance of the German Luftwaffe of earlier times. Hidden from view, some folk could be found drinking far more lager topped with lime juice cordial and Scrumpy cider than they probably should have done. Simultaneously, having had their fill of booze, sausage lovers turned to admiring the vast number of different breeds of pigs as they considered how they were going to get stuck into even more porky delights.

As the evenings in the Mendip Hills wore on, guffaws of laughter, the high-pitched squeal of pigs and the sound of someone singularly and deliberately twanging the strings of a Banjo to the tune of 'Duelling Banjos' from the film 'Deliverance' did nothing more than raise a few eyebrows by people in nearby villages. In some respects, it's a pity such 'Porky party-goers' didn't open the event to the world, just as the Glastonbury Festival's organisers had done. Some European cousins reputed to have an insatiable appetite for 'Swine-Fleisch' und alles Wurst would almost certainly have relished the prospect of being able to get getting stuck into all things auf dem swineflisch.

Our continental friends, if they had indeed attended such an event, would most likely have returned home having had the time of their lives smugly thinking their local Burgermeister only had the option of gaily prancing around in Lederhosen to the sound of an Oompah Band (frontal physique allowing) while dancing with every Jungfrau known to man. But, at the same time, our intrepid home-goers, mindful of the often-quoted phrase in German-speaking countries of 'Man weiß selten was Glück ist, aber man weiß meistens was Glück war (man seldom knows what happiness is, but usually only what it was), could boast of a Gloucester Old Spot experience, forever wondering if the term also referred to a very unpleasant medical condition. Ein, Zwei, Drei, Super! Bis zum nachsten Mal. Until the next time - Pet. Oink! Oink!

The book, 'German In Twenty Lessons', awarded to me for being top of the course way back in Denbury Camp all those years ago, still serves me well.

An Indulgence

I realised I was getting older when: -

- The realisation that the years between my father's birth (1894) and my present age spans three centuries.
- I became invisible to women.
- Touch-typing unintentionally brought up the character next to the intended one due to arthritic disfigurement of fingers.
- Instead of young ladies at the supermarket checkout averting their gaze and subconsciously touching their hair when being gawped at, would address me as 'Luvvy' or 'Me-dear' and ask if I would like some help with packing and not giving a sod about how their hair looked.
- Looks of astonishment from bus drivers when offering money instead of flashing a free bus-pass.
- Fiendishly consuming flatulence-inducing food before trips to the supermarket.
- Automatic 'Seniors' rates applied at barbershops without being asked.
- Being pulled over in my Volvo car of twenty-plus years at port security only to be told where I would find the bonnet release catch.
- Entering a massage parlour accompanied by a man wearing a turban carrying a flute and basket in case there was a need for extras. Gertcha!
- Recovering from surgery with a prosthetic hip only to find my middle-aged son at the end of the bed staring up at me through my hexagonally shaped feet, worrying that he might have inherited the same fate.
- Waking up in yet another hotel room shouting 'Wurthefukarwe' having dreamed of the London

Underground train network and Borneo's nomadic tribe.

I have no wish to espouse virtues or philosophy of any kind other than to draw conclusions garnered from my own life's experiences. My advice to anyone reading this book is simple: -

- Believe half of what you see and nothing of what you hear. Some religions, politicians and commercial retail businesses fall into this category. Some years ago, a survey of the Christian clergy members revealed that nearly half of them did not believe in Jesus Christ's resurrection. Jesus Christ!

In recent times, a British Labour Party politician vowed to reduce traffic volumes by ten per cent during his term in office – he failed. However, what the lascivious minister did succeed at getting down on several occasions came with a bit of help from his secretary. Oops! The same guy had an aversion to raw eggs, and if anyone was brave enough to offer him one in the form of a missile, the most likely outcome would have been to receive the full force from five of his other digits that were also capable of leaving a legacy. Gertcha!

There is a bakery in Wells Somerset that calls itself 'Burns the Bread', although I suspect that doesn't happen very often – if ever.

An Undertakers in Burnham-on-Sea also in Somerset has the rather interesting name of 'Burnham Funeral Services', could easily be misconstrued as meaning they don't muck about at crematoriums. I'm sure they must also offer burials and other means of sending us all on our way.

- For most of us: 'You are what you eat and become what you think. H'mm.
- Be the master of your own destiny, and live the life of your choosing, free from anyone or any organisation wanting to control your life for you in whatever guise it

presents itself. Stand up to bullies and face your fears, even if you need help doing so, mindful that bullies will always require the victim's permission. I wished someone had told me that when I was young.

Whatever the reader of this book's social or economic background, my advice would be never to allow oneself to be stereotyped into how you think others see you. Metaphorically put, if somebody says you should be a 'Van driver's assistant' but you think otherwise, just walk away; it might be easier than you think.

- Always keep your perceived enemies close.

- Finally, embrace change. From my own experiences at an early age, I learned that change, expected or otherwise, can provide new opportunities.

When writing this book, the United Kingdom had left the European Union and had set off on an uncertain future, both politically and economically. Well, I have to say that whatever reasons people of our great nation chose to vote, for or against leaving the European Union, as a nation, we are where we are, and we've just got to get on with it. Just as my path through life had its ups and downs, so too leaving the EU has and will continue to do the same. Looking forward provides endless opportunities if we're prepared to look for them. From what I gather, great British inventions account for the vast majority of innovations in use in the world and include anything from snow skies to the internet. There's no reason to expect that will change, although my hope is that going forward as a nation, we do not continue to sell our ideas to others as we have done in the past through individual greed and self-gratification. Spreading ideas and wealth around the world for the right moral reasons, within a system that allows everyone down to the poorest man and woman wherever they are, an opportunity to make something of him or herself, instead of living in poverty or reluctantly having to rely on welfare benefits, has got to be a good thing? All of us are good at something; just keep searching.

Sylvie-Agnes Bermann, a former French career diplomat who served as an ambassador in the United Kingdom during Brexit, scornful of the British in a very negative way, said, "The British nation does not cry over spilt milk; they will bounce back because they are dynamic while having the talent".

So, come on the people of Hammersmith, London, and the entire United Kingdom; whatever your background, upbringing, race or religious creed, now's the time to bring your lights out from under a bushel.

I recently read an article in the media that the best times of anyone's life were seventeen and seventy. Well, here I am, settling into my seventies, mindful that both parents and two of my siblings have passed away. Time has allowed me the luxury to reflect on my own life's experiences. I can tell you that at the age of seventeen, life was starting to look good; I was free of Faroe Road and free from the bullies who had unsuccessfully attempted to make my life a misery, unwittingly holding me back in all kinds of ways.

Despite my betterment endeavours, I never did become a 'Captain of industry' by any stretch of the imagination - but it was never a concern for me. I am debt-free, own my own house in the country, wear a clean pair of socks without holes, my arse no longer hangs out the back of my trousers, I eat well along with being able to put a bottle or two of wine on the table, and, answerable to no-one except my wife and family, others who are affected by my presence, and, of course, the law of the land. Perhaps my mother was right after all when she referred to me as a 'Goody-bloody-two-shoes'.

Would I change any aspects of my life? Perhaps. Do I have any regrets? None, other than wishing I had been encouraged to face up to my fears. I arrived at this juncture in my life alongside my loving and devoted wife of almost half a century, without whom the outcome might well have been very different. I have two happy and satisfied grown-up children who have achieved far more than I was ever able to do, and for that, I shall be eternally grateful. My son is the Head of Department as a teacher in a large secondary school, despite his school reports as a child suggesting he was 'thick' and would underachieve. My daughter, who, despite refusing to go to university, became one of the youngest people in the country to qualify as a Certified Accountant within a world-renown company of accountants at the ripe old age of twenty-one; not bad considering some of the 'Catcher of Rats' genes from their great maternal grandfather might well be coursing through their veins. Both are married to exceptionally talented and lovely people, giving my wife and me adorable grandchildren who I hope will make the most of what life has to offer. I'm happy with all of that.

I've always tried to find ways of earning just enough money to put worries aside and be able to get on with life, even if that meant sometimes going without. For a final spin of the dice, perhaps I should consider hawking this book around Hammersmith to see what the guys there think of it before moving on to Buckingham Palace – of course!

Finally, as I continue to age, I am under no illusion whatsoever that my life could change in an instant, but for as long as I am able, I'll pick myself up from whatever befalls me and carry on, hoping against hope that when I do finally fall off my perch, I do not come back as a…

…Sheep!!!

Oh, and just one more thing; the reference to the boy called Toby back in Faroe road who became averse to dog excrement and all things ring-shaped, was actually a boy named Terry; I just wanted to protect his identity. I've no idea why I've told you that.

Vive la France, Viva Espana, God bless America. God save the Queen. God almighty!   Amen